Workplace Counselling

Workplace Counselling

A Systematic Approach to Employee Care

Michael Carroll

SAGE Publications
London • Thousand Oaks • New Delhi

First published 1996
Reprinted 1999, 2002

SAGE Publications Ltd
6 Bonhill Street
London EC2A 4PU

SAGE Publications Inc
2455 Teller Road
Thousand Oaks, California 91320

SAGE Publications India Pvt Ltd
32, M-Block Market
Greater Kailash – I
New Delhi 110 048

British Library Cataloguing in Publication Data

A catalogue record for this book is
available from the British Library

ISBN 0 7619 5020 6
ISBN 0 7619 5021 4 (pbk)

Library of Congress catalog card number 96–068421

Typeset by Mayhew Typesetting, Rhayader, Powys
Printed in Great Britain by Selwood Printing Ltd., Burgess Hill, West Sussex

Contents

Figures

Tables and Boxes

Acknowledgements

I would like to thank Cathy Carroll, Elizabeth Mann and Michael Walton for their reviews and comments on early drafts of the book: their contributions have been immense. Many others, far too numerous to mention by name, have helped shape the contents, both directly and indirectly: I hope they will see their influence throughout these pages. Susan Worsey, editor at Sage, was ever hopeful, cheerful and encouraging – what more could one ask from an editor?

The book is dedicated to Robert Graham, Lawrie Gilbert and David Whiteley, all of whom died in 1994, and to the three courageous partners they left behind, Phyllis, Alexa and Anne. I want to acknowledge their work and contribution to life and people.

Preface

This book takes one context – the workplace – and considers counselling provision there. Its focus is the interface between counsellor, client and organization. The three work together or are in conflict. While the book focuses primarily on workplace counselling, much of it is applicable to counselling in other organizational settings; for example, medical and educational. When an organization pays counsellors to see clients on its behalf, whether those clients are employees, customers or members of the public, then particular sets of relationships are set up that are the theme of this book.

Considering organizational aspects as part of individual counselling provision has been new learning for me. I was taught that counselling involved two people who met privately to enable one of them to deal more effectively with his/her life. Great emphasis was laid on the fact that the involvement of any others in the counselling relationship was intrusive. Counselling, by and large, was concerned with the internal world of the client, with the external world and its problems left to social workers, welfare officers and information-giving services. Rarely, if ever, would counsellors intervene in the external life of clients.

From my counselling work I became painfully aware that many individuals were not responsible for what had happened to them. As part of the wider community, they were often pawns in political games which left them powerless, defenceless, depressed and confused. Nor could they be made responsible for their reactions, despite Victor Frankl's assertion that we all have the right to choose our reaction to what happens or 'is done' to us (1959). While it is important to support and work with individuals crushed by others and by systems, it also seems worthwhile to see if systems can be changed. I was beginning, in Egan amd Cowan's terms (1979), to move from 'downstream helping', where individuals are pulled from rivers and resuscitated, to 'upstream healing', which looks at the systems and organizations that push them into the river. Sick companies produce sick employees, as dysfunctional families produce dysfunctional family members, as sick societies produce sick citizens. Not all subscribe to systemic approaches to life and relationships. Our Western culture upholds, by and large, an individualistic approach where our ideal is the strong and self-sufficient person who survives alone and is able to meet life's problems without help from others. No wonder counselling has had problems adapting to other, non-Western cultures, especially those with a strong sense of family and extended family identity.

My interest in counselling in organizational settings, and in particular counselling in the workplace, began about 10 years ago. At that time, I was asked to train and supervise the work of the Welfare Branch of the Metropolitan Police. This taught me that the organization has a vast effect on the way counselling takes place and helped me see that the individual side of counselling is only one side. In 1991 I organized and ran a two-year Diploma in Counselling at Work course for TDA (Training Development Associates). This was a pioneering programme, and my attempts to find material in this area were thwarted; there were few pathways. I had to think through what was needed and make the best of what was available, both from my own experience and that of others. Throughout this time I was supervising counsellors who were constantly dealing with particular organizations: educational establishments, GP practices, private organizations, public services, religious establishments. Furthermore, for the past seven years my wife, Cathy, has been the in-house counsellor for Shell International. She was involved in researching in-house counsellors' perceptions of their roles and responsibilities (Carroll, 1994). She translated theory into practice and never allowed my lofty thoughts and ideals to get too far from reality.

From all this experience I am convinced that working as a counsellor in an organization brings its own issues. Questions are raised that are not considered in other counselling contexts. Who to involve, when to involve them, who to speak to, who not to speak to, when do responsibilities to the organization come first, which roles to engage in, and which roles are compatible with other roles? Managing counselling provision and negotiating with organizations are not skills that come naturally to counsellors, nor are they built into counselling training. It is to be hoped that they soon will be.

Readers will not find all chapters of equal importance to them and their work. They may want to pick and choose what is applicable to their particular situation. Chapter 1 provides an overview of what employee counselling means, its many faces, and looks briefly at the history of workplace counselling, in particular at this history in Britain. Chapter 2 offers a review of counselling models used in workplace counselling. Chapter 3 is my attempt to summarize the critical points, debates and trends happening in workplace counselling. Understanding some of the questions may help to work towards possible solutions. Chapter 4 is a central chapter in this book. It summarizes how organizations can impact upon and influence employee counselling. This chapter contains my reasons for writing this book: to try to understand how various organizational cultures create their own dynamics (some conscious and some unconscious) which impact on individuals in many ways. Chapter 5 returns to counselling provision and sets up a model of introducing counselling into the workplace. Chapter 6 outlines a model for practitioners working with individual employees. It is a systematic model over five chronological phases and will allow counsellors to monitor their own work. The final four chapters pick up themes within employee counselling: Chapter 7 is centred on the theme of evaluation and concentrates on methods of evaluating both individual counselling and counselling systems; Chapter 8 focuses on the important dimension of ethics and professionalism in employee counselling; Chapter 9 proposes a possible training curriculum for counsellors who work or will work with employees; and Chapter 10 helps counsellors in the workplace understand and use supervision effectively. I argue here that supervisors need to be aware of the contextual dimensions of counselling when working with supervisees from organizational settings.

Throughout the book I present models and frameworks that deal with the ideal. Reality falls far short of this and, like 'stars we never reach but which still guide us', these models can be used to help us reflect on our work and adapt it rather than become sticks with which to beat ourselves. We need to accept where we are if we are to move to where we want to be.

This is an exciting time for counselling. From the past it has inherited the three main forces of psychodynamic, humanistic and cognitive-behavioural approaches, and from the present comes the fourth force in counselling: cross-cultural or multicultural counselling. Perhaps the fifth force in counselling will be a new awareness of context in counselling and the impact of the environment on counselling provision. When that happens workplace counselling will be seen as an important area of counselling provision.

1
Understanding Workplace Counselling

> The role of the organisation is to support the process of employee empowerment through promoting mental health education, counselling and other information services to the workforce.
>
> N. Tehrani, *Counselling Psychology Quarterly*

Approximately 30 years ago, Alvin Toffler (1970) predicted the rise of leisure time and his *Future Shock* envisaged employees with two-thirds of their time devoted to leisure pursuits. Not only has this not happened (except for unemployed people most of whom have not chosen to be unemployed), quite the reverse is true. The modern workplace seems to demand more employee time than ever before, there are fewer resources with which to do the work and more and more employees are suffering from 'presenteeism' (needing to be seen to be at work while overstressed doing the job). Levels of stress seem to be at an all-time high. A National Opinion Poll (*The Daily Telegraph*, 11 September 1995) reported that a third of workers feel so insecure in their jobs that they are afraid to take time off sick, 70 per cent feel more in jeopardy than they did two years ago, and 44 per cent are afraid to criticize their bosses. As employees struggle to cope, more and more employers, as well as health experts, are struggling to find new ways of managing workplace stress and its inevitable implications.

The workplace today

Statistics bombard us daily on how stressful the workplace has become. Not only have learned journals published their research studies, but stress has become such a constant feature in the popular press and glossy magazines that Newton (1995: 3) remarks wryly, 'Copy on stress would seem to be located in almost every editor's filing cabinet. Production is easy: include a stress check question-naire, offer a ten-point plan to help readers attain "stress fitness", and make a few telephone calls to some academic luminaries on file.' Stories abound about 'twice the work in half the time', about 'downsizing' (or 'rightsizing' if you want to give it a positive bent), about 'flatter' organizations, about massive redundancy and what happens to the survivors of redundancy. There is a constant reminder that the changes in organizations are putting extra stress on those employees who remain and that employers are becoming worried by the legal implications. O'Leary (1993) and Cartwright and Cooper (1994) have documented some statistics around mental illness in the workplace:

- One in five of the working population suffers some form of mental illness each year (approximately 6 million people).
- Some 90 million working days are lost each year as a result of mental illness.
- When asked about the 'true' reason for absence from work, over half the employers felt that emotional/personal problems and stress were to blame.
- Between 30 and 40 per cent of all sickness from work involves some form of mental illness or emotional stress.
- Alcohol abuse is estimated by Alcohol Concern to cost about £2 billion per annum, with the cost to industry being put at approximately £1 billion.
- Approximately 20 per cent of any workforce are affected by personal problems that impact on their work performance.

There are several reasons why employers should be closely involved in the physical and mental well-being of employees (O'Leary, 1993, 1994). It makes sense to have a healthy and high-performing workforce. Not only does it create happier individuals who provide quality service, but it contributes to overall profits. Combining care for employees with the drive for profit ensures that both objectives can be met. However, there is some incongruence in this. While 94 per cent of companies surveyed by the Confederation of British Industry (CBI) in 1991 felt that mental health should concern them, only 12 per cent actually had a policy (O'Leary, 1993). Furthermore, the legal and ethical responsibilities for managing the welfare of employees has come to the fore. A number of cases regarding 'unreasonable' stress have made employers acutely aware of their legal responsibilities in the area of helping employees deal with mental health issues (Health and Safety Executive, 1995). There are reasons to believe that there may be an increase in the number of employees making stress-related claims against employers.

What are employers doing to face the effects of mental illness/ stress/physical illness in the workplace? More employers are providing facilities to help employees increase their level of physical fitness and reduce instances of physical illness (colds, back injuries, coronary heart disease). These may be either in-house facilities or the use of other facilities in the locality (O'Leary, 1994). There has been a large increase in the provision of counselling facilities for employees and their families. This includes employee assistance programmes (EAPs) with a variety of provision, including personal, couples and family counselling, legal and financial services, information and advice. Some companies offer in-house counselling, others external, and in some instances there is a combination of internal and external. Health education organized in the workplace is increasing. Workshops, short training sessions, and days on specific topics, including alcohol awareness, stop smoking campaigns, stress management, taking care of your heart etc., are all ways of helping employees to manage their physical and mental well-being.

Why workplace counselling?

There are various reasons why employers are turning to counselling as one method, among others, of caring for their workforce. Employers' responsibility for the welfare of their employees is one reason. More and more employers realize that illness and productivity do not go well together. A healthy workforce produces. Furthermore, as more and more health services have longer waiting lists or have limited availability on the National Health Service (like counselling and psychotherapy), companies are moving in to provide it speedily. The fact that employees are taking legal action is another reason for the introducion of counselling. A number of legal cases have made history on these points. Employers have three responsibilities towards employees, breaches of which can result in employees suing successfully: (1) a duty to take care (which inevitably arises in the employment situation), (2) a breach of that duty, and (3) foreseeable injury. In the US there has been an increase of 5–15 per cent in compensation claims for work-related stress, and in Australia it is reckoned that 35 per cent of the cost of compensation pay-outs to government employees followed stress claims (Labour Research Department, 1994). One way of anticipating risk and providing relief from it is to offer counselling services. Employers are turning to counselling as one way of helping to manage the mammoth changes taking place in organizations. Change is never easy: it disrupts, disorientates, causes grieving and takes time. Support is needed for individuals and teams as transitions in organizations are managed. Counselling is one way of supporting employees as they cope with organizational change. Counselling can be seen as a way of improving mental health. Employees do not leave their problems aside as they turn to face their working day. Egan (1994) has noted the financial cost to organizations of psychological and social problems, and lists the kind of everyday problems that can be costly to the organization: a poor relationship between two key members of a production team, a middle manager who is becoming dependent on alcohol, a high-level manager distracted by an impending divorce who loses a significant account, a secretary grieving for a dead relative who mislays an important letter. When these individual problems (and when are they not the order of the day?) are seen in the context of a large workforce, and when they go unnoticed and undealt with, then, collectively, the cost can be immeasurable.

Counselling also highlights the value of people as organizational assets. More and more organizations are becoming aware that people are truly their best assets. Most have said it for years; perhaps they are beginning to believe what they have inscribed in their mission statements. Pfeffer's (1994) research into successful organizations showed clearly that the most important ingredient was the way they cared for their employees. The direct link between care for people and the drive for success and/or profit is a major factor in convincing employers to install counselling services as a further way of managing their workforce constructively.

Counselling services within the workplace are being viewed not just as 'crisis' points or for severely disturbed individuals, but also as a preventive service. Counsellors are in a unique position within the organizational setting to offer the kind of training and education that prevents mental illness. From their work with clients, they can gain an overview of the ills within the organization and can create training packages to forestall further injury to employees. In the long run, preventive measures are more cost-effective.

When surveyed, top executives insisted that 'corporate social responsibility' was the main reason why they wished to install an EAP (Corneil, 1985). Obviously, they saw such programmes as beneficial to themselves and to the wider community. Organizations are realizing that a 'wholeness' approach needs to be adopted towards employees: that physical, mental, emotional and spiritual well-being go together and that people need to be worked with as people. Emphasizing one element is not enough. Counselling provision is part of that overall package, where it is accepted that individuals need professional counselling help at stages of their lives and that for the majority this is a worthwhile venture that enables them to deal with transitions and crises.

Overall, counselling can be cost-effective. Although it is difficult to ascertain what financial investments are made and what money is saved, it is possible to work out the economic cost to industry if the mental health of individuals is not sustained. We know the cost to industry of alcoholism, of absenteeism, of stress: we have never costed the effects of depression or broken relationships, never mind the day-by-day emotional and mental problems faced by most individuals.

Counselling can itself be a source of organizational change. Rather than being just an appendage to a company, counselling can bring the values, the energy of change, the vitality of acceptance, a realization of who we are and what we can be, to the very dynamics of workplace life. Counselling values are about the importance and process of change, how people are empowered to manage their lives, how social responsibility is built into life, and how decisions can be made. Counselling can influence organizational culture to work towards the ideal strong and adaptive culture that serves the company.

These are some of the reasons why employers introduce counselling into the workplace. Cooper (Magnus, 1995) has divided the reasons into three categories: according to his research, 76 per cent of employers see counselling as a caring facility; 70 per cent expect counselling to help employees deal with workplace change; and 57 per cent view counselling as a means of managing stress. Workplace counselling makes sense when it is realized that employees spend about one-quarter of their lives in work settings; that, for many, key relationships are part of their work; that personal identity is often bound up with jobs; and that almost all people integrate personal and professional lives to a great extent. Having counselling available in the workplace means that problems can be dealt with fairly quickly and can be worked through in the very environment from which they often emerge.

The history of workplace counselling

The historical development of employee counselling gives an insight into the various reasons for establishing counselling provision. In brief, there have been three phases in the history of workplace counselling.

The human relationship era

The history of workplace counselling begins in the US and is intertwined with the arrival in industry of medical, psychiatric and social work provision. Oberer and Lee (1986) trace the relationship between industry and the management of resources to the early nineteenth century where the basis for the relationship between management and workers was first laid.

Counselling in the workplace, specifically, has existed since the early 1900s though in quite different formats from those we understand by workplace counselling today. By 1913 there were about 2,000 welfare workers in industry (Carter, 1977). There is some evidence that the first counselling programme in industry was initiated by the Ford Motor Company in 1914. The Engineering Foundation of New York commissioned a research survey of emotional problems among employees before 1920. The discovery that 62 per cent of employees were discharged because of social rather than occupational incompetence resulted in the introduction of preventive measures. Two companies, Metropolitan Life Insurance (in 1922), and R.H. Macey (in 1924), employed full-time psychiatrists. Anderson, who was the first psychiatrist for Macey, provided the first book connecting psychiatry with industry, simply entitled *Psychiatry and Industry* (McLean et al., 1985). Even though psychiatric services were available in and to industry from the 1920s, it was not until 1948 that the first training programme in occupational psychiatry was introduced (McLean et al., 1985).

This first era in employee counselling emphasized human resources and human relations as key factors in effective management. It also focused on the link between the working problems of employees and organizational behaviour (Swanson and Murphy, 1991). Tehrani (1995) has traced the roots of British employee counselling to the late nineteenth century with the introduction of welfare officers whose job it was to monitor the physical and mental well-being of employees.

The alcohol awareness stage of workplace counselling
A lull in mental health provision seems to have taken place between these endeavours and the 1940s. Mayo was a key figure in researching employee needs, criticizing industry for not paying adequate attention to the psychological needs of employees and himself establishing a counselling service in 1936. It is interesting, today, to note some of the characteristics of this service, before Rogers (1961) outlined his client-centred approach. Dickson, the head of the counselling service, described it in 1945:

> Our personnel counseling program has been set up in our Industrial Relations Branch as a service to our employees and supervisors. At the present time we have forty counselors equally divided between men and women . . . every counselor is assigned a territory comprising some 300 employees to whom his entire time is devoted. He has no other duties or responsibilities. Each counselor has access to the shops and office locations to which he is assigned and spends a considerable part of each day contacting people while they are at work . . . their contacts with employees are of two kinds: off the job interviews, and on the job contacts. The off the job interviews are held in an interview room where the employee may talk in privacy . . . the on the job contacts take place at the employee's work place, in the aisle, at the drinking fountain, or in the rest room . . . we began this work back in 1936 . . . as this work

progressed, we became more and more aware of two things. First, frequently the complaint as stated was not the real source of the individual's trouble. Consequently, action based upon the manifest content of the complaint did not assure us that the difficulty would be eliminated. Secondly, our attention was arrested by the observation that, given an opportunity to express themselves freely, many complaints were restated by the employees or disappeared entirely ... we decided that the counselors should devote their attention exclusively to bringing about adjustments and changes in employee attitudes through the interviewing method itself. As we saw it, the counselor's role should be at all times that of a neutral party. It was seen that in order to maintain such a role in an industrial situation, the counselor had to be free from all activities which were incompatible with this position. This meant that the counselor should not take action upon complaints or grievances nor should he at any time intercede on behalf of the employee, supervisory, or management. Only in this way could he maintain his role of interviewer and keep himself from becoming entangled in the system of personal relationships with which he was dealing.

In the interview situation our first objective is to put the employee at ease. We accomplish this principally by being at ease ourselves and occasionally leading the interview during the warming up period. As soon as the employee starts to talk, the interviewer encourages him to continue by an occasional nod of the head and displaying real interest in what is being said. Occasionally the counselor will restate what the employee has said in order to encourage him to continue his train of thought or reexamine what he has said. These restatements are always addressed to the feeling the employee expresses rather than to the logical content of what he says. The counselor never interrupts, he never argues, he never gives advice. His function is that of a skilled listener and the attitude he displays encourages the employee to talk about anything which may be of importance to him. The counselor, when he listens, is seriously trying to understand what the person is revealing about himself. (1945: 343–45)

This programme began in 1936. In 1940 there were 20 counsellors, in 1948 there were 55.

When a new phase of interest emerged directed at employee health, the earlier emphasis on 'attendance, production, health and disciplinary problems' gave way to issues of 'alcoholism, accident, psychosomatic accidents, the ageing worker, executives' emotional problems, techniques of management, and structuring of the work environment' (Lee and Rosen, 1984: 277). In fact, alcohol concerns dominated much of the counselling provision from this stage until the 1960s. The term 'employee assistance programme' (EAP) was coined by the National Institute of Alcohol Abuse and Alcoholism as a way of widening provision to include problems other than alcohol. The 1940s witnessed the beginning of the EAP era of workplace counselling with such provision centred principally on alcohol issues in industry.

During this era, a whole range of people became involved with employees: ex-alcoholics, psychiatrists, social workers, occupational and industrial psychologists and personnel officers, covering a variety of approaches from psychometric testing to job appraisal, and from alcoholism to family problems. Presnall (1985: ix) summarized the trend: 'Employee Assistance is a phrase now used to describe a unified approach to intervention and assistance for a wide variety of related human problems in the workplace.'

The second era in workplace counselling put in place services for helping employee growth. There was still an emphasis on 'unhealthy' employees and how to help them return to effective work, and the main providers of help tended to emerge from 'medical' backgrounds with the 'medical model' uppermost in their minds. According to Reddy (1994: 62), 'managed care' characterized the EAPs of this era. He outlines some of the movement:

> Thus, although EAPs were originally a shopfloor initiative with strong support from labour unions, it was not long before they were adopted by management. They were next converted by natural evolution into the now conventional 'broadbrush' service. Alcohol, like any form of substance abuse, is rarely due to a single cause, nor is it the sole symptom of distress. The new service changed its name from OAP (Occupational Alcohol Programme) to EAP (Employee Assistance Programme) and covered a wide range of mental health conditions.

Presnall (1985: xv–xvi) saw the 'persistent' and 'pervasive' workplace needs which give rise to employee assistance programmes as fourfold:

1   To do more about problems in the workplace.
2   To act upon the realization that the workplace is both a human-problem breeder, and a problem-resolver.
3   To humanize the workplace.
4   To develop new work practices based on the awareness that areas are interrelated in the workplace, i.e. health, wholeness, work, relationships, etc.

Internal and external counselling provision

The third phase in employee counselling was ushered in with the advent of employee assistance programmes (EAPs) which moved beyond dealing solely with alcohol issues. Still with an emphasis on drink and drug problems, they moved swiftly in the 1960s, 1970s and 1980s to provide a range of services, legal and financial help, stress management, telephone counselling and face-to-face counselling. It has been estimated that there were in the region of 10,000

EAPs in the US by the late 1980s (Swanson and Murphy, 1991). Reddy (1994) suggests that around 1 million UK employees, and in many instances their families, were covered by EAP provision by the end of 1994. Counsellors and counselling psychologists were now part of mental health teams, and individual counselling became a major part of EAP services. So rapid, and successful, have been EAPs that Tuthill (1982) depicts this as 'a hundredfold increase in a quarter of a century' (quoted in Lewis and Lewis, 1986: 3). This increase is not confined to the private sector alone. In the US it is not unusual for educational institutions and voluntary/nonprofit-making sector companies to provide counselling for their employees.

Despite the rise in the number of EAPs, there is still little agreement on what constitutes an overall programme. Services differ from one to another as providers adapt to different organizational needs and cultures. Sonnenstuhl and Trice (1990: 1) suggest a description of EAPs that they see as applicable in most instances: 'We define EAPs as job-based programs operating within a work organization for the purpose of identifying troubled employees, motivating them to resolve their troubles and providing access to counseling or treatment for those employees who need such services.' Others would view this definition as rather narrow, concentrating, as it does, on the individual. They would prefer that EAPs, while working with troubled individuals, would work also with the organization and management within the organization to prevent employees reaching the stage of needing individual care. Lewis and Lewis (1986: 11) list the differences which distinguish traditional and contemporary EAPs (see Box 1.1).

However, other changes are taking place within EAP provision that more closely ally counselling with organizational culture, management and performance appraisal. For too long counselling has been an adjunct to organizational life rather than an integral part of it. Reddy (1994) has been foremost in showing how EAPs can move from the periphery of organizational life to the heart of it, recommending that they be viewed not as programmes to be administered but as concepts and philosophies about health in the workplace. This is a significant change in conceptualizing EAP provision, moving it away from what is done to employees towards a more general concept of EAP as creating organizational change. Now EAPs are connected to employee performance, to management practice and style of leadership, to training for supervisors, to support at all levels and to training. From here, it is a short step towards seeing EAPs as a help towards individual and organizational change.

Throughout the history of workplace counselling, EAPs have been the most visible form of counselling provision. They were set up as

Box 1.1   *Traditional and contemporary EAPs*

Traditional programmes	*Contemporary programmes*
Emphasis on alcoholism as the basis of the problem	Broad-brush approach: any issue appropriate for service
Emphasis on supervisory referrals	Combination of supervisory referral, self-referral, and referral by others
Problems identified at late stage in development	Services offered at earlier stage in problem development
Services offered by medical or alcoholism specialists	Services offered by generalist counsellors with expertise in chemical dependency and other areas
Focus on troubled employees with job performance problems	Focus both on employees with work problems and on employees/family members with no performance problems
Confidentiality for referred employees	Confidentiality for referred employees; anonymity for self-referred employees or family members

Source: Lewis and Lewis, 1986: 11

either 'internal' or 'external' services, the former as part of an organization and the latter usually as a service specializing in providing EAPs to a number of organizations. There has been some debate on the relative merits of each of these, though latterly Hoskinson (1994) has argued for a movement away from this artificial adversarial approach towards seeing the advantages of both.

What has existed, in the third era of workplace counselling, alongside EAP provision, both internal and external, has been the 'in-house' counsellor. Here, rather than opt for a range of services, companies have hired counsellors to work with their staff. Britain is presently in the pioneering stage of this and the first generation of in-house counsellors has laid the foundations for counselling in organizations (Carroll, 1994). The present-day practice of coun-selling in the workplace places emphasis on an array of services for the employee, on confidential settings and particularly, on a holistic approach to emotional well-being at work.

The history of workplace counselling is bound up with legal and economic as well as humanitarian concerns. While employers have come increasingly to accept that 'counselling may well be the most economical means of improving performance' (Reddy, 1987: 1), the law has intervened to speed up the processes of introducing coun-selling provision. US legislation made employers responsible for 'emotional damage' to employees; and there is some concern ex-pressed today about whether or not stress-related illnesses are valid grounds for litigation against employers. Buckingham (1992: 38) predicts the future: 'Legal action against employers is expected to replace uncomplaining pill-popping as the remedy for occupational stress.' This has already taken place in the United States, where Offermann and Gowing (1990: 103) claim that 'between 1982 and 1986, employee damage suits for stress-related illnesses in California increased five-fold.' The introduction of counselling provision by industry is one way of ensuring that employers are taking reasonable care of their troubled or potentially troubled employees. A recent publication by the Health and Safety Executive (1995), while acknowledging that there is no specific legislation on managing stress at work, uses two foundation laws to guide its advice:

1 employers have a duty . . . to ensure, so far as is reasonably practicable, that their workplaces are safe and healthy
2 employers are obliged to assess the nature and scale of risks to health in their workplace and base their control measures on it (1995: 8).

From these premisses the Executive draws the conclusion that employers have a legal responsibility to make sure that health is not at risk through unreasonable stress levels arising from work. They recommend a number of practical steps for employers to meet their legal duties in respect of stress:

- maintaining good management (which excludes inconsistency, indifference or bullying)
- creating an attitude to stress that takes it seriously where individuals are not punished for what can be an organizational issue
- ensuring that individuals know their job/jobs and have the skills to do it
- setting up stress awareness and stress management courses

- aiding line managers to work with their employees to get help for stress
- providing counselling services
- encouraging employees to consult doctors for help with stress

The history of workplace counselling unveils a progressive movement towards greater employee care on the part of employers. Today, those companies who utilize counselling provision, either internal or external, tend to combine counselling with a broad range of other helping facilities. Perhaps the next stage in workplace counselling is to see it as a helpful mode of organizational change and not just an aid to individuals within the organization.

The many faces of workplace counselling

It would be wrong to think of employee counselling as a uniform concept with the same meaning wherever it is applied. There is no single model covering all instances. Workplace counselling has a number of faces, each face with its own features. Five approaches are presented here (see below) but even they have nuances and differences within each approach which introduce new relationships and cause particular dynamics (e.g. each could be implemented on-site or off-site). The five approaches are:

---

1 Counselling for an organization that employs both counsellor and worker
2 Counselling for an organization where the counsellor is employed by an EAP provider
3 Counselling for an organization where the counsellor is employed to work with consumers of the organization
4 Counselling for an organization where the counsellor is employed to work with members of the public
5 Counselling for an organization which provides a range of specialist services to other organizations and individuals within organizations

---

The organization employs both counsellor and client
Various organizations employ counsellors, either full-time or part-time, to work with their employees. Called 'in-house counsellors' where they are full-time, such counsellors can be part of an existing department (e.g. personnel, human resources, occupational health) or work independently. What characterizes them and their relationships

is that both they and the employees with whom they work are paid by the same organization. However, even within this broad remit, there are variations.

Case example
Carole is employed by the British Council as their full-time staff counsellor. Her main task is to offer confidential counselling for all UK-based staff and those working overseas who have been appointed in London – approximately 1,800 employees. Family members may also use the service. Clients refer themselves by telephoning directly to Carole for an appointment. She is free to agree with individual clients the number of sessions required, how she will work with them and whether an outside referral would be appropriate. Carole works under the umbrella of Corporate Personnel in Staff Advisory Services and her line manager is the head of that unit. However, the sessions are held in complete confidence and her room/office is in a different part of the building. Carole produces an annual statistical report which includes number of clients, number of sessions and presenting problems. This is circulated to members of the Board of Management. The figures are used in conjunction with case-work to monitor general levels of stress and anxiety in the organization and Carole may liaise with management in departments where there seem to be particular difficulties.

Case example
Nigel, on the other hand, is a counsellor in private practice who is employed by a large company to work with their employees on a sessional basis. Employees approach their personnel officer (one is designated as the counselling contact) who gives the go-ahead for them to contact Nigel for counselling. Nigel is restricted to eight sessions with each client and has to negotiate with the personnel officer if there is a suggestion that this time be extended. Usually, with the agreement of both client and Nigel, a further eight sessions can be utilized. After this, clients need to pay for their own counselling. Each year Nigel draws up a set of statistics which he returns to the company showing number of clients, number of sessions, presenting problems, etc. He meets with the personnel officer to discuss findings and see how the organization can implement policies and strategies to overcome some of the issues brought by individual clients.

The counsellor is employed by an EAP provider

EAP providers have increased in Britain in the past few years, e.g. Employee Assistance Resources (EAR), Employeecare, Independent Counselling and Advisory Services (ICAS), Personal Performance Consultants (PPC). Organizations make contracts with EAP providers. They, in turn, employ counsellors, either full-time or part-time, to work with the employees of the various organizations.

Case example
Judy is an example. She is an affiliate to two different EAP providers who refer clients to her. She has a clear contract with the EAP provider whereby she is limited to eight sessions with each client. In particular instances this can be extended. Judy has no contact with the organization itself: the EAP provider does all negotiations. Judy is paid by the EAP, which is in turn paid by the organization.

What characterizes this approach is the fact that the counsellors are once-removed from the organization; all negotiations with the organization take place through the EAP provider.

The counsellor is employed to work with consumers

Some organizations employ counsellors (full-time and part-time) to see those who use their services (e.g. counselling services in educational institutes).

Case example
Margaret works in a student counselling service in higher education, which she and a colleague were instrumental in setting up. She is employed by the Institute to see students, and where appropriate staff, for counselling. The line manager is the Pro-Rector responsible for Student Services. The counselling team have their own counselling suite, and by and large are free to run the service as they choose. They assess all students who come to the service, work with a number of them themselves and refer others to counsellors on placement with the service (who are frequently counsellors in training). In order to ensure accountability both to their employers and to the students who come for counselling, they supervise all the placement counsellors themselves, thereby maintaining managerial responsibility for the counselling work carried out.
They are free to decide what is needed by clients, whether to

work with them short-term or long-term and can refer clients for outside medical and/or psychiatric help. Staff who come are usually referred for counselling outside the Institute, as they are also colleagues. They run a therapy group for students, listening skills workshops for both academic and non-academic staff and workshops for students, such as assertion training and sex education.

The counsellor is employed to work with the public
Some organizations set up counselling provision for needy members of the public. Often self-financing, sometimes within public services such as education or social work, this counselling targets particular groups in the community, for example, young people, children (Childline), abused women, etc.

Case example
Kevin is both director and counsellor with a youth counselling agency. The agency operates a drop-in centre for young people who can refer themselves for a variety of reasons, one of which is counselling. The centre also takes referrals from social workers, from schools, from parents and from GPs. The agency gets most of its funding from the Local Education Authority, employs two full-time staff both of whom are trained as counsellors, and has a number of volunteer counsellors whom they have trained themselves. Kevin has a small case-load of five young people whom he sees on a regular basis. He can work with them either short-term or long-term and is able to see two young people on a long-term (minimum of six months) basis.

Some organizations are set up to provide counselling training and counselling provision as their primary task (for example, the Tavistock Clinic, child and family consultation centres). What characterizes such establishments, and what differentiates them from organizations in the first approach considered above, is the fact that they have been established specifically to provide counselling. Sometimes profit-making, sometimes not, they employ counsellors to work with their clients. Kensington Consultation Centre (KCC) is an example of the former. Set up as a training establishment in systemic counselling and psychotherapy, and a private business, the organization sees clients and employs counsellors to work with them.

Counselling which provides a range of specialist services
Some organizations exist to provide a variety of services, one of
which is counselling, to other organizations. Counselling is often
combined with other services, for example, outplacement counselling
services, executive search, career counselling.

Case example
Cavendish Partners, who specialize in providing outplacement
services, work with clients referred by companies who are
offering them a redundancy package, to help them find a new
position. Counselling is part of that work (Carroll and Holloway, 1993), though combined with a number of other roles; for
example, CV writing and presentation skills. The firm is so
organized that each member supports every client's effort to find
the right job. Cavendish counsellors provide the teamwork to
advise on specialist subjects, conduct video role plays, give input
to brainstorming sessions and cover for the lead counsellor's
absence.

Counselling time is spent listening to clients before the launch
of the job-search campaign. Follow-up sessions, about every 10–
14 days, sometimes reveal the need for more coaching, counselling, modelling, etc. The multiple roles and relationships that
an outplacement counsellor has to perform make the task more
difficult, and counsellors have to be clear about the tasks, the
management of the role and how to integrate counselling with
other roles without damaging any of them.

Each of these different approaches has its own dynamics, its red-
flag points, its particular relationships. This book is concerned
principally with the first and second approaches discussed above.

What is workplace counselling?

A general definition of employee counselling includes one major
component: the organization pays for counselling provision for its
employees. By doing so, it creates a dynamic between three participants: organization, client/employee and counsellor. That dynamic
changes according to the relationships involved. Figure 1.1. shows
the relationship when both counsellor and client are full-time employees of the organization. In this situation, both client and counsellor are inevitably involved in the whole interplay of relationships,
politics and organizational culture that finds its way into, and moves
out of, the counselling room.

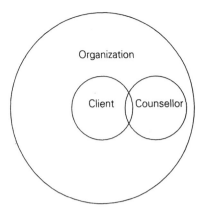

Figure 1.1 *Counsellor and client are full-time employees of the organization*

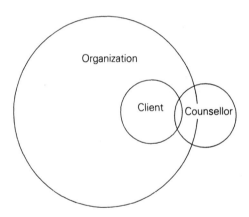

Figure 1.2 *The independent counsellor who works with employees of an organization*

Two other kinds of relationship occur when the counsellor is not a full-time employee and is either (a) independent of the organization but not employed by an EAP provider; or (b) employed by an EAP provider. Figure 1.2 shows the relationship when the counsellor is employed to work with employees as an independent agent: different negotiations need to take place here. Figure 1.3 shows the relationship when the counsellor is supplied by an EAP provider who contracts with the organization. The four main relationships at work within this overall system are:

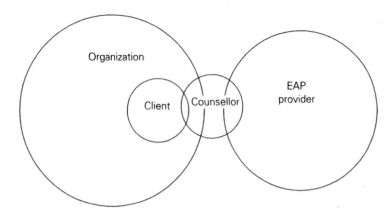

Figure 1.3   *The counsellor employed by an EAP provider*

1   The relationship between the employee/client and the organization.
2   The relationship between the employee/client and the counsellor from the EAP.
3   The relationship between the counsellor and the EAP provider.
4   The relationship between the organization and the EAP.

To these can be added:

5   The relationship between the employee/client and the EAP provider.
6   That between the counsellor who is employed by the EAP provider and the organization.

If we add a further system to this complex web of relationships, that of supervision where the supervisor may or may not be a member of the EAP provider, then we have:

7   Two further relationships: that of the supervisor to the counsellor and that of the supervisor to the organization.

Counsellors, by and large, need to take one of four stances when working with workplace clients, i.e. where clients are paid for by their employing organization:

1   *Counsellors who work as if the organization did not exist.* Counsellors taking this stance engage in counselling as if they were in private practice. They see their responsibilities to the individual client alone. Confidentiality is usually viewed as absolute within the counselling relationship, and clients, by and large, are empowered to deal with their problems, work-related or not. Under

no circumstances would the counsellor contact the organization. Many EAP counsellors work in this manner, leaving all contact with the organization to the EAP personnel.

2 *Counsellors who work as allies of the organization*, intentionally or unintentionally. Viewing their primary role as upholding the welfare of the organization, they see their task as ensuring that employees are working effectively. Such counsellors make it clear that they will refer back to the organization when issues emerge that affect it adversely. They view their counselling as connected to work-effectiveness and their role as supplying a forum in which clients can deal with whatever issues are blocking them from working most effectively.

3 *Counsellors who work as allies of the individual against the organization.* These counsellors consider themselves as advocates of the individual against the organization, which is sometimes viewed as the enemy. Often occurring in power organizations, where both client/employee and counsellor suffer similar repressive regimes, the tendency is for them to combine to combat abuse by the system. Counsellors will rarely contact the organization except to get a 'better deal' for their client.

4 *Counsellors who work at the interface between individual and organization.* Here, counsellors see their role as one of trying to mediate between varying needs. Counsellors move between the organization and the individual.

Before beginning their counselling work with employees, it is important that counsellors clarify their philosophy of intervention and state clearly how they see their role. Considering the organizational dynamics of their tasks may help them clarify responsibilities.

Criticisms of workplace counselling

Despite its many advantages for the workplace, criticisms have been levelled at introducing counselling as part of workplace life. Some see it becoming part of the politics of the organization and used by factions for their own ends. There is no doubt that politics play a large part in workplace life and, given the opportunity, certain individuals and departments would make capital out of owning or not owning the counselling service. I know one organization in the public sector which had great fights about where the staff counselling service should be sited. Human resources had thought up the idea and wanted it placed within their department. Personnel were adamant that it should be placed under their authority and occupational health argued that it seemed most at home close to the medical department. Territoriality (whose turf is it anyway?) can enter the fray, and the fight for space and scarce funds can make the counselling service an unwelcome competitor.

A further criticism of workplace counselling is that it can be too easily used by an organization to shelve its responsibilities towards employees, especially regarding stress. Magnus (1995) brought this to the public's attention recently:

> A report by the London Hazard Centre last year claimed that workplace counselling is being used to get companies off the hook over organisational factors which are the root source of stress. The report says counselling shifts the burden of having to cope with a stressful environment from the employer, who is creating that environment, to the individual, who is cracking under the strain.

Stress at Work: A Trade Union Response (Labour Research Department, 1994) is equally sceptical about the use of individual methods of managing stress and points to 19 international case studies to conclude that person-based methods of dealing with stress, such as counselling and relaxation techniques, were the least useful since they ignore the environment and do not deal with the causes of stress.

It is true that an organization can ignore its corporate responsibility by creating a section to represent what should be the human face of the organization. Sometimes counselling provision absolves the full organization from being compassionate (send them to the counselling service), from facing the implications of what it has done (and when we give them their redundancy notices we will whisk them off to the counselling service to deal with the bad news), and even from avoiding legal action (we have installed a counselling service to help people deal with stress). As Newton (1995) has pointed out, much writing on stress has emphasized the individual's responsibility for recognizing it and managing it, which takes away the focus from organizational responsibilities:

> There is no suggestion in this article (or in most others like it) that you should see work overload as a source of legitimate grievance, or say to your superiors that your workload is impossible. No, you should 'buckle down' and 'own your own stuff', but in our modern world this can be helped by stress management techniques such as time management, prioritizing or delegation. The likelihood that you may be so overloaded that time management and prioritizing are an irrelevance is not seriously considered. (Newton, 1995: 4)

From this perspective, Newton moves to criticize current theories of stress and the use of such provision as individual counselling as a method of managing it. In brief, he criticizes workplace counselling on two counts. First of all it individualizes problems (such as stress), decontextualizes them, and makes them apolitical. Newton looks to the history of EAPs to justify this and sees the Hawthorne Works where counselling was introduced in 1936, as a prime example of employee problems becoming individualized and made the responsibility of the individual. The second criticism of workplace counselling is its way of 'managing emotions' where it could be viewed as a method of organizational social control dictating to individual clients which emotions are permissible and which not within the organization. Newton summarizes this: 'Rather than expressing problems and grievances through a collective channel, through stress management practices they become individualized, a personal problem rather than one which may be shared by a large number of employees' (1995: 146).

Allied to this criticism, a further indictment of counselling in the workplace is that it becomes a tool of management. In the early days of EAPs in the US, especially when they were alcohol-related services, they were viewed with suspicion by unions and workers. Care has to be taken to publicize their confidentiality when counselling services are being introduced. In some organizations, there is great anxiety that going for counselling will be seen as a weakness that will take its toll on career and promotion. And there is some validity in the criticism that counselling helps individuals deal with emotions that ought to be more appropriately directed outwards towards injustice. Several years ago I was involved in a counselling project for unemployed people. The same criticism was raised; perhaps in offering counselling, justified emotions, such as anger and resentment, would be siphoned off rather than directed towards the injustices that caused the unemployed state in the first place.

A final criticism is that counselling is not integrated into the organization but remains on the outside. This can happen all too easily in certain kinds of companies which relegate counselling to the periphery of the organization. If inadequately introduced, the counselling service itself can become dysfunctional. On the other hand, over-involvement of the organization in its counselling service can lead to its becoming a form of social control. In their critique of Western Electric's counselling service, written in 1951, Wilensky and Wilensky make this point quite dramatically: 'The company has developed a network of lower-level functionaries to drain off hostility and has integrated into its structure those forces which represent a potential challenge to its control over the worker' (1951: 280).

It is important to take the criticisms of workplace counselling seriously and to isolate the underlying philosophies that drive the implementation of counselling services. It is naïve to see them automatically as of value to employees. Organizations are certainly not beyond introducing counselling to control their employees or above making organizational problems the responsibility of individual employees. Deverall (forthcoming) suggests that if 10 per cent of personnel in an organization need counselling then the organization is itself in need of help and that individual counselling may be a diversion from the real organizational problems.

Workplace counselling in Britain

In the UK in 1971 the British Institute of Management, from its survey of 200 firms, discovered that 5 per cent offered some form of personal counselling to employees. Orlans and Shipley (1983) surveyed 35 large UK organizations and discovered that all but three had occupational health facilities and, whereas nurses employed within these departments had undergone short-term counselling training, there was not a single case where extensive counselling training had been provided.

Two later surveys (Hoskinson and Reddy, 1989; Reddy, 1993b) indicate that counselling provision in Britain has grown recently. Conclusions drawn from the 1993 survey are quite impressive:

- From 400 replies from companies, 85 per cent saw themselves as providing some form of counselling service.
- About twice as many organizations offer in-house counselling and related activities as those that depend on external counselling provision.
- Nearly 60 per cent of companies provide stress counselling by personnel departments or line managers, or both. The other 40 per cent offer stress counselling in addition or as an alternative.
- EAP have been adopted by some 4 per cent of UK companies. This represents a sharp increase since the 1989 Report. Most of the growth took place during 1992. Indications are that total figures will double over the next twelve months. (Reddy, 1993b)

One of the few pieces of research on counselling in industry was conducted within the Post Office (Cooper et al., 1990). Clients using the counselling service completed a set of questionnaires at their first interview and a second set once their case had been concluded by the counsellor. The results are a clear indication of the value of counselling. 'After counselling, significant improvements are shown on all of these dimensions, indicating significant improvements in clients' mental well-being . . . finally, in terms of sickness absence, the average number of days lost decreases after counselling' (1990: 10).

Overall, there is a growing awareness that it makes practical, humane and economic sense to provide some counselling forum where employees can deal with their personal and professional problems. How this is done varies widely from the use of personnel or welfare officers within the company to the use of in-house counsellors or EAPs, either internally or externally, or both.

EAP programmes in Britain are now well established: Reddy (1993b: 11) summarizes the British scene *vis-à-vis* counselling:

> The evidence from G. Ahern's survey-report is that top management in the UK are aware of counselling but not of the direct relationship of its contribution to business performance in commercial terms.
>
> More than 80 per cent of companies offer counselling for stress in one way or another to their employees. About half of this is resourced externally.
>
> Counselling is currently used more in a reactive than proactive mode. It is introduced on an 'as needed' basis in response to a particular situation or a particular individual.
>
> The requirement is resourced as far as possible through existing staff and by contracting out the rest on an ad hoc basis.
>
> The main obstacles to the development of counselling are said to be budgetary (which means that the cost-benefit equation is not persuasive or understood): and the belief that counselling is counter-culture (which means either that a particular organisation is genuinely not ready for it or that counselling itself is not fully understood).

The emphasis on workplace counselling has impelled Reddy (1993a: 48) to pronounce that 'the centre of gravity of the counselling universe is moving inexorably to the workplace.' Even though counsellors, psychotherapists and counselling psychologists have historically had little involvement in the workplace, there is evidence that that involvement is increasing to such an extent that Gerstein and Shullman (1992) have introduced a new subspeciality within counselling psychology which they name 'organisational counseling psychology'.

While workplace counselling seems to be increasing, with EAPs being used as internal and external provision, there are some worrying conclusions from the Health and Safety Executive funded project on the assessment of UK EAPs and workplace counselling by Highley and Cooper (n.d.). The full publication of this report is due in 1996. However, the key findings are available and some of these make for reflective reading:

- Some 56 per cent of organizations report that there is not enough *independent* advice about workplace counselling available.
- Only 30 per cent of companies carry out any form of needs analysis or stress audit before deciding to introduce counselling.

- Some 70 per cent of the providers' counsellor networks consist of 'counsellors', with only a minority being professionally qualified in some other profession, e.g. clinical psychology.
- Of counsellors surveyed, 11 per cent hold no formal counselling qualifications, and a further 11 per cent hold only a basic Certificate in Counselling. A number of these counsellors state that they are working between 10 and 40 hours per week, carrying out EAP counselling, despite having no formal counselling qualifications.
- The amount of training received from providers is rated by 45 per cent of counsellors as almost non-existent, and by a further 36 per cent as average.
- Eight out of 10 counsellors are concerned about the service the client is receiving, particularly in relation to certain EAP providers who are considered to be providing a 'poor service' for the client, the counsellor and the client organization.
- Most providers, worryingly, do not give counsellors information about client companies, as a matter of course.

These results indicate that there is a lot of work to be done to professionalize workplace counselling in Britain and that perhaps the standards of delivery have not kept up with the demand for counselling provision.

2
Models of Workplace Counselling

Organizations have not quite known where to put this stranger in their midst. A growing number recognise its value. Yet how to position the counselling function, where and how to link it into other organization processes, whilst maintaining its independence, is still unclear to many. Not knowing how to position counselling, many organizations have it 'outside'. From there, it is unable to reach or address many of the issues we raise in this book.

J. Summerfield and L. van Oudtshoorn,
Counselling in the Workplace

Various models portray the tasks and roles of counsellors in the workplace. The following is not an exhaustive list, nor indeed do models exclude each other. It is possible that a number of these can be combined; in fact, it could be said that the effective employee counsellor has access to a range of models applicable to different clients and different situations. The nine models presented here are:

1 Counselling-orientation models
2 Brief-therapy models
3 Problem-focused models
4 Work-orientated models
5 Manager-based models
6 Externally based models
7 Internally based models
8 Welfare-based models
9 Organizational-change models

This chapter will briefly consider each of these models, with more concentration on the organizational-change model as a possible paradigm for the future.

Counselling-orientation models

The counselling-orientation model is characterized by its use of a counselling approach as the key factor in what is offered to employee clients. Counsellors, by and large, subscribe to or are affiliated to, and often trained in, a particular therapeutic approach which they use when working with organizational clients. Historically, this has probably been the most common way of engaging in employee counselling. Individual counsellors were appointed by companies who were more concerned with the individual appointed than the theoretical orientation from which they emerged. Many of these counsellors adapted their counselling theories, skills and practice to workplace counselling.

Subscribing to a particular counselling orientation normally means accepting a specific view of human nature and an explanation of why individuals behave the way they do. This, in turn, leads logically to an assessment congruent with the counselling approach and interventions designed to bring about change. Figure 2.1 gives a brief overview of how behaviours are viewed by various counselling perspectives (Antoniou, 1995). Research in the US (Cunningham, 1994) and in Britain (Carroll, 1994) came to the same conclusions, that EAP practitioners and in-house counsellors, despite being allied to original individual counselling orientations, developed an eclectic style in their work. Both sets of counsellors had become eclectic in response to the demands of the particular job as employee counsellors; for example, the wide range of clients, the number of issues brought, the time-frames available in which they could work.

Several authors have taken particular counselling orientations and reviewed how they might apply in the workplace; for example, cognitive-behavioural therapy (Webb, 1990); neuro-linguistic programming (NLP) (Sanders, 1990); psychodynamic (Gray, 1984a); rational emotive (Gordon and Dryden, 1989); and transactional analysis (Hay, 1989). Summerfield and van Oudtshoorn (1995: 86) have reviewed briefly six counselling theories and looked at their usefulness/non-usefulness in the workplace; for example, they consider that Rogerian counselling is useful in creating new relationships and in its use of respect, empathy and genuineness, but not useful in that it is not focused on short-term problem-solving, is entirely client-led and uses open-ended contracts. Though too brief to do full justice to different counselling orientations, their work highlights the need to evaluate counselling models critically as they are adapted to workplace counselling.

Most counsellors who use particular counselling approaches apply their counselling theory within organizations in the same way as they do when practising independently. There is some understanding of how organizations are assessed using a particular counselling model. For example, Kets de Vries and Miller (1984) have used a psychoanalytic approach to designate different types of organizations, and

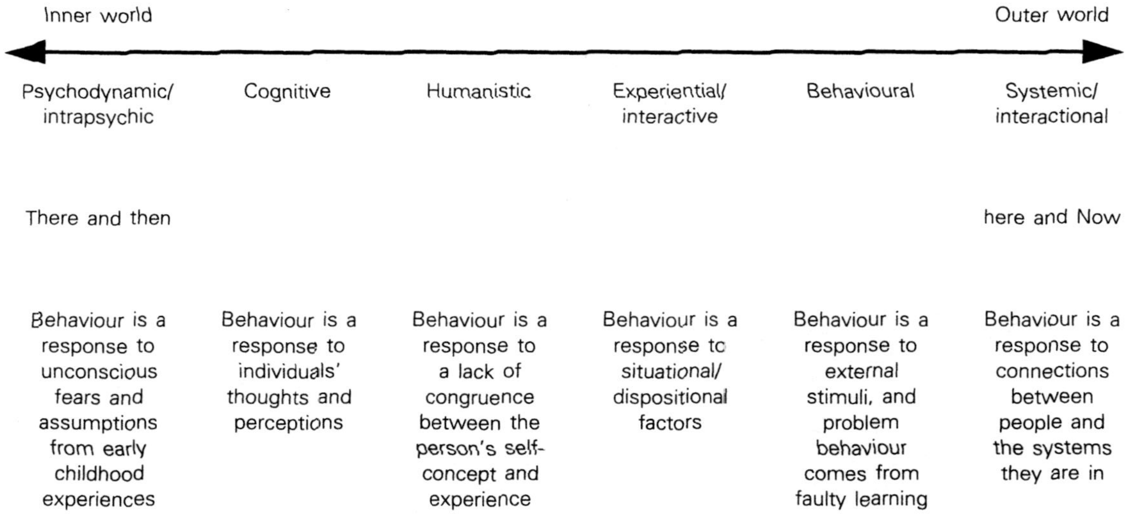

Inner world				Outer world
Psychodynamic/ intrapsychic	Cognitive	Humanistic	Experiential/ interactive	Behavioural	Systemic/ interactional
There and then				here and Now
Behaviour is a response to unconscious fears and assumptions from early childhood experiences	Behaviour is a response to individuals' thoughts and perceptions	Behaviour is a response to a lack of congruence between the person's self-concept and experience	Behaviour is a response to situational/ dispositional factors	Behaviour is a response to external stimuli, and problem behaviour comes from faulty learning	Behaviour is a response to connections between people and the systems they are in

Figure 2.1 *Counselling approaches and behaviour (from Antoniou, 1995)*

Critchley and Casey (1989) have applied the Gestalt model to explain how organizations get stuck at various levels of their development; Stein and Hollwitz (1992) have looked at organizations through a Jungian perspective, and Morris (1993) has adapted rational emotive therapy as a paradigm for organizations. However, most counselling orientations do not have such a typology. Their main interest is still focused almost exclusively on individuals and the organizational dimensions of counselling work are largely ignored.

Brief-therapy models

There is no doubt that brief therapy is the norm in employee counselling. Carroll (1994), in her interviews with employee counsellors in the private sector in Britain, discovered that all her interviewees (12 counsellors from 12 different organizations) saw clients on average for between one and eight sessions. Most EAP practitioners contract for around six to eight sessions with clients. The EAPA *UK Standards of Practice and Professional Guidelines for Employee Assistance Programmes* (1995) sees brief counselling as the norm and builds it into the definition of an EAP counsellor: 'The work of an EAP counsellor is that of crisis intervention, assessment and short-term counselling of the individual clients who are referred to the programme' (1995: 18). However, the choice of brief therapy in the workplace may be guided more by the economics of the situation rather than by client need. It is difficult to know if brief therapy is espoused because of a belief in its value *per se* or whether other factors (waiting lists, number of counsellors, fear of the client spending too much time away from work) play a part in dictating its usage.

Brief therapy has been around for some time and counsellors can be divided into two groups: those that take a particular counselling orientation and apply it in a focused number of sessions, and those that use brief therapy as an approach in its own right not tied to specific counselling theories. In respect of the first, Thorne has become a recent convert to the former using person-centred approaches in an educational setting (Mearns, 1995), which could easily be adapted to the workplace. His comments are worth considering:

> in the face of an ever-escalating waiting list in the university counselling service of which I am director, I found myself pursuing a very heretical line of thought. Whether through inspiration or desperation I do not know, but I dared to think the unthinkable. Could it be, I wondered, that there were some prospective clients for whom short-term counselling was not only a possible option but the most desirable and potentially the most effective? I was strengthened in this wayward reflection by the knowledge that the average number of sessions for clients using the Counselling

Service was only five and that some seemed to go on their way rejoicing after a mere two or three meetings. (Mearns, 1995: 61)

However, as Thorne points out, brief therapy (which he calls 'focused counselling') is not suitable for all clients. Alongside this, there has been an increase in the number of theorists who have devised brief-therapy formats in their own right not particularly tied to individual counselling approaches (see, for example, the work of de Shazer called 'solution-focused brief therapy', 1985).

Occasionally, the impression is given in workplace counselling that brief therapy is dictated by authorities who are still anxious that clients will abuse counselling provision. Some managers fantasize that, given the opportunity, large amounts of time will be spent in personal counselling that neither benefits the organization nor the department. Keeping it short term allays this fear.

For whatever reasons, brief counselling plays a large part in workplace counselling which explains why those who work long term find it difficult to apply their counselling in this context. I supervise a psychodynamic counsellor, who was an affiliate for an EAP, who continually struggled with the eight sessions she was given to work with employees. Inevitably, her diagnosis and way of intervening unravelled issues that needed longer-term work.

Problem-focused models

The problem-focused model of counselling sees the counsellor's role as helping individuals to work with the immediate problems they bring. Whereas these problems may not be entirely work-based, counselling confines itself to working with the immediate issue. One model of this is contained in a training manual for counsellors in the workplace:

- formulate problem
- generate solution
- action plan

Several problem-focused models of counselling are available. Nelson-Jones (1995) developed DASIE, a five-stage model in what he calls 'lifeskills counselling'. The five stages comprise a very helpful problem-solving methodology:

D Develop the relationship, identify and clarify problem(s)
A Assess problem(s) and redefine in skills terms
S State working goals and plan interventions
I Intervene to develop self-helping skills
E End and consolidate self-helping skills

This model is practical and applicable. In this case it is based on a theoretical position that 'most problems brought to helpers are educational in nature' but it can also be used without such a belief. Rather, some workplace counsellors adopt the problem-focused approach because of its immediacy to the issue and its aim of helping employees be more effective as quickly as possible.

Noreen Tehrani (1995) has offered a model of dealing with trauma or stress in the Post Office which could also be seen as a problem-solving method, in this case instances of violence. Folkman and Lazarus (1980) have suggested that problem-focused forms of counselling are more effective in the workplace than are emotion-focused approaches.

Problem-focused counselling emerges for a number of reasons: the limited amount of time counsellors can provide to clients, the number of counsellors available to service a company, the theoretical background from which counsellors emerge, and organizational constraints, e.g. finance. However, problem-solving approaches to counselling are a fairly well-established perspective in their own right and, like brief therapy, will no doubt play a large part in workplace counselling. Many employees come because of a particular issue that may need a single session. They will not thank the counsellor for a psychoanalytic approach that sees their problem as symptomatic of deeper issues.

Work-orientated models

The work-orientated model of counselling is named because it is centred solely on issues blocking an individual in his or her work. Counselling confines itself to the issues interfering with effective employment. Some theorists consider that workplace counselling should only focus on workplace problems and not spend time in other areas. Yeager (1983) is very definite that counselling in the organizational setting is different from counselling in other contexts. 'The approach to assessment in the organisational setting is different than the usual diagnostic clinical testing . . . for a practitioner to approach an organisational context case from the point of view of traditional therapeutic criteria of wellness is inappropriate' (1983: 133). For him, the criteria of counselling are 'performance and productivity' and the role of the counsellor is to get the client/employee fit and ready for work. This, he suggests rather strongly, is not the place to help clients 'self-actualize', or work on personal problems not related to the workplace but 'the main criteria for therapy in the business context is that the method must fix the performance problem and it must fix it fast' (p. 137). The emphasis here is on work performance and a minimalist approach to getting the employee back to work as quickly as possible.

Work-orientated models of counselling pinpoint the immediate problem as a workplace issue and work with it. They do not spend time on the underlying areas of why problems exist, nor are they interested in problems/issues that are not related to the workplace. Their aim is to facilitate the individual to overcome workplace problems and move back to work as quickly as possible.

This is an attractive counselling model for managers who want value for money and want to think that time spent in counselling is for the welfare of the organization through the individual. However, it is not always easy, in practice, to differentiate between what is a workplace problem and what is a personal problem not related to work.

Manager-based models

Though not widespread, there is a tendency in some organizations to view managers as quasi-counsellors for their staff. Since much managerial time and many of their tasks involve working with and managing people (Lane, 1990; Income Data Services, 1992), it is a short step to propel them into the counselling role. Reddy (1993a) has suggested that when managers are using their counselling skills they ought to be recognized as counsellors. And Megranahan (1989a), while warning about the use of clear boundaries, sees no reason why managers should not be viewed as counsellors. Blurring of the boundaries between managerial and counselling roles has continued. In a recent contribution to this field, Redman (1995) sees managers as ongoing counsellors. In his introduction, counselling is regarded as part of everyday life, 'We have all been counselled at some time. We have all counselled somebody else. It probably hasn't been called that, it was just something that happened as part of two people talking . . . if you are reading this book, you are probably a manager and you have probably realised that you do some counselling' (1995: 11). In much the same vein, it could be argued that we are all doctors because we have patched up a wound, all lawyers because we have given legal advice, all car mechanics because we have changed a wheel on our car. Obviously, this is ridiculous and a distinction needs to be made between when we are being helpful in some form and when we are formally being counsellors, doctors, etc.

Nixon and Carroll (1994) have argued strongly against managers taking on a formal counselling role. Not only does it cross boundaries, in their view, but it puts employees in an impossible situation: asking, on one hand, that they share personal issues with their manager, and, on the other, that they be ready for appraisal *vis-à-vis* their careers with the same manager. In short, asking managers to be counsellors creates role conflicts for them and confusing responsibilities for employees. Using interpersonal and communication skills, which are often designated as counselling skills but are in fact generic relationship skills, are part and parcel of all interactive situations whether these be parent/child, between spouses, manager/ employee, etc. The Institute for Personnel Management *Statement on Counselling in the Workplace* has tried to face this issue by explaining that 'Much workplace counselling is not counselling in the modern definition of the term but relates to situations which require the use of counselling skills' (1992: 1).

With the introduction of counselling training for personnel officers, human resource officers, managers, and a host of other individuals in industry and public services, there is the tendency for people to combine a number of roles with employees. This gives rise to innumerable problems. It is small wonder that legislation in the US forbids managers to enter into counselling with their subordinates. With good reason. On the other hand, training in counselling skills for managers helps them to recognize signs of disturbance in employees and no doubt provides valuable aids in their managerial and personal roles (Martin, 1994).

Differences have been drawn between counselling professionally, the use of counselling skills, and the employment of counselling as one role among many. This distinction is used to indicate what managers can and cannot do in respect of their 'counselling' with employees. The significance of these differences is highlighted by the fact that the British Association for Counselling has different ethical codes for the first two. Manager-based models of workplace counselling, in my view, need to treated with caution. Summerfield and van Oudtshoorn's (1995) section on the role of the manager/human resource professional in counselling provision recommends training in counselling skills as a way of helping them to recognize what is happening as well as understanding the limitations of what they can offer within the counselling role.

Externally based models

Externally based models of counselling are those brought in, and bought in, from outside the organization. Usually in the form of an EAP, they are administered and organized from outside. The format used can be any of the above models, or indeed mixtures of them, since EAP providers generally do not employ counsellors on the basis of their counselling orientation. Box 2.1 outlines some of the

Box 2.1 *Strengths and weaknesses of external
counselling services*

Strengths	Weaknesses
● Not part of the politics of the organization	● May not be flexible in what they offer
● Can challenge what is taken for granted within the company	● Have to make a profit
● Can offer training as well as counselling	● May not adapt easily to individual companies
● Can offer clear confidentiality	● Can unwittingly get involved in the politics of the organization
● Can provide a range of services	● May not understand the culture of the organization
● Can offer a number of counsellors with different skills, backgrounds etc.	● May be seen as 'outsiders' by potential clients
● The organization is not responsible for malpractice of counsellors	● May not be able to educate the system to what counselling means
	● Their counsellors may not have had experience of workplace counselling
	● The counsellors may know nothing about the organization from which clients come

strengths and weaknesses of externally based models of counselling: it must be remembered that these strengths and weaknesses can vary according to context and what is a strength here could be a weakness elsewhere. Furthermore, the strengths and weaknesses outlined do not apply to all EAPs and many providers have overcome the weaknesses that are posited here as potential.

There are several formats of external counselling provision used by organizations: some employ established EAPs, others set up an internal EAP, others again opt for employing individuals to work on a sessional basis with employees. Jones (1985: 11) has outlined the characteristics of several EAP programmes:

1 Full-service programmes
   - comprehensive services
   - employees and dependants
   - retirees and dependants
   - disabled and dependants
   - any kind of problem
   - unlimited utilization
   - no cost to utilizer
   - 24 hours per day, seven days a week
   - live answering service, pagers
   - approximately 40 per cent of the utilizers referred out
   - approximately 30 per cent who do not need extensive care or who are not ready to make a commitment to do anything about their problem
   - voluntary
   - confidential
   - professional clinicians as counsellors
   - follow-up and aftercare
   - outreach
   - supervisory training
   - employee orientation
2 Limited utilization programmes
   - provide approximately five to eight free sessions but charge the individual or third person carrier for anything beyond that
   - this can be a fee-for-service arrangement
3 Information and referral-only programmes
   - no face-to-face counselling
   - referrals made by telephone
   - little or no follow-up

Externally based models of workplace counselling have increased over the past decade and it is anticipated that they will continue to increase over the next few years.

Internally based models

In-house counselling provision is the norm in a number of companies (see Reddy, 1993b). A part-time or full-time counsellor, or in some instances a team of counsellors, is employed to work with employees. The counselling service can be part of an already-existing department or an independent unit in its own right. Box 2.2 shows potential strengths and weaknesses of internally based counselling.

Box 2.2 *Strengths and weaknesses of internal counselling services*

Strengths	Weaknesses
• Counsellor is in touch with the culture of the company	• Counsellor can be more subjective in his/her assessments
• Can make assessments in the light of the various organizational systems	• Can be vulnerable if reorganization takes place
• Counsellor has access to the formal and informal structures of the organization	• Counsellor can get pulled very easily into identifying with either the organization or the individual
• Can build up great credibility for the counselling service	• Counsellor can be identified by employees with management and vice versa
• Is able to get feedback into the system from the counselling work	• Can be isolated
• Can adapt counselling work to organizational needs	• Can be used by management to do its 'dirty work'
• Has flexibility to adapt to client needs	• Counsellor is involved in politics of the organization
• Can provide mediation	• Can be used by individuals against the organization
• Is a visible, human face	• More difficult to maintain confidentiality: employees may be worried about leakage of personal information
• Can provide multiple roles	

In-house counselling provision can be set up in a variety of ways: an in-house EAP, with a team of counsellors, with an individual counsellor, as within a particular department, as outside all departments, as part-time or full-time. Internal and external counselling provision can be combined within one organization. Summerfield and van Oudtshoorn (1995), while arguing for the advantages of internally based counselling services in the workplace, present an integrated model combining internal and external provision using the Post Office as an example of this integration.

Welfare-based models

Welfare-based models of counselling combine a number of roles with employees, one of which is counselling. Welfare officers have traditionally been employed in a number of organizations to fulfil several tasks depending on client needs: befriending, information-giving, advocate, home-visiting during sickness, giving legal and financial advice, advising on a range of topics, counselling. Some organizations still have welfare officers (the Civil Service, the Metropolitan Police). Welfare-based models of counselling have been the predecessors of counselling provision in the workplace. Such models were more social work based, seeing counselling as one of many roles enacted with employees. Their strength is their ability to provide a range of interventions, one of which may be counselling. Their limitations depend on the abilities of the welfare officer to work across roles.

Organizational-change models

Gray (1984a: 163) addresses 'counselling which is targeted on the organisation as a whole though is mainly implemented via work with individuals and groups'. It is unclear what is meant by this, whether organizational change is the ultimate aim of individual/ group counselling, or that the result of individual/group counselling will emerge in benefits for the organization. However, it is important to begin to think of counselling in organizational settings as not just directly valuable to the individual and indirectly of benefit to the organization. Perhaps beginning to integrate counselling more specifically into organizational growth, development and, in particular, transition would be a valuable asset to organizations. Critchley and Casey (1989: 11) have found this helpful: 'We do, however, suggest that one discipline may offer another a fresh way of seeing old problems. Just as chemistry is helping physics, and mathematics is helping family therapy, so we find psychotherapy helping organization change.'

In this chapter, organizational-change models of counselling will be considered under three headings: (a) how counselling can change organizational culture; (b) parallel process in organizations; and (c) moving upstream helping.

How counselling can change organizational culture

It was found in a major study of a US bank that the relationship between the bank's service staff and its customers was repeated in the relationship between supervisors and service staff and was repeated in the relationship between top management and supervisors. It is probable, although the research did not go that far, that the pattern was repeated again between the HQ of the bank and its branches. (Hampden-Turner, 1994: 15)

Hampden-Turner goes on to describe corporate culture as a 'hologram' in that all parts of the whole are contained within each segment. This is a fascinating concept when applied to organizations. Relationships will be repeated throughout the organization. Whereas the example above indicates that the relationships moved one-way, it is highly probable that it is bi-directional: individuals, teams and departments deal with others as they have been dealt with, they pass on the relationship either to their customers or to their bosses. One person can make a difference in an organization and can contest the myths and assumptions taken for granted by others.

This I discovered several years ago when I was asked to work with some students in a school. The students were cynical, bored and aggressive and it came as no surprise to find them being treated as less than human by some of the staff. I felt my work was continually impaired by the culture, in which they were expected to be 'hormonally disturbed' (as the headteacher described all teenagers). Several years later, I was invited back to the same school and I entered with trepidation based on my past experience. To my astonishment, and delight, the atmosphere was totally different. I was met with a group of delightful and creative young men and women who were enthusiastic, energetic, challenging and cooperative. It only took me an hour to discover the difference. A new chaplain, a young man, had been appointed to the school about two years previously. With him came a new atmosphere and, because he was not a teaching member of staff, he was able to question some of the myths. He also challenged the culture and slowly began to help it change. He was interpersonally very skilled, very person-centred and non-rigid, trusting the students, and creative in helping them learn. Single-handed, I believe, he had moved the school from one culture to another.

A counselling service can do the same. Counselling services can change cultures because they introduce other ways of working with people and other perspectives for viewing people in relation to organizations and each other. Furthermore, because they work principally in the area of change, they can offer viewpoints on how change takes place, how to facilitate it, and how to deal with the blocks within individuals and groups that make change difficult. Deverall (forthcoming) has used the term 'counselling consultant' to explain how counsellors can be involved in organizational change.

The following are ways in which counselling can be used as a form of organizational change.

(1) *Providing a forum* where people are held, listened to, trusted, respected and helped to make life-growing decisions. Presenting the 'people' side of the workplace as essential, counselling speaks to values and the importance of people within work. This should take place not just in the counselling service but throughout the organization. Humanizing the workplace is essential and counselling understands and practices the necessary values.

(2) *Moving back into the organization to set up training* that will solve some of the problems that are caused by undeveloped management or ineffective systems. Training also in health and health-related issues: stress management, relaxation, time management etc. Educating the organization to eliminate poor practice that causes human distress can bring about change within the organization itself.

(3) *Consulting with managers* about ways of working with individuals and groups within the organization. Egan (1994) has referred to 'the good, the bad, the ugly, and the ambiguous' as examples of personal styles in organizations and recommended that managers learn how to work with such people. Here counsellors can help. With an understanding of personality, how personalities interact, when personalities are dysfunctional, when personality help is needed, they can create a learning organization alert to developing its people. Counsellors can help managers and directors work more effectively with their teams and departments. Creating more efficient sub-systems within the organization can facilitate transition and change.

(4) *Managing individual and organizational change and transitions.* Counsellors are adept at handling change: it is their stock in trade. Understanding the dynamics of transition, they have been compared to mid-wives who facilitate new births, novel beginnings. They know about the loss of letting go, being confused as change progresses, and the difficulty of integrating a new way of being into a old lifestyle. This can be an invaluable asset to the workplace today where change is a matter of course rather than the exception.

Several authors have pointed out the similarities between the way individuals handle loss and the way organizations do (White, 1993). The 'flexible' organization is the one that looks likely to thrive in the modern world. 'Flexibility' is the counsellor's middle name. Of all the characteristics mined from studies on people who make good counsellors, the one consistent feature was 'the ability to deal with ambiguity' (Leddick, private communication).

(5) *Helping with bad news.* Giving bad news has become a commonplace in organizations whether it is about career, redundancy, organizational change, etc. Often this is poorly done by managers who feel guilty about doing it, are not skilled in communication, and have few competencies in allowing employees to deal with their emotional reactions. Helping the organization work with the negative aspects of the workplace can be a culture change and introduce new beliefs into the workplace, e.g. we do not deny bad news in our organization, we give bad news clearly and help our employees deal with it.

(6) *Looking after those made redundant* and those left behind after redundancy. Outplacement counsellors are aware of the damage done to long-serving and dedicated employees by the way they have been made redundant and often how little help is given at that time, either psychologically or emotionally.

(7) *Modelling professional relationships for the organization.* As models of boundary-keeping, as exemplars in ethical and professional consistency, counsellors teach the organization about professional relationships in the workplace. Their service is in direct opposition to much of organizational life which is rife with rumour, scandal, trivialization. 'A call to conscience' reminds the workplace that there are human responsibilities about respect for people, compassion and concern, and at the same time an ability to challenge and bring out unused potential.

(8) *Empowering individuals and groups within the organization.* Much counselling revolves around helping individuals to access and use their own power to solve their problems. Again, this can be a model for organizational life: that management enables the workforce to get in touch with its power and use it effectively and efficiently for work objectives. Counselling has much to offer managers on how to help employees activate their own unused power and potential, how to be non-directive when needed, facilitative when required, and challenging when perceived to be the best way forward. The counselling service will be a model of autonomy, assertiveness, flexibility and decision-making: these are what counsellors are trained to help individuals with. And why not organizations? It is a pity, as Reddy (1993b) points out, that so

many benefiting from counselling are those who are leaving the organization and not those who are developing within it.

(9) *Creating awareness of individual differences.* High on the agenda in counselling training is the awareness that people are the same and different. Being aware of individual differences is a sign of progress in counsellor training. Differences of gender, age, sexual orientation, race, culture and religion all make us aware of the richness of human life. We do not treat people the same: they are different and deserve to be treated differently. This is not about inequality but a deep realization that people have different needs. Workplaces often view people simply as workers.

(10) Helping organizations grow and change by teaching them about *the value of contexts.* Contexts make a difference or, as Bateson (1979) said, 'contexts give meaning'. Understanding the contextual issues gives us insight into what is happening. Systemic understanding helps us realize that we are tied together as human beings, our behaviours affect one another, and change in one section of a company can affect, for better or worse, change in another part of the same organization.

(11) Using counselling modes and methods to *assess and understand individual, group and organizational dynamics* can be a further help to organizational change. Critchley and Casey (1989) have used the Gestalt cycle to understand how blocks occur in organizations; Stein and Hollwitz (1992) have applied Jungian concepts to the workplace; and there are various excellent works on how psychodynamic concepts can facilitate organizational change (Hirschhorn and Barnett, 1992; Obholzer and Roberts, 1994).

These are several ways in which counsellors, and counselling services, in the workplace can dynamically affect the organizations of which they are a part. Cole (1988) has suggested a five-stage model connecting counselling and organizational change:

Phase 1:   Interview individuals with the express purpose of seeing how their usefulness to the organization could be increased.
Phase 2:   Individual counselling for managers.
Phase 3:   Influencing the psychological tone of the organization through small group meetings.
Phase 4:   Team building.
Phase 5:   Cultural change programme for managers to help them build an environment where employees could be strengthened.

Most counsellors in organizations underestimate their abilities to bring about organizational change and are content to work solely with individuals. It is a pity. The whole history of counselling has been taken up with understanding people, empowering them, relating to them in respectful ways, creating autonomy and assertiveness, helping them manage change, make decisions, prepare for the future and live together. Freud summed it up when he saw the meaning of life as 'to love and work'. Hillman (1983) has an apt comment on this when he writes, 'It seems to me we have forgotten half of what he said. Work. We have been talking of what goes wrong with love for eighty years. But what about what goes wrong with work, where has that been discussed?' Figure 2.2 shows the ways in which counselling provision can be integrated into an organization and how it can be a more potent force for organizational change.

Parallel process
One of the most powerful concepts I have come across to help view how counselling might affect an organization is that of *parallel process*. Parallel process (other terms used are 'reflective or reflection process', 'mirroring', 'parallel re-enactment') describes how aspects of one relationship are expressed in another relationship. The example given above by Hampden-Turner (1994) is a good illustration of parallel process: the relationship between staff and customers repeated in the relationship between staff and management. In the early literature, parallel process was seen as a form of transference with the features of transference: an unconscious process, uni-directional, and usually not beneficial to the relationship. However, it does not have to be seen in this way.

So why does parallel process take place? Several reasons are offered. Some view it as a process of communication when words cannot be used: people act out what they cannot say. When someone hurts me I get angry with a friend as a way of acting out one relationship in another. When an employee is angry with a manager she may sabotage an account with a client, unconsciously. She is acting out her anger. Parallel process could also be a way of learning: if the manager is aggressive with an employee then the employee becomes aggressive with a client. They are trying to learn, it is thought, how to deal with aggressive situations. A third explanation is about concealment rather than communication (Bromberg, 1982): managers get anxious about their work and try to hide this anxiety, which then is revealed by acting out the whole process. Doehrman (1976) has reviewed the unequal relationship between two sets of participants as a possible reason for 'mirroring', especially when issues of authority and power emerge.

Applying the notion of parallel process to organizations can help understand some of the dynamics and can provide a method of

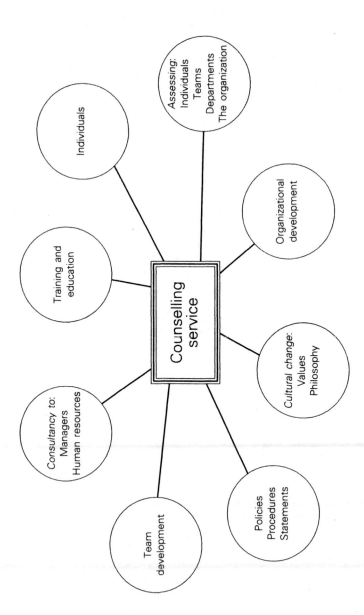

Figure 2.2   *Integrating counselling into an organization*

introducing change (Crandall and Allen, 1982; McLeod, 1993; Hampden-Turner, 1994). Hampden-Turner (1994) tells the changing story of British Airways, documenting the dramatic change in its culture. He concludes, 'By learning to care for its own staff, BA generated the pattern of a more caring culture for the enjoyment of its passengers and the profit of the airline' (1994: 113), and shows the correspondence between levels of the system: 'Hence a skilful and kind encounter between the airline stewardess and a frightened passenger is a microcosm of how the stewardess has herself been treated, which, in turn, is part of a more general attitude towards empowering cabin crews to serve customers better' (p. 15).

Like a cloud, corporate culture descends on the organization and infiltrates every aspect of relationships. Unconsciously, individuals and groups treat each other as they have been treated. And, without anyone realizing it, a cycle or circle of predefined patterns of relating diffuses the organization. This can happen in a school, a company, a diocese, a family and between a couple. We pick up and pass on patterns of relating relevant to this culture. Writers on organizational culture give numerous examples of how relationship patterns move throughout a company.When employees are cared for, they in turn care for others; when abused, they pass on the abuse.

Moving upstream
Several authors have criticized counselling for spending too much time with the individual and not being 'socially' minded (Egan and Cowan, 1979; Smail, 1987). What I want to argue here is that it is not an 'either/or' situation but 'both/and'. Yes, we need to move 'upstream' to fashion the kinds of organizations, and indeed society, that means casualties do not take place. On the other hand, we need to stay 'downstream' and continue to rescue those who have been harmed by systems. In many ways, working as counsellors in organizations is a way of combining both: helping those who have personal problems and at the same time helping create the kind of organizational culture that cares for its employees. At a recent conference in London entitled 'Stress in the Workplace' (1995) delegates were invited to rate organizations on their care for employees and their drive for profit, using a scale of 1–10 (1 very low and 10 very high). It worked out at about 8:4 (the drive for profits was averaged at 8; care for people emerged at 4), with approximately 70 participants in the group. The drive for profit outweighed care for people dramatically. In some way they appeared as opposites: to concentrate on one was to deride the other. Why not combine them?

Setting up a caring environment entails answering two questions: how do we understand the problems people have and where do we apportion 'responsibility'? There are numerous theories of why people have problems, from *medical models* which do not see them as responsible for their past to *responsibility models* that hold them responsible for what has happened. Workplace counsellors need to answer this question for themselves: it determines to some degree how they work with employees. Smail (1987: 67) refers to the 'barbaric fallacy involved in the individualization of fault' where we attribute responsibility to individuals for what has happened to them. Smail continues,

> For as long as we seek the explanation for pain, despair and catastrophe *inside* people, we shall fail to observe that they are in fact the result of our construction of a society serving the functions of power and interest as they operate coercively and manipulatively *between* people.
>
> If you run over a pea with a steam roller you don't blame the pea for what happens to it, nor, sensibly, do you treat its injuries as some kind of shortcoming inherent in its internal structure, whether inherited or acquired. Similarly, if you place the (literally) unimaginably sensitive organisms which human babies are in the kind of social and environmental machinery which we seem to be bent on perfecting, it can be of no real surprise that so many of them end up, as adults, as lost, bemused, miserable and crazy as they do. The only surprise, perhaps, is that so many pass as 'normal'. (1987: 76)

I have spent a disproportionate amount of time on this last workplace counselling model compared with the other models. This has been intentional. While this model can fit easily with other employee counselling models, what I want to highlight is how little it is being used in a clear and intentional manner. Counselling has been underused as a source of organizational change, and workplace counselling needs to widen its perspective and be more creative in applying its rich resources to changing systems as well as individuals.

Conclusion

Cunningham (1994) makes the point that the workplace is too complex to have 'pure' forms of counselling models. Her remarks, made in the US context, are equally applicable in Britain. Combinations of models are the norm rather than the exception. Blended models provide wider choice for employees (some companies have both internal and external counselling provision, and often there may be two or more counsellors working within a company providing different counselling orientations). This brings a richness rather than a dilution of purity. However, there are some models that do not knit well together, e.g. the work-orientated model and the counselling-orientation one.

Workplace counselling can be viewed on a continuum, with varying opinions on its aims and objectives. At one end of this continuum is the extreme position outlined above by Yeager ('the business alternatives will determine the clinical goals' 1983: 133). At the other end is the totally person-centred position of those who counsel employees as if they were working in private practice, but within the organization. It is the personal goals of employees that determine the length of time in counselling, the methods and even the orientation used, and there may be no reference at all to work, work-related issues or how present personal issues are affecting work.

In between these two poles comes a number of points which combine the above with varying emphasis on one position or the other. Some companies predetermine the approach with policies such as the length of time clients can be seen for (e.g. four to six sessions), or by insisting that assessments are first made by a psychologist or a psychiatrist before referral to the counsellor. This, again, may point out the lack of clarity about the precise aims and objectives of workplace counselling. Perhaps this could be viewed as a strength rather than a weakness. It allows for flexibility for counsellors, particularly adaptation to an individual organization, and a multiplicity of approaches that widens rather than restricts choice.

However, there is a problem. Because many companies do not understand what counselling is, and because most providers of counselling are not independent, few organizations are assessed objectively for the kind of counselling best suited to them, the best counsellors for them, and the best means of evaluating counselling provision when it has been introduced. Later chapters will look in more detail at these issues. For now, we ask what are the issues and themes that characterize counselling in the workplace in the modern world?

3

Workplace Counselling Today: Trends and Debates

> Counselling at work needs to address fundamental questions such as, what is the purpose of counselling at work and does it have a role there? Do counselling models and their emphasis on personal empowerment and liberation really fit into an organisational context? It may prove necessary to use ideas and research from counselling, organisational, educational and health psychology, philosophical or ethical perspectives in order to develop new concepts and models about counselling at work.
>
> A. Bull, 'How effective is counselling in the workplace?'

This chapter will summarize and discuss trends and debates within employee counselling. These areas need to be considered by workplace counsellors as a preliminary to beginning counselling employees. The eight areas reviewed in this chapter, some of which will be picked up and dealt with more fully in later chapters, are as follows:

1	What is workplace counselling?
2	The multiple roles of employee counsellors
3	The values of counselling versus those of business
4	Training for workplace counsellors
5	Ethical issues in workplace counselling
6	Stress and workplace counselling
7	The impact of the organization on employee counselling
8	Counselling as a means of organizational change

What is workplace counselling?

Despite recent literature on workplace counselling, and despite the length of time counselling has been part of the workplace, there is still a great deal of uncertainty about what it entails. Perhaps 'uncertainty' is too strong a word – there are many who are very certain about what employee counselling entails. What is definite is that there is no agreed statement on workplace counselling that clearly delineates its purpose(s). As Chapter 2 has pointed out, there are various models of workplace counselling, some of which are based on different underlying concepts of what counselling in this context means. When I shared with one person, who was herself involved in workplace counselling, that I was writing this book, she automatically assumed I would be considering workplace counselling as brief counselling.

The good news about multiple approaches to workplace counselling is that this allows for flexibility and adaptation of workplace counselling to individual organizations. Purposes are not predetermined but negotiable according to the needs and requirements of particular groups. Organizations can involve themselves in a sort of 'pick and mix' exercise whereby they choose which counselling approach, with which features, best meets their organizational demands. They can choose from a variety of counselling orientations, with a number of different roles, either short-term or long-term counselling, or both, and several ways in which the counselling service can be integrated into the organization. They can opt on how to evaluate their counselling service, what criteria for counsellors they will use to appoint members of the service, and they can align counselling provision with organizational culture.

Though much of workplace counselling confines itself to particular ways of working, in principle it does *not* have to be tied to problem-solving, or brief counselling alone, or confined to particular client groups, or working with specific levels (job groups) within the organization. There is much variety of choice.

Where difficulty arises is in determining the *purpose* of workplace counselling. There seems to be a continuum along which purposes run. Figure 3.1 presents a continuum for defining the purposes of workplace counselling. At one extreme, what I have called the 'personal concept of counselling', is the choice of clients to bring whatever they choose to counselling and to use it for their own purposes. These can be personal or professional problems, personal or professional growth, issues involving work, or not involving work. What characterizes this position is that the client determines the purpose of counselling.

Organizational concept of counselling · Personal concept of counselling

Figure 3.1 *Continuum for understanding the purpose of workplace counselling*

Case example

Elizabeth comes to see the employee counsellor. She is in her early 30s, happily married, and needs space and time to see whether or not now is the time for her and her husband to begin having their family. They want children but both are heavily involved in, and enjoying, their jobs. The counsellor suggests coming for several sessions to see if Elizabeth can reach a decision. There is also the possibility of Elizabeth's husband, Philip, joining them for a session.

Case example

Mike has been working for the company for about 20 years, is a capable and valued employee. He comes to the counselling service not because he has an immediate problem but because he has always wanted to be more involved in work with people and is thinking of training to become a counsellor. He would like to be professionally trained. This would not entail giving up his job with the company in the short term while he is undergoing his training, but holds major implications for him about his life.

There are many other examples that could be given where employees are not in crisis, perhaps not even facing difficulties, who would like the opportunity of counselling for personal growth. Some consider this very appropriate for workplace counselling. They see counselling as involving the whole person, not just the problem side.

At the other extreme, what I have called the 'organizational concept of counselling', is the opinion that the counselling service is there to help employees work at least to minimal satisfaction. Its primary purpose is to facilitate employees' work. Since it is workplace counselling, it is basically work-related and considers only problems that concern the work of the employee. This can be interpreted in a broad or narrow sense. Broadly, lots of issues impinge on employees' work: personal problems from home, from within the individual, and any issues within the professional life of employees. Balgopal and Patchner (1988: 95) seem to take this stance when they write, 'It is assumed that employees' problems are private unless they cause job performance to deteriorate. For when that happens, the personal problems become a matter of concern for the company.' Yaeger is another who favours this position, summarizing it as 'the business alternatives will determine the clinical goals' (1983: 133). Narrowly, it can be seen as those issues that directly influence the work of employees in a negative way. Workplace counsellors who hold this stance will only see clients whose work is suffering as a result of their problems. They will utilize a minimalist approach: how much time do we need to manage this issue so that it is not negatively affecting work? The probability is that counsellors holding these views would not work personally with Elizabeth or Mike in the examples above but suggest that they see a personal counsellor (probably at their own expense).

Many companies, because of their lack of knowledge in the area of counselling and/or because of their trust in their counsellors, leave the decision of who is seen for counselling to the counsellor's decision. This seems to have been the position of most in-house counsellors in Carroll's research (1994). There are still, within companies, fears that counselling can take up too much of an employee's time and/or that counselling, of itself, is quite disturbing for employees and will affect their work adversely, especially if it is long term. Finance and waiting lists can, in practical terms, influence the purpose of workplace counselling. All these factors point out the lack of clarity about the precise aims and objectives of workplace counselling. Sworder (1977: 31) has suggested a framework in which problems at work can be assessed:

1 Problems arising within the individual.
2 Problems caused by the work organization acting on the individual.
3 Problems arising outside the individual or the organization: either (a) having visible effects on the work of the individual; or b) not having visible effects on the work of the individual.

While recognizing that there may well be mixtures of the three problem areas, such a framework, at least, gives the employee counsellor a model for deciding when workplace counselling is called for and when it is, or may be, outside the domain of the workplace counselling service.

In summary, it seems clear that organizations and workplace counsellors should clarify the purpose of providing counselling to employees. This will enable counsellors to understand their roles with employees and the organization and help clients with their expectations from the service.

The multiple roles of workplace counsellors

One of the main features that distinguishes employee counsellors from counsellors in other contexts is the requirement that they fulfil a number of roles. Little consideration has been given to how workplace counsellors combine the roles and responsibilities that characterize their work, though Gerstein and Shullman (1992) have counted up to 18 roles for the counselling psychologist in industry, and Toomer (1982) has suggested nine areas of concern for the employee counsellor. To date these have not been articulated clearly, and workplace counsellors are asked to fulfil roles that counsellors in other settings find anathema to their work. It is rare that employee counsellors have one single role with clients; rather, they are often asked to be trainer, welfare officer, home visitor, information-giver, advocate, consultant to managers, personnel adviser, organizational change agent, as well as being counsellor. Carroll's (1994) research is one of the few pieces of work that asks employee counsellors to outline their roles and responsibilities. Her study was clear that workplace counsellors engage in diverse roles within their organizations. From the 12 in-house employee counsellors interviewed, the following roles emerged:

- ensuring counselling provision
- advising line managers on approaching troubled employees
- employee counselling
- training and health education
- advising the organization on policy matters
- managerial responsibilities
- welfare
- casework supervision
- facilitating organizational change
- critical incident de-briefing
- research
- advising on equal opportunities
- publicizing the service
- educating staff about the role of counselling
- developing counselling provision
- monitoring effectiveness
- administration
- referral
- mediating between client and organization

While many fulfil these multiple roles admirably (Carroll, 1994), there is very little help available to determine which roles fit well together and which result in role conflict with their clients. What seems certain is that counsellors at work will not be free simply to be clinicians alone and this will have serious implications about how they are likely to view, experience and be thought about in their roles. While it is fundamental to make clear the various roles and responsibilities that are part of the counsellor's job, there are, unfortunately, few guidelines to indicate the extent of those roles and responsibilities. Interviewing clients for individual counselling is clearly accepted as one. After that, there is little consistency in agreeing primary roles.

Counsellors, by training, can make significant contributions to a number of organizational developments. However, making them consultants to almost every part of the organization may mean overlooking what they do best, i.e. individual counselling provision. It may also fail to recognize the 'boundary issues' or role conflicts that could arise when counsellors take part in a number of organizational activities. Crandall and Allen (1982) point out the possibility of clashes between counselling and organizational roles and name four demands that may be present for the counsellor in an organization:

1 Counselling clients using a particular approach.
2 Being a member of the organization.
3 The demands from clients to collude in their negative stances.
4 Siding with the client when there are unreasonable demands from the organization.

Weaving a healthy path amongst these four can be difficult for the conscientious counsellor since all four demands need to be held together in some form of creative tension.

The workplace counsellor has to ascertain which roles can exist together without compromise, and which roles, though good in themselves, are incompatible in this context. Gray (1984a: 171) talks about the importance of 'role definition, role stress, role overlap, and other people's roles. In attempting to work with the organization, the counsellor is extending or re-defining his or her role.' Nixon and Carroll (1994) have looked at incompatible roles within the managerial framework and insist that being a manager and a counsellor are two roles that do not, and cannot be allowed to, belong together in the same person. Hopson (1977: 30) alerted workplace counsellors to the conflict areas in one of the earliest British writings on counselling at work and made some strong suggestions:

> Whatever the models developed and experimented with in work settings, three prerequisites stand out: the organisation must be crystal-clear about its purpose and motives for initiating or facilitating a counselling service; the counsellor must have a clearly-defined contract with the organisation regarding his job definition, and regarding the issues of confidentiality and loyalty; and the counsellor must also be capable of communicating clearly to his clients the nature of the system and the services he is capable of and allowed to provide.

While admirable in intent, it is not always possible to attain such clarity and agreement, and counsellors who opt to work with employees will find there is need continually to clarify and update the understanding of their service.

Gray (1984a) is adamant that time is wasted when spent solely in individual counselling in organizations. Using the 'upstream/downstream' analogy, he suggests that 'spending all one's time with individual clients can lead to a lack of awareness of the processes of the organisation which provide the opportunities for the clients' particular neurotic, existential or psychotic imperatives to emerge' (1984a: 178). Prominent again, for the employee counsellor, is the consideration of role(s) and how best to apportion time with individuals, with groups, in organizational development, in consulting with management, in training, and so on.

In summary, one of the main issues facing employee counsellors is working out clearly the roles for which they have responsibility. It is clear that some roles may conflict, and equally important that many roles will have to be left aside simply because of lack of time. Decisions have to be made. With the skills that counsellors bring to the job, it is understandable that organizations will want them to be involved in other dimensions of organizational growth. The credibility of the service, boundary and ethical issues, as well as the practicalities of time and emotional involvement, will have to be taken into consideration in making choices.

The values of counselling versus those of business

In his novel *Nice Work*, David Lodge presents the two worlds of education (the University) and commerce (the factory) and uses the theme of 'shadowing' to show the differences between the two worlds. Throughout, the two main characters Robyn (a lecturer from the English department) and Vic (managing director of an engineering firm) struggle to understand and learn about each other's world. They start off with antipathy towards the world of the other and slowly begin to learn how one could influence the other and how values found in one could be of help to the other. Towards the end Robyn has a dream where both worlds meet:

> And the beautiful young people and their teachers stopped dallying and disputing and got to their feet and came forward to greet the people from the factory, shook their hands and made them welcome, and a hundred small seminar groups formed on the grass, composed half of students and lecturers and half of workers and managers, to exchange ideas on how the values of the university and the imperatives of commerce might be

reconciled and more equitably managed to the benefit of the whole of society. (Lodge, 1988: 347)

If we changed the terms above to the two worlds of business and counselling, the underlying themes would be the same. Few texts struggle with the particular problems that arise among the underlying values, philosophies and policies of the world of business and the world of counselling. Some authors have reviewed the conflicting values between counselling and the contexts in which it is applied; for example, counselling in Nazi Germany (Cocks, 1985), and under the apartheid system in South Africa (Dryden, 1990). It is all too easily assumed by many counsellors that counselling will blend easily with whatever context and that the resulting marriage will be one of continual harmony. Warning voices have been raised (Bakalinsky, 1980; Lane, 1990) about introducing counselling into companies without consultation. Some organizations may not be ready for counselling provision. Counselling can be integrated into industry for all sorts of wrong reasons resulting in unclear boundary issues and, in some instances, the 'highjacking' of counselling to cover managerial defects.

Oberer and Lee (1986: 152) articulate a major concern: 'the most obvious [area of difficulty] involves the primary role of business versus the counselor's professional goals.' Is there an inherent contradiction between the aims and purposes of industry and those of the counselling profession? Are counsellors compromised by working within industry? There is no doubt that the aim of counselling is to promote growth, autonomy, to encourage clients to care for themselves, to be assertive, to develop potential. These are not always in accord with particular organizations who do not wish employees to be autonomous. Many organizations want teamwork rather than a concentration on the individual, many require 'passive employees' rather than active ones, and many growth-orientated employees would clash with 'macho managers'. Orlans (1986: 19) highlights possible conflicts:

> One difficulty with counselling within the organisational context is that the values and goals implicit in counselling (especially in non-directive approaches) are not easily reconciled with the economic, rationalistic models which underlie organisational procedures and processes. Counselling is generally concerned with providing individuals with a greater sense of freedom, while an important organisational function is the control of its employees.

Nahrwold (1983) has traced the history of antagonism between counselling and business, showing how social scientists, especially in the mid-1960s 'depicted businesses as amoral, greedy, polluting, exploitive (or even fascist) organizations that sacrifice human values and social responsibilities to increase profit. To counter criticisms portraying them as Dickensian villains, business people in turn have characterised social scientists as naive, bleeding head academics or crypto-Marxist social agitators seeking to overturn capitalism' (1983: 110–11). While acknowledging the strong stereotypes put forward by both camps, Nahrwold upbraids counsellors for an anti-business attitude which is sometimes expressed in the way they dress, and the way they maintain hostile attitudes and professional arrogance. He suggests that the two worlds can exist and blend amicably if common sense, getting to know one another and the roles involved, and an awareness of the politics of the organization, are used with good will.

Besides possible conflicts between counselling values and those of the organization, there may also be value conflicts within employee counsellors themselves where they struggle with their precise roles and responsibilities. Which comes first: the individual client or the organization as a whole? Counsellors are trained primarily to deal with the individual and to put the welfare of the individual first. This may conflict with company norms and even policies. Moving from individual counselling, either privately or in other settings, to employee counselling in the workplace can be problematic for counsellors trained this way.

Counsellors and managers struggle to understand and be changed by the world of the other. Not only are some organizations reluctant to see a role for counselling within their remit but there are counsellors who view industry as simply *against* people and concerned with profit at the expense of individuals. Clashes in values among counsellors, clients, organizations and society have to be faced continually by workplace counsellors who are trying 'to integrate outer-directed business values with the more inner-directed humanistic ones' (Puder, 1983: 96). However, this is a general-ization and not all workplaces would agree that they were either profit-orientated to the detriment of their people, or that they are against the underlying values of counselling. Certainly, there is a growing literature on the supportive and learning organization (Egan, 1994; Hawkins, forthcoming), and Carroll in her research (1994: 56) recounts that in-house counsellors in the private sector found little difficulty in reconciling organizational aims with counselling values,

> Amazingly little of this antagonism or value-conflicts emerged from interviewees. They [in-house counsellors in the private sector] were aware, and indeed accepted, the fact that their companies were profit-making, but also keenly cognisant of the support they received from the organiz-

ation. They saw no opposition between helping people develop, deal with their problems, and the organizational aims of the company . . . employee counsellors seem to be effective bridge-builders between the two worlds.

A key values question that runs through the literature on counselling within industry is: who is the client of the counsellor? Is it the individual client who makes his or her way to the counsellor's door, or is the organization the client? Clarifying roles with the individual client and within the organization becomes something of a difficulty, especially in the light of the expertise expected above. Workplace counsellors have to balance the fact that in many ways their clients are both individual employees and the organization from which they emerge. One of the earliest books on counselling at work in Britain (Watts, 1977: 11) highlighted this area as needing special mention:

> Where counselling takes place within an organisation, however, it has to take account of its responsibility not only to the client but also to the institution, and to operate within boundaries set by the institution. This is especially problematic where the counsellor is employed by the organisation. So long as he works only inside the one-to-one relationship he may be able to avoid being seen by the organisation as threatening or subversive. Yet if he does this, he is inevitably defining problems as emanating from the individual rather than from the institution: where there is conflict between the interests of the two, all he can do is to accept the institution's needs and demands as given, and to help the individual to decide how to respond to them.

In brief, while theoretically there may well be value clashes between the world of work and that of counselling, in practice most employee counsellors are able to reconcile differences and work creatively within organizational settings. However, it seems that some caution is advised in taking for granted that the workplace readily adapts its values to complement those of counselling.

Training for workplace counsellors

Many counselling practitioners move from settings and trainings in working with individuals to working within an organizational context. What are the difficulties of this move? What do they have to unlearn? Re-learn? What new boundaries need to be negotiated? Summerfield and van Oudtshoorn (1995) use the term 'bilingual' to illustrate the need to work in two domains and continually translate elements from one into the other.

There is almost no training for counsellors who either work or intend to work as counsellors within organizations. In Britain, to date, there are only four programmes specifically geared to counselling at work: TDA Diploma in Counselling at Work, Roehampton Institute's Diploma in Counselling in Organizations, Birmingham University's Diploma in Counselling at Work, and the Diploma in Counselling at Work run at the University of Bristol. All these programmes have started within the past few years or are programmed to run within the near future. What training exists tends to be unsystematic, short, and usually arranged for people who will integrate counselling skills into their existing work roles.

Orlans (1986, 1992) has pointed out the notable absence of special training for counsellors who work within organizational settings. She argues that being a counsellor is not of itself sufficient and proposes a general curriculum to cover this area:

> A review of the principles and dynamics of organisational behaviour; models and practices in the design and implementation of Employee Assistance Programmes; ethics and responsibilities in employee counselling; organisational health; the role of legislation; stress diagnosis, management and prevention in the work setting, and the understanding of specialist counselling, AIDS, substance abuse, career counselling, with particular emphasis on their application to the workplace. Such a programme would also need to include the provision of supervised practice, relevant tutorial work and appropriate assessment procedures. (Orlans, 1992: 21)

For those who wrestle with the contents of a comprehensive curriculum for training employee counsellors (Osipow, 1982; Lewis and Lewis, 1986; Megranahan, 1989b; Gerstein and Shullman, 1992; Orlans, 1992; Pickard, forthcoming) there is a tendency for the counsellor to become a jack of all organizational trades. They are asked to be professional counsellors, organizational consultants, trainers, welfare officers, personnel officers, internal or external change agents with expertise in individual work, group dynamics and human resources management. The all-inclusiveness of their tasks could be interpreted as a lack of clarity of the particular aims of workplace counselling. The need to become acceptable to industry could drive counsellors into roles not appropriate to their profession.

On the other hand, we need to heed the warning of Summerfield and van Oudtshoorn (1995: 29) who believe 'that letting loose on an organization counsellors who have neither experience of business in general nor of the organization culture and style in particular is potentially dangerous both to the organization and to the individual clients themselves'.

A more detailed curriculum for training counsellors in workplace counselling will be offered in Chapter 9.

Ethical issues in workplace counselling

There is a growing awareness that many ethical problems face the workplace counsellor which are not applicable to counselling in other areas. A recent spate of articles has begun conversations around ethics and the workplace counsellor (Lee and Rosen, 1984; Orlans, 1986; Bond, 1992; Salt et al., 1992; Sugarman, 1992; Walker, 1992; Carroll, 1994). So particular to the workplace counsellor are some of the ethical issues that there has been a call for a special 'code of ethics and practice for workplace counsellors' (Puder, 1983).

Pryor (1989) puts forward an ethical dilemma where an accountant is referred for counselling and in the session talks about an embezzlement charge which he has never revealed to the company. What should the counsellor do? Employed by the company, and, no doubt, with the company's interest at heart, should a counsellor, knowing there was risk (minor, intermediate, serious?) that this employee might embezzle again (he is in financial difficulty), relay this information to the relevant management? Should this problem be seen from an individual perspective, or an organizational one, or both? Workplace counselling not only contends with the full range of ethical issues emerging from counselling, but another full set of issues arrives on the scene both from within the organization where counselling takes place and between the organization and the counsellor. Business ethics exist alongside counselling ethics and the counsellor needs to be aware of the professional world of business as well as that of counselling.

Various ethical dilemmas arising from workplace counselling have been discussed in the literature:

- confidentiality (Bond, 1992; Salt et al., 1992; Walker, 1992)
- incompatibility between organizational aims and counselling aims (Lee and Rosen, 1984; Orlans, 1986; Sugarman, 1992)
- the loyalty of the counsellor (Carroll, 1995b)
- managing different roles with the same client (Carroll, 1995b)

However, there are other areas not covered. The following list of possible ethical pitfalls/dilemmas is adapted from Lakin (1991):

- If the management pays, how can the counsellor serve the interests of employees?
- Can the targets of the interactions – the employees – share in designing interventions?
- How can the counsellor honestly describe what is proposed to those who are to be affected by it?
- Can employees refuse to participate in counselling without penalty?

- Dare the employee confront a manager/supervisor when the counsellor and the employee have worked on this together?
- What safeguards are there for participants against retaliation from supervisors or aggrieved co-workers for what may take place as a result of counselling?

Workplace counsellors face not only a barrage of possible ethical dilemmas but do so without clear and helpful frameworks for ethical decision-making in work contexts. Most see supervision as an essential requirement for continued efficacy here (Sugarman, 1992; Carroll, 1995a). Sugarman (1992: 28) stresses five focal points for the counsellor where ethical concerns need to be tackled:

- Identifying the extent to which the aims of an organisation compromise counselling's ethical foundation.
- Identifying any point at which the counselling provision benefits the organisation at the individual's expense.
- Identifying any points at which the organisation exceeds its right to control aspects of the employee's behaviour.
- Negotiating what is implied by the term 'confidentiality' and the conditions under which it will and will not be maintained.
- Identifying whether the resources are sufficient and appropriate to doing more good than harm, and in what ways the origins of the resources compromise the aims of the service.

It would be extremely difficult to prioritize ethical issues. However, there is some validity in presenting confidentiality as one of the most crucial that can determine the credibility of counselling within industry. Failure in this area will destroy the reputation of a counselling service. And yet it is not easy to maintain confidentiality with a host of factors in the workplace vying with one another to break it: managers wanting information on employees, personnel asking to be involved, individual clients sharing material detrimental to organizational policy. Because of this complexity, there have been calls for specific codes of ethics geared to each counselling service within each company. Puder (1983) goes into some detail in outlining the content of such a code. Among others, he suggests it should include:

> the philosophy and policy governing the employee counselling program, list the principles regulating program procedures, and include a statement on the limits of confidentiality (what specific situations warrant breaching confidentiality), on the status, retention, and access of program records, on the limits on collection of information, and on the release of information to internal and external sources. The code should specify principles regarding program staff conduct, responsibility, and competence. (1983: 100)

Of great importance from an ethical perspective is how counsellors work where organizational issues seem to impact negatively on individuals. Andrew Swart, who was a counsellor in a university setting under the apartheid regime in South Africa, has talked about how he and his colleagues helped students reflect on their problems (Dryden, 1990). At times they would feed information back to the university, suggesting that some problems were structural problems, they would empower students to confront organizational problems that affected them, and the counsellors needed to examine how they might inadvertently collude with the oppression of the organization.

In brief, it seems that ethical sensitivity as a workplace counsellor means juggling the needs, and sometimes the conflicting needs, of the individual client and the organization. It includes employee counsellors being alert to the dilemmas and contradictions within their own job and the roles they either adopt or are often forced to adopt within the organization. Chapter 8 will look in more detail at ethical issues in workplace counselling.

Stress and workplace counselling

In the past few years strong connections have been made between stress and workplace counselling, with the latter often quoted as a method of reducing occupational stress. And there is no doubt that our awareness of stress, and the increasing legal requirements of the Health and Safety Executive on what is 'reasonable stress', have moved more companies to introducing counselling provision as a way of managing employee stress. In fact, some organizations provide counselling that is specific to post-traumatic stress disorder, and deal with trauma (Tehrani, 1995). Some argue for stress management as the main focus of workplace counselling on the grounds of cost-effectiveness. In the ICAS Report (Reddy, 1993b) on UK organizations' use of counselling and EAP provision, the term 'stress counselling' is used continually, and organizations, in their survey, were asked what provision they made for stress counselling. It is unclear how stress counselling differs from other forms of counselling: is it basic to all counselling (people who come for counselling must be stressed) or is it called 'stress counselling' because occupational stress is the presenting problem of the client?

However, the relationship between stress in the workplace and counselling is only rarely considered in detail: the assumption is made that counselling will help reduce stress. A recent book (Ross and Altmaier, 1994) is subtitled 'A Handbook of Counselling for Stress at Work'. While dealing very well with understanding stress and methods of managing stress and including a small section on cognitive-behavioural techniques, there is nothing to link managing stress specifically with counselling. In fact, in the index there are only three references to the word 'counselling' in the whole book. I mention this book particularly because it is symptomatic of work in the field of stress management. There are lots of ways of helping people manage stress (Ross and Altmaier, 1994 outline these very well) but these are more educational than counselling. I realize that many counsellors see training as part of counselling, especially those who come from a more behavioural background. However, I want to argue here that educational methods and skills training are, in my view, only one limited aspect of counselling, and what principally distinguishes counselling from other methods is its ability to help individuals marshall their own resources by using the counselling relationship. Having said this, it seems to me that counselling is a good method of helping employees use stress creatively. Stress is itself useful in energizing and motivating us. It is when it becomes debilitating that it paralyses.

While stress will continue to be a workplace issue, kept centre-stage because of legal issues, we still have some way to go in showing how counselling is effective in managing stress for employees. As was pointed out in Chapter 1, the use of counselling in stress management has been criticized for ignoring the organizational causes of stress. Two documents have looked at the organizational aspects of stress: the Health and Safety Executive's *Stress at Work* (1995) and, in particular, *Organizational Stress in the National Health Service* (Opus, 1995) which is concerned with outlining the underlying organizational causes of stress.

This debate can too easily become polarized: stress is either an individual problem that needs to be tackled by the person or stress is an organizational issue that needs to be solved at an organizational level. It is a pity to lose sight of either: stress is both an organizational and an individual problem and managing stress can never be reduced simply to one or the other. Counselling will certainly not be effective if organizational aspects of stress are not recognized and confronted. On the other hand, managing organizational stress will remain ineffective if individuals cannot cope with and harness reasonable levels of stress.

The impact of the organization on workplace counselling

There is virtually no literature on the impact that organizations have on counselling provision. Few doubt that 'organizational culture' influences most of what takes place within companies, and even though there are suggestions that different types of culture will influence counselling services, there has been little research or writing to help prepare, introduce, maintain and, where necessary, terminate counselling provision in different company cultures. McLeod (1993: 273) has formulated a list of challenges faced by counsellors working in non-counselling agencies:

- being pressured to produce results desired by the agency rather than the client
- maintaining confidentiality boundaries
- justifying the cost of the service
- dealing with isolation
- educating colleagues about the purpose and value of counselling
- justifying the cost of supervision
- avoiding being overwhelmed by numbers of clients, or becoming the conscience of the organization
- avoiding the threat to reputation caused by 'failure' cases
- coping with the envy of colleagues who are not able to take an hour for each client interview
- creating an appropriate office space and reception system

While organizations may impact on the practicalities of counselling relationships (number of sessions, location of counselling service, etc.) there may be other ways in which that influence is less obvious. How do the values of the company, conscious and unconscious, infiltrate the counselling service? How much, unwittingly, do counsellors manage the emotional lives of their clients and fit them to company culture? How often are problems individualized and made the responsibility of the employee when they should be viewed as organizational problems?

Of course, organizations not only have a visible profile and culture, they also have a very powerful informal structure which influences what happens in the organization. Egan (1993a) warns against underestimating what he calls the 'shadow side' of organizations and offers six categories to help managers recognize 'shadow-side realities' (p. 34):

- organizational stupidities
- organizational messiness
- the idiosyncrasies of individuals
- vagaries of the social system
- organizational politics
- culture

These, too, will influence the counselling service. Counselling managers in organizational settings, like line managers, may need to assess and work with these 'a-rational' aspects of the organization and be able to know how to work with them effectively.

Whatever the context, and whatever the organizational culture, workplace counsellors have to deal with a number of demands from organizations. Bureaucracy is part and parcel of everyday life in organizations, as are issues of communication and information flow, red tape and accountability. Learning how to work with these, as well as dealing with the frustrations that are part of them, can be worthwhile skills for counsellors in organizational settings and, while not solving the problems, can at least make life more tolerable.

Chapter 4 will look in more detail at the impact of organizations on counselling. Suffice it to say, at this stage, that not to consider the impact of organizations is to be unaware of how organizational culture can imperceptibly impregnate the counselling service with its values and requirements.

Counselling as a means of organizational change

This theme was considered in Chapter 2 where it was also viewed as a model for workplace counselling. However, it will undoubtedly become a key issue for debate and negotiation within companies and institutions as counselling provision becomes more acceptable and settled within them. Several points will be added here and further issues considered in Chapter 4 where the impact of organizations on counselling will be reviewed.

Reddy (1994) has lamented the fact that EAPs in Britain, to date, have not been more active in closer integration into organizational life. He emphasizes that EAPs can be seen not as 'devices' but as central to company life: 'employee assistance is more about a concept than about a programme – certainly about any single programme. It is more a philosophy about how employees can be supported, in the interest of health and performance, and more a philosophy about how their needs can be identified and met, than it is any particular *device* to meet them' (Reddy, 1994: 64). In particular, he moves to pinpoint the performance management dimensions, supervisor training, and support to managers as key elements in integrating EAPs into the workplace. Though EAPs are wider than counselling provision, it seems to me that the same tenets apply, and Reddy's summary of how company and EAP are connected is applicable to employee counselling in general:

> The introduction of an EAP offers a new opportunity to: refresh super-visory and management development training throughout the organiz-ation; give supervisors and managers a sense of the counselling values and techniques which are now available to them; underline or re-focus

their responsibility for day-to-day performance management; and teach them how to handle the more personal aspects of below-par performance and refer appropriately to the EAP. . . . The full EAP has in fact a triple role: counselling the individual; consulting for the line manager or supervisor; and training. This full potential has not yet been exploited in Britain. (Reddy, 1994: 67–8)

Workplace counsellors have yet, like EAPs, to exploit what they bring to organizations. They have skills for contributing to a 'preferred culture' (Egan, 1994), where concern for people is matched with attaining the objectives of the company. They epitomize the process of change and decision-making, are experts in transitions, and give away the knowledge, skills and strategies of empowerment, growth, dealing with people problems and difficulties, as well as working with systems. And there are particular areas where counselling skills can be adapted to help individuals and organizations; for example, performance reviews, career development and growth, relocation counselling, retirement counselling, alcohol counselling and outplacement counselling (Masi, 1992).

Conclusion

The trends and debates in employee counselling that we have focused on in this chapter are not the full extent of issues within workplace counselling but they will probably be the agenda for discussion in the foreseeable future. Chapters 1–3 have concentrated on understanding the workplace and how models of workplace counselling can be defined. Debates, discussion, themes and critical issues in workplace counselling have also be reviewed. In a sense this has been the 'theory' side of workplace counselling. Chapter 4 will now consider the impact that organizations have on counselling services before we look at models for workplace counselling in Chapters 5 and 6.

4

The Impact of Organizations
on Workplace Counselling

> Our thesis . . . is that in order to fully understand the devel-
> opment of a therapeutic relationship one must pay attention to
> the organisational context in which the helping occurs.
>
> R. Crandell and R.D. Allen, 'The organisational
> context of helping relationships'

> As every organization is an entirely unique system (there is no
> pure type), it follows that no two will have exactly the same
> needs. If counselling is to make a positive impact on the culture
> and performance of an organization, it needs to out of, and
> respond effectively to, these special needs.
>
> J. Summerfield and L. van Oudtshoorn,
> *Counselling in the Workplace*

Bateson's (1979) famous dictum 'The context gives meaning' is
particularly relevant when we review the impact that organizations
have on counselling provision. The context in which counselling is
offered influences what happens between counsellors and clients. The
extent to which this occurs is debated, with extremes on both sides.
Some see individual problems solely as contextual issues: organizations create problems within individuals, individuals take on the ills
of the contexts in which they live and relate. In *The Neurotic
Organisation*, Kets de Vries and Miller (1984) ask the critical question: 'What are the connections between organisational and human
pathology?' Taking a strong psychoanalytic approach, they argue for
close links between these two, suggesting that 'an integrated syn-
drome of pathology' (p. 17) can exist in an organization and that the
personalities of top people are reflected in the culture and policies of
organizations. Systemic approaches to counselling also interpret
human problems using relationship terms: individual problems
emerge from the situations in which people find themselves. Considering the amount of evidence for the role of social support as an
essential ingredient in the well-being of people and the effectiveness
of counselling (Pearson, 1990; Mahoney and McCray Patterson,
1992), it is not surprising that some advocate counsellors taking

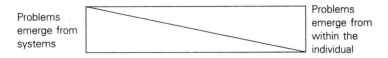

| Problems emerge from systems | | Problems emerge from within the individual |

Figure 4.1 *Continuum for explaining workplace problems*

more responsibility for changing social systems rather than work solely with individuals.

Others give little credence to the impact of the organization on counselling and consider the counselling relationship as an insulated alliance where people are empowered to work with and within the systems to which they belong. Gestalt approaches to counselling and many of the cognitive-behavioural orientations, for example, rational emotive behavioural therapy, concentrate on the individual so much that for them the context often matters little. Sorting out the person, empowering the individual, educating and training in managing skills deficiency, are methods of dealing with human problems. The role of the counsellor from these perspectives is to work with the individual who will then deal with his or her environment. Traditionally, psychodynamic orientations in counselling have stressed the 'internal' or intrapsychic dimension of problems, opting to focus on how the individual can gain control rather than how the environment can be changed to support the individual.

Figure 4.1 which represents different views on a continuum that analyses problems, at one extreme, as being totally the result of organizations and systems and, at the other end, as emanating from intrapsychic issues within the individual. It seems to me that there is a direct relationship between these two and that both are true: problems are caused by systems and problems emerge from within individuals. Both organizations and individuals are affected by this and some individuals cause havoc in organizations just as some organizations destroy the individuals who work within them. While institutions affect individuals, it is not deterministic; individuals can resist at times and take individual stances. Counsellors in organizational settings seem, to me, to best serve the interests of organizations that employ them and individuals with whom they work by taking an open stance of how problems occur in life. Being open to the possibility that they can come from the organization or the individual gives counsellors better space within which to work and more freedom to make helpful assessments of how this individual came to have this particular problem. From a research point of view, we know little of the relationship between organizational processes and counselling outcomes (McLeod, 1993).

In this chapter, I will argue that organizational contexts make significant impact on the counselling relationships within them. There seems to be some evidence that the values within an organization are linked to organizational culture as well as policies and management style (Pheysey, 1993). For example, Perry (1993) traces the history of the relationship between the development of counselling in women's organizations and its impact on those organizations' structures. She points out how values for women are often reflected in the way the organization is structured, how workers relate to one another and how female-managed organizations adopt more cooperative and collegial styles than do male-managed organizations. Such styles and systems will percolate to all levels of the organization influencing individuals, relationships between individuals, groups, departments and the overall organizational ecology.

There are several ways of considering how individuals relate to and are influenced by the organizations in which they work; for example, Brack et al. (1993) have applied chaos theory to organizational development. Two of the major approaches will be reviewed here: the psychodynamic and systemic approaches to organization.

The psychodynamics of organizations

Foremost among theories considering the interface between individuals and organizations is the psychodynamic approach. Based on the work of Freud with individuals and groups, and moving into understanding of the dynamics of small groups through the work of Bion (1961), the same ideas were applied to institutions and organizations (Obholzer and Roberts, 1994). In the UK, the Tavistock Clinic has been at the forefront of applying psychoanalytic concepts to organizations and has been innovative in combining these with ideas from systemic approaches.

Briefly, psychodynamic approaches to organizations view organizational development as similar to individual development. Like individuals, organizations are living organisms that have a sort of 'collective unconscious' (not the same as Jung's collective unconscious) side that motivates and drives the organization. This unconscious side is the 'shadow' or darker side of the organization and has vast influence on the individuals and groups that go to make up the institution/organization. Understanding these forces allows managers and consultants to interpret what is happening. Some of the principles underlying psychoanalytic approaches to understanding organizations are as follows (from Obholzer and Roberts, 1994):

1   Organizations, like individuals, develop defences against diffi-
    cult emotions which are too threatening or too painful to
    acknowledge. Menzies' (1960) hospital study showed how
    nursing tasks were organized in such a way as to deflect insti-
    tutional anxieties around pain and death.
2   The organization, its processes and procedures, and the social
    groups within the organization, defend individual workers against
    the anxieties of the workplace, many of which are unconscious.
3   Being a member of the organization makes it extremely difficult
    to understand the organization: members are emotionally
    caught up in the dynamics and anxieties of the organization
    which does not easily allow for objective viewpoints.
4   Irrational processes are very much at work within organizations
    and affect individual involvement and work.
5   What happens to individuals and groups in an organization,
    and what they talk about, may be symbolic ways of referring to
    the unconscious processes at work within the organization.
6   Organizations are places of great ambivalence. At one and the
    same time they want:

    (a) to bring problems to the surface and to deny problems;
    (b) to love the organization and to hate it;
    (c) to change and to remain the same;
    (d) to care for people and to sacrifice people for profits.

    These ambivalences remain side by side within organizations
    and can easily give mixed messages to employees.
7   Individuals are often attracted to particular organizational
    cultures because that culture provides the setting in which they
    can work with their own unresolved issues. The culture can also
    fit in with their type of 'personality' and parallel their defence
    systems. Deverall (forthcoming) uses the image of organizations
    as lions and foxes, each type with a different culture, to illus-
    trate how they appeal to diverse personalities.
8   There is a two-way traffic between individuals and organiza-
    tions: organizations create the individuals they want, projecting
    into them their healthy and unhealthy aspects, and individuals,
    in turn, make the organization into what they need it to be for
    them.
9   Many problems brought to counselling by individuals are
    expressions of organizational pathology. These problems will
    not be resolved by working at the intrapsychic level.
10 Institutions are 'containers' for individual anxieties. In so far as
    the organization cannot or does not contain these anxieties, the
    individual will project them onto parts of the organization.

11 Being part of an organization will bring out the difficult and hated side of an individual. This will be seen when it is projected onto parts of the organization: interpersonal relationships, team and staff settings, departments, individuals, the whole organization.

12 'Troubled' or 'difficult' individuals within organizations often play out an important representative role: 'this unconscious seduction of individuals into performing a function on behalf of others as well as themselves happens in all institutions' (Obholzer and Roberts, 1994: 131). Focusing on individual pathology, or individual relationship problems, can miss the organizational dimension.

Organizational dynamics

It is a short step from understanding these dynamics to seeing how they are played out in organizations and how they infiltrate counselling services in the following ways.

Splitting In splitting, individuals draw a line down the middle of a person (or organization) and make two realities out of one. Instead of being able to live with the anxieties of loving and hating an individual at the same time, they make two parts and love one and hate the other.

Case example

Jill came to counselling because she was accountable to two bosses, both male. One she loved and was very loyal to; the other she could not stand and saw everything he did as bad and ineffective. She had split them, one into the all-good, who could do no harm, and the other into all-bad, who could do no good. Recognizing this dynamic can help the workplace counsellor work with Jill, knowing well that Jill might do the same to her, the counsellor, but helping Jill recognize both sides of issues.

Organizations also split. One department can be the flagship where everything good occurs; another the scapegoat where everything bad takes place.

Projection Projection is a method of making others responsible for how one feels. An employee can project his or her feelings onto the organization, as the organization can project itself onto the individual. Management and employees can often do this to one another.

Case example
For some time, Nigel had been getting poor appraisal reports. They pointed out that he was difficult to work with, moody, interpersonally aggressive, and that his working teams spent a lot of energy trying to manage him as well as deal with their tasks. When he is made redundant, he is furious and tells the outplacement counsellor that he has been sacked because the organization cannot deal with creative and different people like himself. This could be an instance where Nigel is unable to accept his own shortcomings and projects them onto the organization.

Case example
Elaine has been a happy and valued member of the personnel team and has always pulled her weight. Recently, rumours have been circulating about mammoth redundancies within the department. This has raised suspicion among its members who have not been able to talk about what is happening in an open way. Elaine has become stressed and has had to take time off work, which is unusual for her. The counsellor suggests that she may well be carrying the stress of the department and expressing it in her illness.

'Projective identification' is another form of projection. This is explained well by Halton (1994: 16):

> Within organisations, it is often easier to ascribe a staff member's behaviour to personal problems than it is to discover the link with institutional dynamics. This link can be made using the psychoanalytic concept of projective identification. This term refers to an unconscious inter-personal interaction in which the recipients of a projection react to it in such a way that their own feelings are affected: they unconsciously identify with the projected feelings. For example when the staff of the . . . Unit projected their depression about closure onto the consultant, he felt this depression as if it were his own.

Often, the recipient of the projected feelings acts on them as if they were his/her own without understanding the process by which he or she expresses these feelings. So Joan comes complaining of depression, low energy, uncertainty about the future. It might not be a surprise to find that her department is going through change and the very feelings she talks about are the ones within the department. Perhaps, and this is the kind of question the counsellor will ask,

Joan is expressing and acting out the happenings within the department that cannot be expressed there.

Transference   Individuals transfer onto the organization unresolved feelings towards others in their lives, particularly parents. James acts towards his boss in much the same way as he responded to his domineering father. Even though his manager is far from domineering and has quite a participative style of leadership, James finds himself confronting him on his manner of leadership.

Similarly, the organization transfers its unconscious anxieties and feelings onto individuals who take on this pathology. In a process called 'scapegoating', particular individuals will act out the difficulties of the team, the department, the institution or the organization. This can be reflected in the roles individuals adopt in groups or the illnesses they take on or the emotions they express.

Working with psychodynamic concepts
The key elements for the counsellor who would try to understand and harness the psychodynamics of organizational life are to:

- Listen to the symbolic messages in what is said and how problems are articulated by clients.
- Assess the defence mechanisms of individual clients as a way of understanding what is happening between them and the organization.
- Decide what needs to be worked with: the internal world of the client, the interpersonal world, or organizational issues.
- Monitor one's own (the counsellor's) feelings (the countertransference) as a way of understanding what is happening to whom.
- Monitor the culture of the organization to foretell some of the problems likely to occur with individuals who work within its ambience.

Systemic approaches to organizations

Systems approaches to individuals and organizations work on the principle that there are connections between individuals that automatically create systems. People are not isolated; in subtle ways there are links between us all that influence how we think and behave. McCaughan and Palmer (1994: 12) explain systems thinking as: 'describing and explaining the patterns of behaviour that we encounter in the life of organisations . . . a system is a pattern of interaction, between persons and groups, which can be represented by one or more feedback loops – that is, by closed loops or sequences of interaction that link and integrate all the components of a system.'

Key concepts in systems thinking include the following:

1 Circular causation: human behaviours cause each other, not in a linear fashion as when a billiard ball hits another, but in a circular movement. Mother nags teenage son to do his homework, teenage sons gets more withdrawn, mother increases her nagging, son gets further withdrawn. Causation here is circular, one behaviour influencing the consequent one.

2 In open systems there is a continuing relationship between the organization and its environment.

3 Recursive systems models indicate that organizations are constantly re-making themselves (as do human bodies).

4 Organizations are dependent on their ability to learn in order to survive.

5 Within a systemic framework, organizations and individuals are connected by dynamic feedback loops. The organization moulds the individual through its culture, creating a corporate identity.

6 Individuals in an organization 'co-create' their world with all its meanings, difficulties, problems, relationships, etc. This co-creation is dependent on understanding and sharing contexts. Contexts give meaning, and behaviours have different meaning when viewed in different contexts; for example, kissing one's partner may be very acceptable at home but kissing one's patient may be unethical for a doctor. Problems sometimes arise because contexts are viewed differently.

The workplace counsellor who wants to work with systemic ideas would:

- Understand problems as context-specific rather than within individuals. Whose problem is this (or who is problematizing this issue)?
- Ask the right questions to arrive at answers to:
  Why is this situation the way it is?
  How can we reframe the problem and see it from new perspectives?
  What is the hidden order of the organization and what are its messages, overt and covert?
  Of what is this problem a symptom?
- Recognize the patterns emerging.
- Perceive the meanings ascribed to issues, organizations, problems etc.

Briefly, the psychodynamic and systemic approaches to organizations, which are not the only ones indeed, show how our understanding of organizations helps us to make sense of what happens
within them, particularly how they affect individuals who are
employed by them. These are far from simple concepts and the
whole relationship between individuals and the organizations in
which they work is complex. Other factors need to be considered:
the stage of development of the organization (is it just established,
well established?); the effects of the wider community on the
organization (economic and political forces); and the state of the
external environment within which the organization is operating. All
of these come together in what is termed 'organizational culture'.

Organizational culture

Organizations, like individuals, come in all shapes and sizes, with
different cultures and a multiplicity of ways in which they structure
their lives. 'Culture' is a term often used to describe differences in
organizations: different cultures reflect the contrasting ways in which
organizations manage their internal and external relationships.

Just as individuals have their own personalities which include
temperament, interpersonal style and their particular way of engaging with the world, so organizations have their personality (their
culture) which determines, to a large degree, the behaviour of their
employees. Organizational culture is about the ecology, the ethos, the
personality, the atmosphere of a company or institution. It is
reflected in 'the way we do things around here' and encompasses
values, beliefs and attitudes that are shared by members of the
organization. Sometimes these shared values come directly from the
organization and are enshrined in mission statements and policies
(e.g., on equal opportunities, sexual harassment etc.), but much of the
culture is passed on to newcomers invisibly. They soon learn how
'things are done around here', either by observing and doing or by
making the mistake of doing it 'wrongly' and being told what is the
accepted way of behaving. Organizational culture emerges in dress
codes, language, authority and power, permission to do things, sexual
expression, management style. Egan (1993a) has referred to what he
calls the 'shadow side' of organizations to show how a whole domain
of invisible networks exists in most organizations. These networks
facilitate informal communication, relationships, decisions and are
often as powerful, if not more powerful, than the formal channels.
Egan makes the point that effective managers know and manage the
'shadow side' as well as the formal side of organizations.

Organizational culture is a powerful influence on its members, and newcomers are socialized into the prevailing culture very effectively and often unconsciously. They learn, by osmosis, how to act and behave and relate and communicate and dress in ways that are accepted within the organizational context. By agreeing to do so, they are accepted within the culture. Individuals who do not conform stand out and have to be dealt with by the organization. Some are accepted as eccentric and live within the organization, others are laughed at, some are seen as the rebels, and some represent the anti-culture lobby for the organization.

Understanding the culture of an organization, institution or even a group, gives valuable insights into why individuals within these groups act the way they do, the norms that dictate behaviour, and also help us devise interventions to help people who become ill, mentally or physically. It may be that organizational culture demands behaviour from people that makes them ill; for example, the amount of time worked, how emotions are managed, and sometimes totally suppressed.

Different organizational cultures and counselling

Like trying to classify individuals into types (e.g. introvert, extrovert), several authors have attempted to classify organizations by culture. This has both strengths and weaknesses. One of its strengths is that it helps us understand, in a broad way, how to compare and contrast different organizations. It allows prediction of what might happen if we know the culture into which some things are being introduced. The weakness is that we can take the culture, like diagnostic categories for individuals, as absolute. We can, too easily, label the organization without realizing that cultures vary in content, in strength and in intensity (Pheysey, 1993), and that many contain varieties of different cultures rather than being stringently uniform.

The following classifications need to be seen in this light: as possible ways of understanding organizations, theoretically. They do not exist in 'pure' forms in any organization. The only way to know the culture of an organization is to live within it and experience its ecology. I will present five ways of depicting organizations to show how culture can be viewed from different perspectives and then offer an overview of what seems to be the most popular classification. These are by no means the only classifications: Critchley and Casey (1989) use the Gestalt cycle to outline six forms of organization that have different ways of getting stuck: the suppressed organization, the hysterical organization, the knowing-and-angry organization, the frightened organization, the task organization and the exhausted organization.

Table 4.1 gives an outline of five approaches to organizational cultures. A format used by van Oudtshoorn (1989) and Pheysey (1993) and originating from Harrison (1972) is the one I will use here to look at types of organizational culture with particular reference to how they might view and implement counselling provision. Harrison (see Summerfield and van Oudtshoorn, 1995) has offered a more recent version of these cultures which he calls the transactional, the self-expression, the alignment and the mutuality cultures. However, I will stay with the original typology: it seems to fit better with counselling provision. Harrison (1972) isolated four types of organization:

1   Role culture
2   Achievement culture
3   Power culture
4   Support culture

Role culture
The role organization is characterized by the fact that 'things get done around here' by people who take on roles and see others in role terms. Because people are defined in terms of their roles and responsibilities, these organizations tend to be somewhat hierarchical with rules and regulations to maintain roles. Authority exists to make sure that people maintain their roles, stay within them, sort out role conflicts, and principally ensure that the roles are geared towards the specific aims of the organization.

Case example
Sawlands Secondary School is a good example of a 'role culture'. The Headmaster, who is called Headmaster, not Mr Neilson, sees his role as maintaining good order and authority within the school. The Deputy Head (Mrs Harlow) is never called by her name but is called Mrs Deputy Head. Throughout the school, individuals are called by the task they do. Relationships are sorted out by role. The Headmaster is keen that the school be seen as a 'football team' (his analogy) where everyone has a part to play in the successful maintenance of the team. There is an extensive reward system for pupils from the Sports Personality of the Year to academic achievements throughout each year. The Headmaster maintains quite formal relationships with the staff and is proud of the fact that he is a just and fair person who will evaluate each situation on its merits: he likes to say he runs an orderly ship.

Table 4.1 *Organizational culture from five perspectives*

Hawkins and Shohet (1989)	Randall et al. (1980)	Kets de Vries and Miller (1984)	Cooke and Rousseau (n.d.)	Harrison (1972)
Personal pathology	Founder's syndrome	Paranoid	Humanistic/helpful	Role culture
Bureaucratic	Charismatic leader	Compulsive	Affiliative	Achievement culture
Watch your back	Compulsive collective	Dramatic	Approval	Power culture
Reactive/crisis-driven	The bureaucrats and the	Depressive	Conventional	Support culture
Learning/developmental	bored	Schizoid	Dependent	
	The love-is-all		Avoidance	
	The nothing-but-the-task		Oppositional	
			Power	
			Competitive	
			Competence/perfectionistic	
			Achievement	
			Self-actualization	

The strong and effective role organization is one where individuals know their role and how that role connects to the other roles within the organization. Administration is for the service of the organization and services it well. The degenerate form of the role culture exists where individuals are sacrificed to the organization. There is such an emphasis on role that roles become artificial rather than personal and/or real. The system can become closed when information is not allowed in from outside and conserving the past becomes a norm irrespective of the value of innovation and change.

In looking at the position of counselling within a role culture, Lane (1990: 542) writes:

> While resistant to counselling, if they develop it, counselling is likely to become a system in its own right, detached and accountable to its own professional code, but having little impact on organisational process. Some general statistics and advice may be passed back to management, but organisational change is not a feature of the service, nor can it be.

Role cultures may introduce counselling but will tend to see it as a 'fix-it' operation where individuals out of role can be helped to return to full role operations. Unfortunately, counselling can be viewed as punitive within role organizations and may be used by managers to sort out their troubled or troubling employees. Counselling will be viewed as a way of moving employees back into role, of managing role conflict, solving role confusion and generally creating harmony by defining clear role boundaries. Because role organizations tend to be 'rational' in their approach there may be little time for or appreciation of emotion/feeling. Counselling will be seen as problem-solving, is likely be short-term and may be cognitive-behavioural.

Achievement culture

The achievement culture concentrates on the work to be done rather than roles. People will cross roles to get the job done and swop responsibilities when needed. Such organizations tend to be small where individuals are trusted to get on with the job and react to what the job needs.

Decisions in achievement organizations are made laterally rather than hierarchically as in the role culture. Individuals are driven and motivated by their enthusiasm for the job, or because they have a stake in the company. Collaboration is the order of the day, and employees are encouraged to think of new ways of doing work.

Case example
Coombs and Coombs, an advertising firm, is just such an organization. It tends to employ creative and energetic individuals (men

and women), and you can find employees in the office as late as 10 o'clock at night. Last year, with one large order, a small team worked through the night, almost forgetting the time in their excitement at a new package they were designing. George Coombs is as likely to be found making coffee for some of the team as he is designing a logo: everyone is expected to market the business as well as produce for the clients. Close friendships are rife throughout the firm and lots of laughter emanates from the offices.

The strong achievement organization is an exciting and creative place to be. Change is part of life: the fact that it was done this way last year is no reason for doing it the same way this year. Rules, regulations, policies are under constant review. Consultation takes place on all levels. The weak achievement organization sacrifices the team to the individual. Innovation and creativity can be cherished for themselves and not harnessed to the welfare of organizational objectives. The organization can become chaotic rather than organized.

Lane (1990: 542) has pointed out how the achievement organization is likely to view counselling:

> Counselling, if seen as a highly professional resource, may be both provided and dropped as need arises. Where established on a long term basis it is likely to generate high levels of company referrals, not just individual ones. The organisation is likely to demand accountability for results and see counselling as part of the goal of performance. Its impact on company policy is therefore greater.

Despite their supportive and friendly atmosphere, achievement organizations find it difficult to cope with counselling. For them weakness is unacceptable, and whereas they stress the importance of the individual over the organization, it tends to be the healthy and working individual. As soon as individuals fall behind in the rapid, hectic world of the marketplace, there is a tendency to send them off to have them sorted out. Achievement organizations tend to move towards external counselling provision which keeps counselling at a distance.

Power culture

The power culture is one where dominance rules, where strength and control are cherished values, and where individuals know their place in the pecking order. Usually hierarchical, leaders are seen as making key decisions, handling individuals without feeling, and keeping clear and tight control on what happens. Motivation is seen as extrinsic and rewards are often monetary or benefits. Such companies may be patriarchal where the organization protects the individual as well as demanding outstanding loyalty from him/her. The organization values uncritical obedience, loyalty, hard work and, in turn, offers clear rewards.

Case example
Greenfields Police Service is a power culture organization. Policemen and women are fairly well guaranteed a job for life provided that they do not blot their copy-book. Obedience is expected and there are rules and regulations to guide behaviour at all levels. Employees are not expected to question authority or any changes brought in by management. Such changes will certainly not be discussed with the rank and file.

The strength of power cultures is their ability to 'get things done', and in emergencies are very useful to have around because of their decision-making ability. They protect their employees and reward them well. The weakness of power cultures is their view of human nature. They subscribe to the view of individuals as weak and needing motivation. As a result, they can be very punitive when someone does not live up to expectations or is not as loyal as he/she is expected to be. They, like role cultures, will sacrifice the individual to the organization.

Counselling may be introduced to power organizations as a way of helping weaker employees manage their jobs. It can be allied to welfare with a number of roles – information, advocacy, medical services – or the counselling provision can be external to the organization. Lane (1990: 542) connects counselling and power organizations:

> Counselling, if it has a role at all, is likely to be external, and medicalised. . . . Some of the longest established counselling services are within such positive power organisations. Such services are likely to see counselling as part of a welfare function, in house, confidential and with no impact on organisation change.

In general, power cultures are somewhat embarrassed by weakness and tend to deny or ignore it by relegating it to the sidelines of the organization. I was asked by the Vice-Chancellor of a sizeable university to talk to his Board about introducing counselling into the university. When I blithely referred to counselling for staff and students he stopped me and told me that the service was for students. He expected his staff to manage their own problems and if they could not then they needed to re-consider whether or not the university was the best job for them.

Support culture
The support culture organization stresses the value of relationships, mutuality, communication, and looking after its people. The emphasis is on collaborative work and rewards tend to be intrinsic: the satisfaction of working in the organization. Individuals are trusted to do their work, and support systems are in-built to help employees do their jobs well and reduce stress. Training is part of the job and employees are expected to be continually developing.

Case example
Outreach Youth Counselling Service is a good support culture. Set up as a comprehensive information, advice and counselling service for young people, it employs about 20 staff, full-time and part-time. The team meets as a full team once a week, supervision for counsellors takes place twice a week with an outside supervisor, and support groups within task areas have been organized. Decisions are made collaboratively.

The strong support culture cares for its employees deeply and recognizes, not just in words, that they are the best assets of the company. It sets up support at all levels of the organization so that individuals and teams can work effectively. Individuals will feel they belong to a nurturing group. The degenerative support culture will forget its task and concentrate on team and individual growth. The latter may become so prominent that the task of the organization suffers. Navel-gazing could well become the order of the day with the personal needs of individuals outweighing all other considerations.

Counselling services are seen as a natural part of support cultures. People are expected to have personal and work-related problems and need a forum where they can work with these. The organization will be eager to know what the problems are and how organizational structures can be changed to help people with their problems. Lane (1990: 542) sees support organizations as: 'unlikely to see counselling as a formal service but rather part of the skills within the organisation. Counselling services have difficulty in establishing themselves in such organisations, but sometimes appear as specialist additions, unlimited areas, such as AIDS, or career counselling.' Support cultures are scarce within the private sector. Many of the organizations talked about by Perry (1993) seem to fall within the support culture; for example, organizations set up for counselling women.

Summary

In brief, understanding the ecology of the organization will help articulate what may be expected and what needs to be done within that particular organization. As a result of such an assessment, a counsellor may decide that he/she is not ready or able to work within its ambience. For example, if a power culture organization wants to set up a counselling service it will do so in a way that does not allow for organizational change and will expect the counsellor to work with clients in such a way that they emerge as more dedicated members of the organization.

Counsellors are not, usually, management consultants, and not, usually, in a strong position to assess the well-being of an organization and its effects on its employees. Perhaps an area of training for those who would work as counsellors in organizational settings is precisely the skills required to assess the willingness of a company to introduce counselling and whether it is the answer to their employee problems. Egan and Cowan (1979) have drawn the distinction between 'upstream' and 'downstream' helping that is very pertinent to those working within companies. They see little point in hauling out individuals who are drowning, resuscitating them and sending them back 'upstream' where they once more become casualties of the system. Better, they insist, to go upstream and help the system so that it does not become an agent in the dysfunction of the individual. Lane (1990: 544) wants answers to a 'minimum of four questions . . . before a counselling service is introduced into an organisation. What problems are emerging that give rise to the demand for counselling? What factors influencing the situation are amenable to change? What problems is counselling expected to resolve? Is counselling an appropriate solution?'

Counsellors, by training, think interpersonally. In organizational settings, they are asked to think both interpersonally and organizationally. This can be quite a mind-shift. Counsellors are asked to be of benefit to the organization as a whole not just to individuals within it. They need to widen their perspectives: 'Employee counselling should not be tackled on a piecemeal basis, but should be coherently and effectively integrated with assessment, training and consultancy endeavours to form part of a coherent overall strategy for the whole organisation' (Clarkson, 1990: 4). Reddy (1993b: 65) has connected what he calls compatible organizational climate with counselling provision and designates the following characteristics:

- Full support and visible commitment from both top management and unions.

- Integration with good management and personnel practices.
- A willingness to deal also with the environmental sources of stress.
- Integrated initiatives in counselling skills training for internal counsellors.
- Acceptance of their responsibilities towards subordinates by supervisors and managers.
- Training for them to confront and deal with problems as they arise.
- A statement of policy and procedure from management and full information about the service to each employee.
- The appointment of one individual within the organization with clear accountability for the proper management and resourcing of the EAP.

One further aspect of organizational life will be considered here before looking in more detail about how to introduce counselling into an organization: the emotional side of organizations.

The 'emotional' workplace

Lest we think that the workplace is a mechanical, rational forum where everything runs according to plan, and reason, Joseph Heller (1966: 72) reminds us of the other side:

> I've got bad feet. I've got a jawbone that's deteriorating and someday soon I'm going to have to have all my teeth pulled. It will hurt. I've got an unhappy wife to support and two unhappy children to take care of. (I've got that other child with irremediable brain damage who is neither happy nor unhappy, and I don't know what will happen to him after we're dead.) I've got eight unhappy people working for me who have problems and unhappy dependants of their own. I've got anxiety: I suppress hysteria . . . I've got old age to face. I've got the decline of American civilization and the guilt and ineptitude of the whole government of the United States to carry around on these poor shoulders of mine.

Employees do not switch into rational mode when they enter the workplace. They come as persons, they bring their home problems, they relate to each other, sometimes effectively, sometimes destructively, they respond with levels of feelings to their workplace, the policies, the people, the changes. The workplace teems with feelings. We ignore them at our peril; not to recognize their force and their worth is to underestimate a valuable source of energy and a powerful force for either destruction or growth. Many experts on organizations, as indeed some on counselling, write as if feelings

were irrelevant to the workplace and portray the ideal as an emo-
tionless arena ruled by rationality. Emotions, even if granted
existence alone or as part of our thinking, will not be permitted
expression or any influence on organizational policy or development.
Hochschild (1993: x) asks a key question: 'Is emotional expression
an unexpected departure from workday routines, or is it part of the
inner wiring of them?' Can we doubt that they are part of the 'inner
wiring'? People at work are happy, sad, depressed, excited, enthusiastic, lustful, vengeful, resentful, bored, playful, worried, anxious,
hurt, hopeful, furious, isolated, frightened – to mention but a few
emotions that course through their veins. And those feelings have
vast influence on their work, their work relationships, their motivation and morale. Managers are all too aware of how powerful
feelings can be and indeed how difficult they are to manage.

Case example
Lucinda is a middle-manager who has, in her own words,
'busted a gut' in the past year on two projects. They have taken
up all her days and seen a number of midnights as well. She has
been told at her recent appraisal that she will not be considered
for promotion and it has been hinted that she has no promotional future with the company. She is furious, hurt, resentful,
and has vowed that never again will she put so much energy into
a company that appreciates what she has done so lightly. She is
particularly peeved that her boss who is noted for his lengthy
lunches seems to be getting the credit for her work.

Case example
Jeremy is head of Personnel. And very difficult to work with. He
has periodic bouts of severe depression when he is quite
unapproachable. During these bouts he can be vindictive,
hurtful, and paranoid when he thinks individuals are putting
him down. His department revolves around his moods, and his
secretary's first job each day is to determine how he is and let
the rest of the department know what is possible that day.

Case example
Imelda and Peter have never got on even though they have to
work together as part of Human Resources. She thinks he is
arrogant, opinionated, sexist and he considers her a wimp who is

always moaning about life and who cannot take stands. They
have given up public fighting but their feelings are expressed in
passive-aggressive behaviour. He makes jokes behind her back,
while she makes sure that his role in their work is diminished at
all opportunities.

The three examples above, all about emotions, are not just inner
feelings but active influences on behaviour. None of them will add
to the workplace and some of them could have quite serious
detrimental effects on work, morale and productivity. Hochschild
(1983) coined the phrase 'emotional labour' to connote knowing
about and managing one's own and others' emotions. Organizations
manage emotions in many ways. Some buy employee emotions and
sell them to customers: Fineman (1993: 18–19) comments on this:

> A shop assistant's smile without warmth, or a waiter's glum or disdainful
> expression the instant he turns away from his customer, reminds us that
> emotional performance can be a fragile affair. As hierarchical control and
> surveillance bears down more firmly on the *detail* of emotional perform-
> ance, emotional labour becomes more demanding . . . the difficulties
> occur when work-laboured performances stick; they become situationally
> unspecific. The 'handle-em-tough' executive carries the mask home. The
> 'sincere' salesman cannot switch off his patter when with his friends. The
> limelight never fades; work demeanour and self merge.

Whether the emotions of employees are for sale to customers or
not, most organizations regulate the expressions of feeling. Emotional maps are part and parcel of companies, public and private.
They are ways, some conscious, some unconscious, in which the
organization dictates what feelings are permitted, how feelings can
be expressed, and what circumstances allow for which feelings.
Different jobs permit the expression of different feelings: while a
manager might express negative feelings towards an employee, it is
not permitted the other way around; and while it might be acceptable for a female employee to 'flirt' with a boss, it would not be
acceptable for the occupational doctor to sexualize an interaction
with an employee. As Fineman (1993: 20) puts it 'emotions, as social
currency, vary in their rates of exchange and validity.' Corporate
culture has rules about emotions ('the way we deal with emotions
around here') and how they are mobilized and managed, what is
acceptable, what not.

Putnam and Mumby (1993) suggest ways in which organizations
can facilitate feelings to the betterment of the workplace. Specifically
they recommend:

1 Training for employees to understand the complexity of emotions in the workplace and how they fashion life there. Rather than control emotions this allows for expression of work feelings.
2 Emotions and feelings could be geared as adapting to the social context rather than be prescribed beforehand. This gives freedom to employees to choose their reactions, e.g. it might well be appropriate for a secretary to articulate her feelings of being used by her boss rather than put on a plastic smile which hides her resentment (as dictated by the manual).
3 Seeing feelings as serving a communicative role that develops community. Using emotion as a way of building relationships and teams can help mutual understanding. Building in team development using the expression of feeling might be more helpful than trying to build teamwork rationally.
4 Seeing emotional expression as an alternative for dealing with covert control. This gives a further option for dealing with situations that cannot be solved rationally. Heller points out the dilemma in his novel.

> People in the company, for example, do their best to minimize friction (we are encouraged to revolve around each other eight hours a day like self-lubricating ball bearings, careful not to jar or scrape) and to avoid quarrelling with each other openly. It is considered much better form to wage our battles sneakily behind each other's back than to confront each other directly with any semblance of complaint. (The secret attack can be denied, lied about, or reduced in significance, but the open dispute is witnessed and has to be dealt with by somebody who finds the whole situation deplorable.) We are all on a congenial, first-name basis, especially with people we loathe (the more we loathe them, the more congenial we try to be). (1966: 47)

Rather than denying what is happening emotionally, employees can be helped to deal with it. Often the workplace organizes ways of siphoning off emotions in an acceptable way: some of these do so, some just add to the resentment and hidden negative feelings, e.g.

• emotional events such as days out, dinners
• ritualized events such as drinking parties, office events, sports
• individual events that are permitted or at least tolerated

Organizations will have different ways of staging emotional events.
Despite the reality of emotions in the workplace and their expression, whether allowed or not, there is still a myth that the workplace is governed by rational events and thinking. Feelings are seen as irrelevant to the workplace. Putnam and Mumby (1993) argue the opposite. Rather than being a deviation from what is seen

as worthwhile in organizations, they see emotion as 'the process through which members constitute their work environment by negotiating a shared reality' (p. 36). The shared reality allows them to express their feelings in a team rather than simply individually.

There has been some criticism of workplace counselling as a method of individualizing emotions and providing a forum where they can be dissipated rather than used for organizational change. This does not have to happen if counselling is used as a way of empowering individuals to be in touch with their feelings and express them when and how they choose.

Conclusion

The organizational context in which counselling is offered to employees has vast influence not just on the administrative side of counselling but on the interpersonal dimension as well. Counsellors need to be aware of that influence and be able to manage it effectively. Otherwise, pathology can be chased around the system and organizations may never be aware that the counselling they have set up is part of the problem, not part of the solution. Matching counselling provision to organizational culture is essential if the service is to survive and prosper and meet the needs of the particular environment. With this in mind, Chapter 5 will review how to set up counselling services within organizations.

5

Setting up Counselling in the Workplace

'No!' said Robyn hotly. 'That's not the answer. If you try to make universities like commercial institutions, you destroy everything that makes them valuable. Better the other way round. Model industry on universities. Make factories collegiate institutions.'

'Ha! We wouldn't last five minutes in the marketplace,' said Vic.

'So much the worse for the marketplace,' said Robyn. 'Maybe the universities are inefficient, in some ways. Maybe we do waste a lot of time arguing on committees because nobody has absolute power. But that's preferable to a system where everybody is afraid of the person on the next rung of the ladder above them where everybody is out for themselves, and fiddling their expenses or vandalizing the lavatories, because they know that if it suited the company they could be made redundant tomorrow and nobody would give a damn. Give me the university with all its faults, any day.'

'Well, ' said Vic, 'it's nice work if you can get it.'

D. Lodge, *Nice Work*

Setting up and maintaining a counselling service in the workplace, whether in-house or external, needs careful planning: a haphazard effort may result in the wrong kind of provision for the organization and a poor introduction never quite recovers from its bad beginning. Like the quotation above, where Vic and Robyn argue the relative merits of their own workplaces, so the introduction of counselling into the workplace is about the merging of two worlds. As in all mergers that succeed, there is a need for clear negotiation, for understanding the world of the other, and an anticipation of potential pitfalls. It went wrong in one large, multi-national financial establishment that was keen to have counselling for its employees. Perhaps because the organization (and in this instance Human Resources who had been given the task) knew little about counselling, or perhaps because it was not high on the list of 'things to be done', they decided to hire an in-house counsellor, give him/her a counselling room/office and let him/her get on with the job. A counsellor was duly appointed (they did not have a counsellor on the interviewing panel) and within a few weeks she had disappeared into the organization. She was psychoanalytically trained and worked long-term, she saw only a few clients, and because of her concerns around confidentiality she never involved herself in the organization. She refused any invitations to be involved in training, to sit on any committees, or be part of any policy-making groups, insisting that it would endanger relationships with clients. Within a few months the word on the shop-floor was that if you went to see her you were inevitably in for long-term (minimum of six months) counselling. This inhibited quite a number of people. The service was discontinued at the next annual review.

Without carefully thought-through decisions on policy, procedures and marketing, problems will inevitably arise. In the example above, counselling provision had not been thought through clearly with an eye to policy for the organization, procedures to make it effective and marketing to keep it viable. Wrich (1985: 172) has suggested that it is not clinical incompetence that is the danger point for EAPs:

> Suffice it to say that we have not seen a single EAP fail because of a clinical issue. Failures we have seen have been due to issues of administration, politics, a lack of sufficient evaluation, or inadequate communication of evaluative material. Invariably, the problem causing the failure could be traced to the initial program implementation process.

This chapter sets out to offer a step-by-step guide on how to set up a counselling service in the workplace. It is not the only way to do so and one model is offered for consideration which consists of six stages:

1 Preparation for counselling
2 Assessing workplace counselling
3 Contracting for workplace counselling
4 Introducing counselling into organizations
5 Terminating the relationship between organization and provider
6 Evaluating workplace counselling

The final stage, evaluation, will be dealt with in Chapter 7.

Preparation for counselling

Before beginning the process of assessing organizations, it is helpful to have structures already in place. I am calling setting up these structures the pre-assessment or preparation stage. It is essential that both an organization and a counselling provider (either external or one that hopes to be internal) have a number of facilities organized in advance.

The organization

I would suggest that an organization which has never had a counselling service before begin by thinking through carefully what it wants. This can be done by:

1 Setting up a small, representative team from within the organization to steer the discussions and negotiations for providing a suitable counselling service for this group. It is crucial that this group be representative and, if staff councils or unions are part of the workforce, that they have delegates on the team.
2 Engaging an independent consultant (who understands counselling) to work with the team to help the members assess what they want. This consultant ought not to be employed by a counselling provider or be one who would be involved in the counselling work itself with this organization. He/she could monitor the whole process and, indeed, could well evaluate the service at a later date. But the value of the consultant to the organization, at this stage, is to facilitate its search and provide needed education when necessary.
3 Finding out what the organization needs from counselling: internal or external provision, a combination of both, what minimum requirements are needed from a counselling provider, what qualifications counsellors should possess, what facilities are needed for the service, what budget is available to manage the service, and whether the counselling service is to contribute to organizational support and change. It is essential that the counselling provision is seen to be congruent with prevailing management practices.
4 Reviewing the cost of counselling and investigating the costs of different forms of counselling provision.
5 Checking how committed the key people in the organization are to counselling. Hoskinson (1994: 3) has put this well, 'One of the most important components . . . is the organizational investment or *commitment* to provide such services systematically, uniformly and to professional standards – and to perhaps position the service as in the interests of *both* the well-being of the employee *and* the performance of the business.' Actively engaging that support from key people in management, as well as within unions and particular departments, is an effective way of ensuring that the counselling service has a chance of success.

6 Drawing up a list of potential providers to be interviewed. Potential providers can be discovered by asking other companies who have organized counselling and use providers and by getting lists of counselling providers from the Employee Assistance Providers Association (EAPA).

At this early stage, before the search has begun for a counselling provider, the organization will have defined what it means by counselling, whether or not counselling will be part of a wider provision, including such elements as advice, welfare, information, etc., or stand on its own, and will have reviewed the motivation of the organization in seeking to implement counselling as part of its resources. When the organization begins the assessment part of the search, it will already have a clear concept of what it wants and where it is headed.

The counselling provider
Before beginning the process of assessing and negotiating with an organization, the counselling provider (this could be an EAP provider, a group of counsellors or an individual counsellor) needs to have a structure in place that informs an organization about the service and provides a basis for negotiation. This structure should include the following:

- explanations of how the service works (theoretically)
- a clear programme of services offered
- supervision arrangements
- methods of keeping statistics and giving feedback
- how the relationship between individual clients, counsellors and the organization is agreed and maintained
- clarity around contracts
- clarity about insurance
- issues of referral, emergencies
- other roles

Preparations involving the above will help prevent misunderstanding and will offer guidelines for both parties.

Counselling providers need to have policy statements outlining their purpose, the provisions they offer, restrictions and limitations, and finances involved, where applicable. Wright (1985) has outlined the policy and procedures necessary for an EAP, which is applicable to counselling provision in general. Such policy statements ideally contain:

- The purpose of counselling.
- A statement on counselling philosophy in the workplace, i.e. how counselling is seen as beneficial in the workplace, why it is

needed, and what benefits it will provide for both individuals and the company.

- What is needed to provide counselling within an organization: support by highest authority, budget, premises, a steering committee, a contact person within the organization, supervision for counsellors, publicity etc.
- How counselling within an organization provides other resources: training, consultancy, welfare etc.
- Who is covered by counselling provision: employees, family, dependants, etc.
- How referrals take place: self-referral, referral by others, recommended or mandatory.
- A confidentiality statement, which clarifies when confidentiality could be broken with or without the consent of the client.
- What to do in emergencies.
- How counselling services can be evaluated.
- The criteria for the background and training of counsellors.
- The roles and responsibilities of different groups and personnel: steering committee, the counsellors, managers, departments, employees.
- The code of ethics to which the counselling service and counsellors subscribe (see Clarkson, 1994, for help in setting up a code of ethics for the counselling office).

Policy statements need to be clear enough to be understood and flexible enough to adapt to different organizations. By providing sample policy statements, counselling providers show that they have thought through organizational issues and are prepared for negotiation. Good preparation on the part of the organization and of the provider goes a long way in helping clear negotiation. It also shows how seriously both parties take the exercise. Preparation forces organizations and providers to spend time thinking through what they want and what they supply, and forces them to articulate these in statements and policies.

Assessing workplace counselling

This is a crucial stage in setting up counselling in an organizational setting. It involves the organization assessing those who would provide counselling and it entails the provider evaluating the organization. It must be recognized from the outset that the uniqueness of each organization demands that the counselling provision be 'tailor-made' to suit size, culture, the nature of the work of the organization, its location, its particular workforce. There is no single model that covers all these: examples can be seen from the organizations that have an existing counselling service. Summerfield and van Oudtshoorn (1995: 16) suggest 11 questions to help organizations decide about the right kind of counselling for them.

1 Who or what has driven the initiative?
2 What do senior management want from the provision?
3 What does the human resource function want from the provision?
4 What do individual employees, including management, want from the provision *for themselves*?
5 For each of the above three interest groups, what are the priorities?
6 What structures/support systems are already in place?
7 What are the logistical and economic constraints?
8 What level of quality assurance is required, and how will quality be monitored?
9 How will the programme be marketed?
10 How will the programme be evaluated?
11 How will the programme fit in with the organization's culture?

Assessing the organization
Maynard and Farmer (1985: 31) have posed some essential questions in assessing the organization:

What do we have to know in order to decide

1) what the company wants from its program,
2) who should be involved in the planning stages of the program,
3) how and where the program should be integrated into other company functions and systems, and,
4) what specific implementation activities should be conducted and in what order?

These and a number of other areas need consideration to understand how best to enter and set up counselling in a particular organization.

What is the organizational culture of this group? How is that culture expressed? How might this particular company respond to counselling? Having some idea of what kind of culture is involved should help ascertain what kind of counselling provision is best suited to this group of people (see Chapter 4). There are various ways of assessing the culture of an organization. Spending time within it, talking to different groups and individuals, reviewing policies and statements, being acquainted with the organizational decision-making process and reviewing the power structure are all ways of getting a feel for the ideology of an organization. More formal psychometric assessment is also available; for example, the *Organizational Culture Inventory* published by Human Synergistics (Verax, 1991), or *Diagnosing Organisational Culture* designed by Roger Harrison and Herb Stokes (n.d.).

What are the counselling needs of employees?   Some sort of needs analysis should open up the kinds of problems employees face: stress within work, personal issues brought into the workplace etc. It may also help to evaluate whether or not counselling is the best method of meeting these needs. It could be that organizational change consultants may deal more effectively with what is happening, or involving an outplacement counselling firm may be more effective.

Cooper and Cartwright (1994) have suggested a 'stress audit' as a helpful way of assessing some of the organizational needs. One method of doing this is to use the *Occupational Stress Indicator* (Cooper et al., 1988) which has been used as a diagnostic tool. Data from this instrument can be used to assess employee needs and to match those needs to helpful interventions whether these be counselling, training or other.

Why is the organization looking for counselling just now?   How will the provision of counselling affect what is happening? Answers to these two questions will often reveal whether or not counselling is required for a particular area (e.g. a Building Society that is mostly interested in helping employees deal with armed raids), and what kind of counselling might best help (e.g. post-traumatic stress disorder counselling).

How does the organization understand counselling?   An awareness of how counselling is described will help dispel myths – e.g. counselling will create a happier workforce – and will also face unreal expectations or real expectations that cannot be met by counselling provision.

How committed to counselling provision are the top people?   Wrich (1985: 171) is clear that support from the top is essential: 'many attempts to establish an EAP never really get off the ground specifically for lack of active management support from the very top of the organization on down.' He goes on to clarify that support is not just about not opposing the venture, and uses terms like 'active advocacy', 'casting a positive vote', 'providing a substantial contribution' to describe what support means. It is also a good idea to identify the individual or group who initiated the idea of counselling: their active support could be invaluable in the future or, indeed, it might unearth reasons for suggesting counselling not in keeping with what counselling is about. It is worthwhile trying to understand how employees might view the introduction of counselling by top management. It some instances it might be seen as a method of social control or as a way of preparing for major change with job losses.

What facilities will be provided for counselling? Rooms to see clients, secretarial support, confidentiality provisions, budgets etc. are a few areas that need to be considered carefully by the organization. Is the organization aware of what is needed financially to run a counselling service effectively? Wrich (1985) has pointed to the need for adequate funding for the venture and has offered advice on what services may be most cost-effective for different sizes of organization.

Who is the organizational contact with the counselling service? Who is line manager if the service is internal, and who will be the contact person with the external provider? Managing the service is a key factor in how well it works. Hoskinson (1994) suggests that this management function is best supplied by an 'advisory committee'.

How will counselling be integrated into the organization? It is too easy for counselling services to become appendages to organizations rather than being integrated into their lives. Organizations can be helped to see how counselling can do more than simply deal with individuals in crisis and can be a process for organizational change (see Chapter 2).

Deverall (forthcoming) has summarized the areas that should ideally be covered when an organization is interested in introducing counselling as follows:

1 The age and history of the organization.
2 What does the organization do?
3 How well is the organization performing financially relative to the market, to past performance and to public opinion (especially if it is not a profit-centred organization)?
4 What is the size and geographical spread of the organization?
5 Personnel statistics, e.g. personnel turnover, remuneration etc.
6 Statements, policies, plans.

7   What is the management style of the organization?
8   Has the organization been the subject of takeover?
9   Who is the organizational contact with the counselling provider?

At this stage of assessment, counselling providers can take one of several stances. First, the company is ready for a counselling service and has the infrastructure (attitude, motivation, personnel, budget, facilities) to begin negotiations. A second stance is that the company is not ready for counselling provision but needs more help from a consultant to build up awareness of what counselling means and how it might be integrated into the organization. It is important throughout this process that counselling providers retain their freedom to refuse to provide counselling if they consider that the situation is wrong and that counselling has little chance of succeeding.

Assessing counselling provision

As counselling providers (or counsellors) will want to assess the organization and its readiness for a counselling service, so organizations will want to assess the group or individual(s) who will provide their counselling. What should they look for? I suggest the format on page 89 can be used (this is what the counselling provider has in place before counselling begins). Good providers will have this available for organizations and will meet to clarify issues and/or give further information and answer questions. Deverall (forthcoming) suggests the following areas for assessment:

1   How many counsellors are available and what is their availability?
2   What are their qualifications?
3   Do counsellors have experience of working in organizations?
4   Are qualifications uniform or diverse?
5   What are the value systems of counsellors and are they uniform or diverse?
6   Where are counsellors located?
7   Where will counselling take place?
8   What sort of service is being offered? Is it 24-hour, remedial, developmental, long-term/short-term?
9   What will be the cost to the organization?

Contracting for workplace counselling

The assessment stage allows both participants to find out information about each other and make initial judgements about suitability. The next stage is to draw up a more formal contract or agreement that covers roles and responsibilities as well as the practicalities of working together.

Francek (1985) has offered guidelines for contracting within organizations that are applicable to counselling provision. Some of these are offered below, adapted specifically to counselling provision:

- expect the unexpected
- expect resistance
- anticipate the objections
- know about counselling and its strengths and weaknesses within organizations
- recall earlier meetings
- be knowledgeable about the organization
- understand human nature and the basic reluctance to buy
- be prepared with alternatives
- know what is negotiable and what is not
- be professional (don't allow personal reactions too big a sway)

Contracts can include as much or as little as participants want. Some cover essentials (see Appendix 1 for a short contract). Contracts will include agreement on:

- the philosophy of the counselling service: this will include the purpose of the programme, the elements involved, who can use it, how confidentiality is defined and understood and what qualifications counsellors will need
- objectives to be attained
- policies
- procedures
- the contact person within the organization and/or steering committee
- publicity of the service: this will include announcement of the programme and material for each employee
- the responsibilities of all parties (counsellors and organization)
- provision for supervision and training
- evaluation of the counselling service, record keeping, reports and feedback
- counselling budget and financial responsibilities
- integration into company policies
- a code of ethics for the counselling service

Bull (1995: 8–9) has summarized areas that require consideration when setting up a service that can be used as a useful checklist (see Box 5.1). What is essential at this stage is that both parties to the counselling agreement are satisfied that they have discussed

Box 5.1   *Setting up a counselling service*

- identify the needs of the staff and the organization
- compare service costs with those of alternative strategies
- agree services to be provided
- obtain the backing of key people and groups within the organization
- establish guidelines for access to the service, i.e. type of referral
- establish lines of accountability
- establish boundaries for confidentiality
- devise methods of data collection and record keeping
- ensure a confidential location for counselling
- establish a continuing strategy for publicizing the service
- identify local referral network
- agree number of sessions and with whom
- establish administrative support
- agree hours of service availability
- provide external clinical supervision
- ensure counsellors have professional indemnity insurance
- establish quality assurance systems
- evaluate service

Source: Bull, 1995: 8–9

and negotiated all aspects of implementing counselling into the organization.

Hay (1992) uses the work of Eric Berne to highlight three levels of contract that are applicable to workplace counselling:

1 Administrative contracts which outline various arrangements concerning such issues as responsibilities, payments, timing, publicity, etc.
2 Professional contracts which revolve around policies, objectives, tasks and roles of various individuals and groups and methods of implementation and evaluation.
3 Psychological contracts which are based on respect and trust and are more concerned with the various relationships involved. Unhealthy psychological contracts exist where there are unresolved issues between participants, underlying dynamics and politics that influence behaviour. Psychological contracts allow different parties to deal with any blocks, individual or group, conscious or underlying, that might harm the programme.

Often it is the third of these that is most neglected and in the long run can have the most influence. It is recommended that all three be considered in some detail when negotiations around workplace counselling are taking place.

Introducing counselling into the workplace

Contracting to bring counselling provision into the workplace, however, is only the beginning: the really hard work starts in working out and implementing a strategy for introducing counselling to the organization. This involves a number of areas.

Managing the counselling process

Many counsellors, well trained in clinical work, have little expertise in counselling management, that is, how to set up a counselling system that works within another system. These are skills beyond the skills of working with individuals and groups in a therapeutic way, and demand the ability to think systemically and practically about the full implications of counselling work. This, too, needs to be part of the training of organizational counsellors. Counselling management covers such areas as:

1 What physical arrangements are needed to provide confidential counselling to clients in this setting? Where will the counselling room be placed? How will it be furnished? Klarreich (1985) reckons that, after confidentiality, location of the service is the most important ingredient in successful workplace counselling. Suitable counselling rooms and adequate office space will enhance not only the service but the image of the service.

2 How will clients contact the counselling service? Can they be referred by others? Will the counsellor accept referrals and appointments from sources other than the client, e.g. colleagues, managers, supervisors, disciplinary boards, personnel, etc.? And what are the circumstances in which referrals will be made?

3 How will the counselling service be advertised/publicized?

4 In what circumstances would a counsellor not accept a referral, for example, when a manager wanted to give a formal warning and insists on counselling to help the employee change their behaviour?

5 What happens when the client contacts the service? Who is the first contact? What information does the first contact require?

6 How is the client assessed, and what referral points are appropriate?

7   What does the client (and the appropriate manager) need to know about the counselling service?
8   What kind of contract is made with the client?
9   What notes are kept on the client, where are they kept, who else besides the counsellor has access to these notes? How long are notes kept after the counselling has terminated?
10 What happens when the client terminates counselling?
11 How are statistics kept within the service and how are they publicized?
12 How will the counsellor organize his/her time in respect of clients, publicity, training, contacting?
13 Will clients be seen for a specific number of sessions, will some be long-term?
14 If the counselling provision is within a department (e.g. occupational health, personnel), what are the relationships involved? What contact will the department have with clients, what will they need to know about the clients, if anything?
15 What contact will the counsellor have with referral agencies? When will a client be referred for specialist help?
16 What methods will be used to evaluate the counselling service?
17 When will the counsellor contact other professionals (e.g. a doctor, psychiatrist, social worker) with or without the client's permission?
18 What insurance (indemnity) is appropriate for the counsellor to have (personally and/or organizationally) and what should this cover?
19 What supervision arrangements are essential (desirable) for the counsellor to have?
20 What will the counsellor do in the case of an emergency?

This may seem a 'hefty' agenda for the beginning counsellor who needs to have worked through most of these areas before beginning to see clients. However, these items by no means exhaust all the areas necessary to be set up. Not to have thought them through and worked out some answers will result in boundary issues, clients feeling unsafe and unsure, and the counsellor making up answers as the occasion arises. Counselling management is a prerequisite to good counselling provision, and seeing clients is part of an overall safety structure provided by good counselling practice.

Publicizing counselling services

There is little point in having a counselling service in an organization if it is not known by all employees, and if the image intended is not the image in the minds of consumers. Fisher's research (1995) highlights some of the views of counselling that need to be avoided: 'There is still a lot of suspicion about personal counselling, and it's still seen here quite a lot as a failure if you need counselling . . . the very concept of counselling sends most people into a corner saying where's the crucifix and garlic.' Marketing the service is crucial on several points. It needs to ensure that all those for whom it is intended know of its existence, how to contact it, and what it will provide. It will be essential to have an 'announcement' day or event formally to introduce the service and its personnel. In one company (Klarreich, 1985) a letter endorsed by the executive director of medical services was sent to all employees. Publicity is also a way of explaining what counselling does. Employees need to know what will happen when they present themselves in the counsellor's room, what are the limitations of the service, what confidentiality means in this context.

Francek (1985: 24) has indicated that marketing EAPs is a complex process and has isolated a number of factors to be considered: 'In truth, the diversity and complexity of the targeted organisations, coupled with the need for versatility and adaptability on the part of the marketing experts, suggest a dynamic interplay that makes simple solutions next to impossible.' He recommends that the organization be assessed to understand how to publicize within the particular group and culture. How does communication typically take place, where do individuals and groups meet, what is the best method of accessing the information flow within the organization? Good assessment should uncover how best to publicize: individually, through groups, newsletters, meetings, etc. It will also reveal the key individuals within the organization who need to know what counselling is about and how to refer to it. Francek (1985) uses the term 'organizational networking' to describe setting up relationships with all levels of management, and all departments, within the organization. Working with the 'shadow-side' of organizations is a further skill to help promote services (Egan, 1994).

Clear strategies for publicity need to be outlined: what needs to be said, how it is best communicated with the group, how it will be said, what particular groups will be targeted for publicity. This will differ from organization to organization: the size of the organization may be one variable in how publicity will take place. Once the strategies are clear, they can be implemented and monitored to see how well they are working. Evaluating publicity will help counsellors know where knowledge about the service is located. It may be, if only women are coming for counselling, that publicity will target male employees.

High visibility and good work are the best promotional methods.

Interviewees in Fisher's (1995) research talked about ways of publicizing their counselling service: 'I think we have to go and make some positive personal relationships, with more senior managers . . . I see it as fundamental to my role that I am known to as many key stakeholders as I can be.' In the long run, satisfied clients will take over as the main publicizers of counselling, and referral by clients themselves is ideal. However, other strategies can help. It is always helpful to update information as a way of periodic publicity. This can be done through individuals or departments, as well as in-house magazines. Making presentations on the counselling service to different groups is a further method of publicity and often a way of establishing personal contacts. Including the counselling service in policy statements – for example, equal opportunities, sexual harassment, stress management, health and safety policies – is a way of indicating how the service has been integrated into the organization at all levels.

Obviously, how counselling is introduced to the organization as a whole is a critical task. The right publicity gets across the image intended. Publicizing counselling services rarely rates highly on counselling training courses. The skills of the publicist are not the same as those required for working with clients. What is needed in publicity is:

- the ability to produce clear written formulations: brochures, policies, statements
- good oral skills in presenting the service
- very good interpersonal skills to facilitate meeting key people in the organization and establishing personal contacts
- assertiveness skills to ensure that the service has a high profile
- organizational skills to assess how best to publicize in the organization

Terminating counselling with an organization

Contracts are either renewed or ended. In some instances, counselling comes to an end. This can happen for several reasons: the company has decided to change its counselling service, the counselling provider is not renewing the contract, mergers have taken place, a company is closing down. Whatever the reason, it seems important to prepare for this termination effectively.

Termination with individual clients should be considered carefully. Even though the formal contract has ended, provision must be made for individuals who are still in counselling. Generally, dates will be negotiated for ending, referral may take place as a result.

Ethically, it is clear that service to individual clients must be ended in a satisfactory and measured manner.

Termination time is also a good opportunity for feedback. Companies can be asked for information on the counselling service, why they are not continuing counselling provision, and how they found working with counsellors. Likewise, counsellors can give feedback to the company on what they have learnt from working with it. If the contract and contact between the two parties has been good, they will already have shared many of these issues and surprises will be unusual.

Employees, in general, need to be told about ending the service. Just as the service was introduced formally, so termination is best done formally. A letter from the chief executive or managing director will give the news with an explanation of why the decision to end has been made. A small group can be set up to deal with the practicalities of ending: what happens to notes and files, who owns what and what counsellors have a right to take away from the company.

Conclusion

The first five stages of introducing counselling into an organization are not sufficient on their own. Effective counselling adds evaluation as a way of monitoring the quality of its service. This will be considered in Chapter 7; but, first, Chapter 6 will offer a model for counselling individual employees.

6

An Integrative Model of
Individual Employee Counselling

People rarely plan to fail, but often fail to plan. (Advertisement)

Workplace counselling can be deemed to be any activity in the workplace where one individual uses a set of techniques or skills to help another individual take responsibility for and to manage their own decision-making whether it is work related or personal.

Institute of Personnel Management, *Statement on Counselling in the Workplace*

This chapter will present a systematic five-stage model of setting up, maintaining and terminating a counselling relationship with an employee in an organizational setting. There will be a pre-assessment stage during which counsellors prepare for counselling work with employees, and employees prepare for counselling.

There are few systematic models for workplace counselling that outline the stages and processes of counselling in this context. Most are adaptations from individual counselling, often from private practice where there is a clear dyadic relationship. Counselling in organizations is more of a triadic relationship with client, counsellor and organization in a three-way relationship. Models that involve more than two people in counselling (couples and family counselling, systemic approaches to counselling) are the closest models to counselling in the workplace.

In this chapter, workplace counselling will be divided into five stages as a map to guide counsellors (see Table 6.1). The five stages of the integrative model are:

Stage 1:   Preparation for workplace counselling
Stage 2:   Assessment
Stage 3:   Contracting/referring
Stage 4:   Engaging in workplace counselling
Stage 5:   Terminating workplace counselling

These stages do not have to be followed rigorously. They are meant to be flexible and simply act as a guide. Above all, workplace counsellors are flexible and adapt their time and therapeutic

Table 6.1   *Five-stage model of workplace counselling*

Stage 1 Preparation	Stage 2 Assessment	Stage 3 Contracting	Stage 4 Engaging	Stage 5 Terminating
Preparation by: Counsellor Client	Understanding clients	Agreeing to work together	Managing the personal, adminis- trative and organiz- ational sides of counselling	Agreeing a termination date
	Methods of assessment	Contracting on: Practicalities Roles of client and counsellor Role of the organization		Working towards termination
	Agreeing and assessment			Process of termination
	Considering interventions		Re-entry of employees	Final session
	Agreeing counselling	Referring, if appropriate	The tasks of workplace counselling	After termination
	Sharing information			

relationships to particular situations. There are times when a stage-related model makes no sense; for example, when an employee comes for a single session. The five-stage model above needs drastic adaptation at times: often there is a crisis or an emergency that bypasses stages in the model and focuses immediately on the presenting problem. The whole concept of termination takes on a different meaning when employees come for a one-off session to deal with an immediate issue and may well do that several times within the course of a year. So flexibility, which includes the needs of clients as well as the adaptability of counsellors, pertains in applying this model. However, having an overall model for workplace counselling gives an overview of the process. This enables employee counsellors to know and understand where they are in the counselling process and to make choices about what is best for individual clients, and what will not be appropriate in the circumstances.

The values of this model are:

1   It is atheoretical: it can be used with various counselling orientations or with an integrative approach, and many of the models outlined in Chapter 2.

2   It is a process model: it allows the practitioner to follow counselling throughout its many phases, and can be used to monitor what is happening with individual clients.

3   It is a competency-based model: workplace counsellors can see the skills against which they can measure themselves and their array of competencies.   .

Preparation for workplace counselling

The pre-assessment stage is presented here as an ideal: it is what 'should' happen before clients are seen, and indeed before the counselling service is established. In reality, such provision is rarely in place before counselling begins – which is a pity. It is difficult for workplace counsellors to create new ways of working out of their own experience rather than having a working model to guide them even before they begin. Certainly, we know enough about counselling and workplace counselling to be able to define and outline working models before counselling services are established.

Preparation for the service allows counsellors to think through and operationalize before they begin to see clients. By doing so they can have a system in place that can be further adapted in the light of their experience. Like all models, pre-prepared policies and checklists are our servants and not meant to imprison or depersonalize the therapeutic endeavour. Throughout the five-stage model, I work on the principle that the counselling relationship is at the heart and core of counselling, whether expressed as working alliance, real relationship, transference, reparative or transpersonal (Clarkson, 1995). The relationship is more important than the technology of counselling, and models, policies and structures are all ways of serving the relationship. However, professional relationships are not haphazard; if not negotiated, they, like all relationships, end in game-playing.

The counsellor prepares for workplace counselling by organizing:

- Clear policies regarding the roles and responsibilities of the counselling service to clients and to the organization. This policy indicates the interaction between all three systems: clients, counsellors, organization. Preferably, this is worked out in a document. An example of this kind of policy is included in Appendix 2.
- A clear structure for managing the counselling process (see the section on the administrative side of counselling later in this chapter).
- A focused counselling location set up and ready for counselling. The type of location will differ according to circumstances. Some workplace counsellors are peripatetic and move from site to site according to need and may not have a permanent room or office. An example is a major building society which has a full-time employee counsellor who meets with employees who have been victims of armed robbery and needs to be where the robbery has taken place.
- An understanding of the objectives of workplace counselling: the counsellor is clear about workplace counselling and what aims

are being achieved (see Chapter 3 on 'What is workplace counselling?'). Clarity here is essential if counsellors are to be focused in their assessments and interventions and in what information they offer their clients. Lack of clarity on the counsellor's side can result in expectations from client and organization that may not be the intention of the counselling service.

- Information they want from clients to help with (a) assessment, (b) counselling, and (c) evaluation of counselling. Forms will be created to contain this information (Appendix 3 gives an example of an in-take and progress form and Appendix 4 offers an individual evaluation form).
- A network for referral.
- Appropriate insurance by the counsellor.
- Information to give clients, before counselling and during it.
- An understanding of what model of counselling is being used.
- Personal supervision for client work.
- A system by which employees are clear about how to refer self or others.
- Methods of advertising the counselling service.
- Evaluation of counselling and the counselling service.
- A method for keeping statistics and presenting reports.
- Clarity around what information will be given to the employing organization.

Particular organizations may demand that other areas be thought through carefully. For example, a counselling service in a bank has made it clear that should counsellors come across embezzlement in their counselling work that they must divulge this to the relevant authority. This is obviously something that needs to be communicated to potential clients.

Clients prepare for counselling by knowing:

- what is available: name, phone number, place of counselling service
- what counselling is about
- the parameters of confidentiality
- the roles and responsibilities of each person in the counselling system: counsellor, organization, client

Careful planning for counselling means extra safety and containment for clients. They know that the 'rules' are not being made up as counselling progresses but that there are clear structures and strategies, some of which are already determined, some of which are negotiable. Lack of clear structure can result in extra suffering.

Case example

Gerald is an example of a counsellor who had little thought-through preparation for his counselling work. He was hired to set up an in-house counselling service for a Health Authority. With his very first client he moved straight into dealing with her problem. It was only when he got a bad cold and had to remain off work, thereby missing their next appointment, that he realized that he had no way of contacting her to keep her counselling confidential. All he could do was get someone to put a notice on his door explaining his absence. The client was furious, having negotiated time off for counselling and having travelled from another site to meet Gerald. Joan, on the other hand, having carefully outlined her understanding of counselling, was able to refer Jenifer who came for counselling to help her personal development. She was dealing very well with her life, was happy with her work, but wanted to look at ways in which she could develop her 'inner life'. Joan considered that this was not 'appropriate' for workplace counselling but knew counsellors to whom she could refer Jenifer. Gerald had not thought through the implications, Joan had clearly defined her understanding of workplace counselling.

Assessment

Assessment is the means by which: (a) clients decide if they wish to continue to see this counsellor; (b) counsellors make an initial formulation of why the client has come for counselling; and (c) counsellors/clients decide to work together or an appropriate referral is made. Even though, when put in stages, assessment seems like a lengthy process, it can, in reality, be shortened as appropriate. Obviously, a client coming for a one-off emergency session with the workplace counsellor will not go through all these stages. However, even short-term counselling (e.g. six sessions) will cover a number of these areas:

---

1   Understanding clients and their issues
2   Methods of assessment
3   Agreeing an assessment
4   Considering interventions
5   Agreeing counselling
6   Sharing information

Understanding clients and their issues

Although the words assessment, diagnosis, and formulation of problem are not terms acceptable to all counselling theories, it is my belief that counsellors of all persuasions inevitably make judgements about clients. That 'judgement' formulates and defines what they consider to be the problem(s), whether or not counselling is the appropriate intervention for the client, and whether or not the workplace counsellor is the best person to work with the client. It must be stressed that assessment takes place within a counselling relationship and is not, in my view, an expert applying psychological technology to clients. Torjman (1985) has distinguished between what she calls the 'what' of the interview, generating information to make an evaluation, and the 'how' of it, the manner of communication, the rapport established, the sensitivity of counsellors and the creation of a safe environment.

Assessments are sometimes formulated by counsellors exclusively (and it is to this exclusivity in particular that some object). It puts the counsellor in the 'expert' position, and often relegates clients to subjects within an illness category, for example, schizophrenia. It tends to utilize established categories of assessment (e.g. the *Diagnostic and Statistic Manual* of the American Psychiatric Association (1987) and the *International Classification of Diseases* of the World Health Organization (1992)). On the other hand, many counsellors work with their clients to arrive at an agreed understanding and articulation of what they consider the issues to be and how to work with them. The following are three examples of counselling work within an organizational setting.

Case example

John approaches the employee counsellor and explains that he is Head of Purchasing. He is obviously exhausted and stressed. He explains that his department is undergoing mammoth reorganization, that they have lost two of their seven members and that these will not be replaced, and that extra work has involved him in working up to 12 hours a day. For the past two months he has usually spent Saturday morning in the office. He is falling behind in his projects at work, and at home he feels he is perpetually grumpy and out of sorts.

Case example

Eleanor bursts into tears as soon as she sits down in the counsellor's room. When she calms down she explains how embarrassing it is to tell someone that she has no friends, either at work or privately. She is 32, still lives with her elderly mother, and leads a very restricted social life. She would dearly like to get married and have children but never seems to meet a suitable man who is interested in her.

Case example
Jill tells the counsellor that she has worked as a departmental secretary for five years now and up to a year ago loved the job. A new male boss was appointed then and she has been subjected to his sexist jokes and innuendoes. Within the past two months he has three times approached her sexually and she has resisted. She feels she is being sexually harassed but is 'only a secretary' and considers that if she takes public action on this that she may be seen as a trouble-maker and get the sack.

In working with each of these three people, counsellors will consider questions to arrive at some conclusions:

- What is happening to this person?
- How do I understand what is happening?
- How does the client understand what is happening?
- Are issues within the person (personality), in the situation (situational), and/or organizational?
- What is the best help for this person just now?

Methods of assessment

There are several formats available for assessing clients in the workplace. The choice of which of these to use will depend on several factors: the beliefs and orientations of counsellors, the needs of the workplace, the setting of the counselling service and the amount of interprofessional involvement. Methods of assessment can be roughly divided into two areas: those that assess the individual and those that assess taking an organizational aspect.

Four methods of *individual assessment* will be presented here. These are not the only methods, by any means, but give a flavour of the kinds of methodologies available.

Formal assessment using an existing formula   In the US the *Diagnostic and Statistical Manual of Mental Diseases* (DSM) is the most commonly used method of diagnosis. Because much counselling that takes place is paid for by insurance companies, many of these insist that there is clarity around the diagnosis. DSM IV is used in medicine, psychiatry, clinical and counselling psychology. In Britain, the ICL (*International Classification of Diseases*) tends to be more popular.

Psychometric assessment Some counsellors use psychometrics as a way of understanding clients; Bayne (1991), for instance, has outlined several helps in which using the Myers–Briggs Inventory with clients can be helpful. Not only does it tell the counsellor about how to relate to clients (there can be a difference depending on how introverted/extroverted is the client), but it gives a measure that can be used to see if change has taken place as a result of counselling. Other tests – for personality, depression, decision-making and stress – can be utilized (see Anastasi, 1982; Hood and Johnson, 1991; Carroll and Pickard, 1993).

Interpersonal assessment Many counsellors rely on the relationship between themselves and their clients and the use of transference and counter-transference as their guide in assessing clients. Monitoring what is happening in the therapeutic relationship gives insights into the client's personality, interpersonal style, characteristics and way of handling conflict. Counsellors rely on the initial relationship between themselves and their clients to realize information to help them make a clear assessment of what is happening to clients.

Case example
An example of this kind of assessment is seen in work with Joe. Geraldine, the workplace counsellor, was aware from the very first contact with Joe that he was highly nervous and anxious. He did not look directly at her, kept fidgeting in his chair, and was disorganized in his thinking and his explanations of what was happening in his life. She was continually confused by what he said and needed to clarify almost all details of his story. She had already discovered for herself his difficulties in maintaining relationships when he got around to telling her that his problem consisted in not being taken seriously by his bosses at work.

Assessment of presenting problems and underlying psychological needs Crouch (1992) provides a helpful distinction in clarifying what is happening with clients. He draws the distinction between particular problems and psychological concerns. The former usually present difficulties with which the client needs help: a relationship concern, a financial difficulty, a bereavement. Psychological concerns, on the other hand, are underlying patterns in a person's life that give rise to present problems: the inability to hold down a close relationship, not being able to get on with people in authority. Psychological concerns generate problems. Using this as a background, clients can be seen to come for help for a number of reasons:

- to increase healthy ways of living
- to build up ways of coping that have broken down
- to establish ways of coping that have never been there

Understanding what clients' needs are, and how psychologically 'healthy' they are at this time in their development, can be of help as counsellors enquire about how to work with them.

Four further assessment models are presented where the emphasis is also on the *organizational aspect of assessment*.

Workplace assessment   Because counselling is in the workplace there are further aspects of client problems that deserve consideration:

- Is the problem within the individual?
- Is this a problem that the client has irrespective of the organization? Could it be an interpersonal problem he/she has had since childhood? Depression that has been around for a long time?
- Is the problem due to the specific work situation the client is in? Sexual harassment, bullying, difficult manager, poor team relationships, bad work environment? Could there be an interplay of dynamics specific to the work environment, or come directly from the work itself to the client and for which the client has little responsibility?
- Is the problem due to factors outside work? An unhappy marriage, problems with children, family, medical illness?
- Is the problem due to the organization? Poor management overall, change within the organization, redundancy, reorganizing, downsizing?

Assessment of level of client need   Drum (1987) has developed a schema around levels of need within educational contexts which could be used effectively within other organizational settings (Table 6.2). The use of Drum's work enables workplace counsellors not

Table 6.2   *Sevel levels of client need*

Level	Description	Intervention type
1	No existing need possible susceptibility	
		Preventive
2	No known need probable susceptibility	
3	Emerging need or challenge	
4	Clearly existing need or challenge	Developmental
5	Deteriorating unmet need emerging crisis	
6	Recurring crises or problems	
		Psychotherapeutic
7	Entrenched dysfunctional life patterns	

Source: Drum, 1987

only to assess individual needs but to set up a process whereby they can integrate various levels of work: face-to-face counselling for crisis situations, counselling and education for developmental needs, and publicity and preventive measures for employees in general.

Assessment of individual and/or organization   Clarkson (1990: 4) contains one of the few models that applies assessment within an organizational context. Who needs help and what help is needed:

1   Is the individual dysfunctional?
2   Is the individual growing?
3   Is the organization dysfunctional?
4   Is the organization growing?

Clarkson devised a quadrant between the two axes of individual/ organization and development/breakdown (Figure 6.1).

Assessment of client within the organization   Torjman (1985) offers a five-step approach (more in keeping with problem-solving models of workplace counselling) to assessment which combines individual and organizational assessment issues:

● Obtain a clear description of the situation troubling the employee.
● Determine who sees the situation as problematic.
● Why has the situation become problematic?
● How often has the situation occurred and for how long?

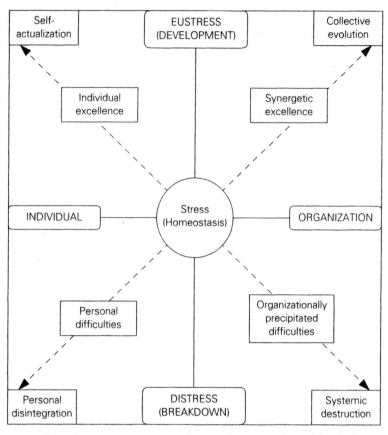

Figure 6.1   *Assessing individual and organizational stress (from Clarkson, 1990: 4). Reproduced with permission of* Employee Counselling Today

- What efforts have been made to deal with the situation?
- What solutions are possible and what helping resources may be required?

Appendix 5 offers an example of an assessment format.

In summary, it is essential that workplace counsellors have clear methods by which they articulate how they understand what is happening to their clients. It is equally important that those methods take the workplace into consideration in assessing clients and do not presume that all problems arise from within individuals. Their understanding of workplace counselling will determine to a large extent how they assess and how they use assessment with clients. That understanding, and sometimes other factors such as the department of which they are a part, will influence what information they need from clients. Counsellors are also aware that assessment continues throughout counselling. An initial assessment is just that, the first formulation of what is happening. More information, further insights, and some counselling work can change initial assessments.

Agreeing an assessment

It seems obvious that client and counsellor will work towards a common agreement on what is happening to the client. This does not always happen. Sometimes counsellors formulate an assessment and never share it with clients. Cognitive analytic therapy is a good example of a counselling methodology that works with clients so that, together, counsellor and client can arrive at a statement that summarizes what is happening to the client. Formulation takes place in terms of a dilemma: you are *either* pleasant to people and liked *or* assertive with people and have no friends. Another example of this kind of articulated assessment is: you can *either* talk to your boss about this problem and take the risk of damaging your career *or* keep silent and watch unethical practice take place. From the point of view of both client and counsellor, there is an agreement on what is a key problem for the client, there is an agreed articulation of this in a form of words, and there is already an agreed agenda for the counselling work.

By and large, clients are relieved when some definition of what is happening to them is offered. Franks (1993) saw this as one of the major curative factors in helping: that an understanding (even an hypothesis) of what is happening to the client is shared with them. Certainly, this gives clients more say in the discussion, it helps them to understand that they too have resources and are not totally dependent on an 'expert' who understands them more than they understand themselves, and motivates them to be more actively involved in finding solutions to problems which they have had a say in articulating.

If a formulation of the issue, problem or difficulty can be agreed between counsellor and client (looking at personal, interpersonal and workplace implications of the issue), then this goes a long way in setting up appropriate interventions. This can be important even if the client is coming for a single session. It gives focus to the work and it motivates clients to be more personally involved when they know they have helped define their problem.

Considering interventions

Counsellors tend to err in seeing most issues in 'counselling' terms and do not always consider other interventions as well as they might. There are many forms of intervention, all of which have valuable contributions to make: medicine, psychiatry, clinical psychology, social work, advice and information services, legal and financial services, teaching and training services, personnel and a host of other helping agencies. As suggested by Malan (1976), it is worthwhile to think:

- *Medically*: does the client need medical help? Not all problems are psychological. I know one counsellor who attributed the headaches of a client to stress when later it was discovered he had a brain tumour. Another workplace counsellor who had a medical background recognized the signs of diabetes in a client who came to talk about tiredness. A quick referral to the company doctor verified the symptoms.
- *Psychiatrically*: does the client need psychiatric help? There can be a tendency for counsellors to be wary of psychiatrists and not utilize their services. With severely disturbed clients (I know of one instance of a suicidal client and another with bulimia), psychiatric assessments can give valuable assistance especially if hospitalization or specific medication is required.
- *Psychodynamically*: are there underlying issues for this client? It is too easy to assess problems only in presenting problem terms without considering possible underlying causes. Thinking psychodynamically simply means considering the possibility that what is presented is a symptom of deeper issues. The decision can then be made about which to tackle.
- *Practically*: what does the client need to help him/her just now? Thinking practically can result in giving information: did you know that there is a group specifically to help dyslexic people, have you thought of doing a course on assertiveness, have you found out your legal position on that situation etc.?

Matching intervention to client is a key skill for workplace counsellors. Getting it wrong can result in wasted time and strong feelings on the part of clients. Turner (1985: 76) has emphasized its importance: 'Matching is the deliberate and consistent attempt to select a specific candidate for a specific method of intervention in order to achieve specific goals. For it to work, there must be an adequate evaluation of clients, of methods of intervention, of goals, and a rational method for aligning candidates, interventions, therapists and goals.'

Agreeing counselling
Presuming that, as a result of assessment, data intake and reviewing possible interventions, both counsellor and client agree that

counselling is the preferred intervention, then counsellor and client should agree on which counsellor is best suited for this individual. In many instances, it will be the workplace counsellor, the person who did the initial assessment. But within a counselling service there may be a choice of counsellors and allocation can be made, with the agreement of the client, on a number of factors:

- *Gender*: sometimes clients will choose a same-sex counsellor in the hope that it will facilitate understanding. This can be very important for clients and it is a mark of respect by counsellors to offer them choices. Running a youth counselling service for several years made me realize that such a choice will always be viewed as positive and made me aware of how often clients will choose same-sex counsellors. At some developmental stages, same-sex counsellors for women is recommended (Wray, 1992).
- *Race and culture*: like gender, race and culture can be difficult issues to work with and giving clients the choice of similar-race counsellors is a great sign of respect for individual needs. Having said that, the practicalities of having same-race counsellors may be difficult to implement.
- *Sexuality* can be another reason for offering choice of counsellor. Hitchings (1994: 131) has noted the importance of a good match between gay clients and counsellors: 'Gay and lesbian clients deserve to work with psychotherapists who have resolved, to as great an extent as they can, their own homophobia, so that gay and lesbian affirmative models of psychotherapy can be most effectively utilized.' It is essential in the workplace, where homophobia can be rife – among individuals, groups and institutionally – that gay individuals have the freedom to have counsellors who can work with them effectively.

Referral to a counsellor outside the company may also be possible. Some companies have EAP alongside in-house counselling provision. Specialized counsellors (e.g. marriage guidance, AIDS counselling, eating disorders) may be available through them or through other resources.

Sharing information

Once agreement has been made to engage in a counselling relationship, then the counsellor will share information on the service and answers questions from the client. This may have taken place at an earlier stage. However, once they have decided to meet, there will probably be other issues that need clarification. Counsellors may need to explain:

1 What counselling is about: it can be too readily accepted that clients understand why they are coming for counselling. This could be far from the truth. Clients come to counsellors for many reasons.
2 How counselling works: meetings, expectations of clients etc.
3 What information is needed from both clients and counsellors. Clients may want to know about the counsellors, about the relationship between counsellor and organization, about the length of time of counselling, about qualifications and experience. The counsellor will want to know about the clients: some factual information (name, marital status, how to contact them, medical and social history), about the presenting problem which precipitates the client's coming to counselling, and any other information that allows the counsellor to ascertain which interventions would be most helpful for this client. (Appendix 3 includes an example of an in-take form for workplace counselling.)

In conclusion, the assessment stage of workplace counselling is a key element in its overall success. It demands particular skills in diagnosis, in formulating problems, in understanding the workplace, in negotiating with clients, and in matching interventions to client needs. From the employee counsellor's perspective, it demands a clear understanding of what workplace counselling is about, how to utilize assessment effectively, and how to get the best help possible for this client with this problem.

Contracting/referring

The third stage of counselling in organizations is the contracting phase. Counsellor and client agree to work together or agree that the client needs referral to another counsellor or agency. This stage of counselling contains several components:

1 Agreeing to work together
2 Contracting on
     practicalities
     roles of client and counsellor
     role of the organization
3 Referring, if appropriate

Agreeing to work together
This is a formal agreement whereby counsellor and client agree to work together within a counselling relationship.

Case example
Phil, the employee counsellor, and Jason, a middle manager who was worried about his annual appraisal which talked about his lack of skills in working within the team, spent their first session looking at the problem and formulating it, and Jason went away to think about the possibility of 10 sessions of counselling. On his return, he shared that he felt this was a good way ahead and accepted an initial contract for 10 weekly sessions. Phil and he then talked about counselling, what it meant and they looked at Jason's difficulty in coming at the same time each week. They finally agreed to set subsequent sessions after each session. Jason had done an introductory course in counselling and asked Phil about his way of working and wanted particularly to understand what confidentiality meant in these circumstances. Eventually the details of their sessions together were finalized and Jason received answers to his questions.

Contracting
The contract or agreement outlines the issues which have been negotiated and agreed, and include:

- confidentiality
- when information would go back to the organization, with or without permission of the client
- what information will be kept on file by the counsellor
- who will have access to notes
- who will own counsellor notes
- what is counselling and what is expected from clients
- how to contact the counsellor
- what to do if a session needs to be cancelled
- supervision arrangements by the counsellor
- where to meet
- how often to meet
- what to do if either cannot keep an appointment
- what to do if either wishes to terminate counselling before the agreed date
- number of counselling sessions

Some counsellors insist on written contracts: most have verbal agreements.

Referring clients when appropriate

Instead of working together, counsellor and client will agree that a referral is required. This conclusion will have implications for action in the following areas:

(1) *Who will make the referral?* Will the client contact the appropriate agent or agency or will the counsellor set up the referral? As long as there is a clear method, with agreed responsibilities for who does what, there are no rules about which method is best. Sometimes counsellors will contact the referral agency and make a formal referral, possibly with a written letter. The client will then telephone to arrange a meeting time. At other times, clients simply need knowledge of the referral group and can set up help for themselves. In some instances this is done together. If a company has both internal and external counselling provision, the in-house counsellor can telephone through a referral. The EAP will provide the name and phone number of a suitable counsellor with whom they have checked availability. The in-house counsellor contacts the client and hands on the name and telephone number; the client then makes his or her own arrangements.

(2) *What will be the contact between the referral agency and the workplace counselling service?* Again, this is an open question and has to be agreed between all three parties: counsellor, client and referral agency. In some instances, it is appropriate that the referral agency write a report, for example, referral for a psychiatric assessment which is shared with the counselling service. At other times, there will be no contact between referral agency and workplace counsellor unless finance is involved, in which case it may be sufficient to have a letter indicating services rendered (the client attended for 10 sessions). It may be that there will be no contact between employee counsellor and referral agent (where the client chooses private counselling to deal with long-term issues).

Contracting in workplace counselling helps all parties involved – counsellor, client, client's department, the organization, the referral agent/agency – to be clear about the rules, roles and responsibilities involved in engaging in counselling. This clarity provides safety for clients where they know their rights; it also provides guidelines for counsellors so that they are acting professionally and ethically and providing quality services.

Engaging in workplace counselling

Engaging in workplace counselling, besides the actual contact with individual clients, contains a number of other elements: identifying clients who need counselling, assessing clients for counselling, working with clients as counsellor, working with employees and the organization in other capacities. This fourth stage is when the actual counselling sessions together occur. A number of issues pertain here:

> 1 Managing the personal dimension
> 2 Working with the administrative side of counselling
> 3 Working with the organization
> 4 Fulfilling other roles/tasks within the organization

These four main dimensions of workplace counselling are represented in Figure 6.2.

Employee counsellors need to be skilled in more ways than solely clinical work: 'Many counsellors, well trained in clinical work, have little expertise in counselling management ... these are skills beyond the skills of working with individuals and groups in a therapeutic way, and demand the ability to think systemically and practically about the full implications of the counselling work' (Carroll, 1995b: 27). By and large, counselling is a private affair between consenting adults behind closed doors. Two individuals meet, form a working relationship, and combine efforts towards helping the client deal more effectively with his/her life. We can call this the personal or the interpersonal part of the counselling process: what takes place when counsellor and client are together. Most of the time in counselling training, and the greater part of the literature and research in counselling, is concentrated in this area. Counselling theories, types of therapeutic relationship, counsellor interventions and strategies, various skills, and ways of conceptualizing and assessing client problems all focus on this aspect of counselling work.

Besides this obvious side of counselling, there are two other dimensions that do not get quite as much attention: the administrative and

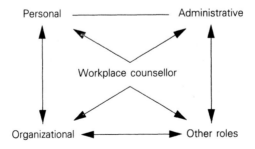

Figure 6.2 *Four dimensions of workplace counselling*

Table 6.3   *Five-relationship model of workplace counselling*

Relationship	Contribution to the organization	Human motivation	Some signs of dysfunction
Unfinished	Grit in the oyster	Completion, resolution	Fixed, disruptive patterns of relationship
Working alliance	Achieving, organizational	Doing competence, productivity	Task-dominated culture, sterile, driven work climate
Developmental	Developing the organization	Growth learning	Neediness, over- or under-protection of staff
Personal	Developing the organization as a working community with a healthy culture	Intimacy, friendship, community	Conflict and competition, fake *bonhomie*, loss of task focus
Transpersonal	Developing wider organization, human resources	Being, meaning, connection	Meaninglessness, *anomie*, ennui, disregard of ethics

Source: P. Clarkson (1995) *The Therapeutic Relationship*. London: Whurr

organizational aspects. Effective counselling takes all three areas into consideration in setting up, maintaining and terminating counselling.

The personal side of counselling

Essential to counselling in general, and to workplace counselling in particular, is the value of the personal/interpersonal dimension of counselling. Setting up a counselling relationship and establishing rapport with clients is crucial to effective counselling. The value and centrality of the counselling relationship and its content have been well documented (Gelso and Carter, 1985). Clarkson (1995: 330) has used her five-relationship model of counselling in organizational consultancy to understand how different relationships affect work environments. Table 6.3. includes her assessment framework for relationships at work. Clarkson (1995: 330) suggests that employee counsellors can provide the kind of relationship needed by workers, depending on their needs. Obviously, this will require both short-term and long-term work, but will clearly contribute to organizational development, especially working with those dysfunctional relationships that cause havoc in the workplace.

The personal side of counselling takes place in the counselling room where the right kind of therapeutic relationship is forged by counsellors who are able to engage in the kind of relationship that best serves the client at the time.

The administrative side of counselling

The face-to-face encounter between counsellor and client needs to be administered so that this professional relationship remains professional and safe for both parties. The administrative side of counselling (the arrangements around the counselling work) is about good house-keeping, involving a number of areas before, during and after the actual counselling contact.

First contact between client and counsellor

1 How do clients contact the counsellor? Are they expected to write or phone? Or, in the modern office, to use e-mail?
2 Do they contact a secretary, an answer-machine (what is the message on the machine?), the counsellor in person, or someone else?
3 What information is given to the client at this first contact?
4 What happens in the intervening time between first contact and first meeting? Does the client receive any further information?
5 Where do counsellor and client meet? How is this setting arranged, organized, furnished, and made safe for both clients and counsellors (panic button?).
6 Are counsellors covered by the insurance of the organization or do they need to have their own indemnity arrangement?

First meeting

1 Do clients have clear directions on how to get to the location of their counselling session?
2 Who meets them? What is said to them? Where do they wait before seeing the counsellor? What arrangements are in order should they come early?
3 What information is needed at this first meeting: by counsellors, by clients?

After the first meeting

1 How are notes written up?
2 Where are they kept?
3 Who has access to these notes?
4 How are referrals handled, if needed?
5 How do clients pay for counselling, if that is appropriate?

During counselling

1   How are emergencies dealt with?

After termination

1   What happens to notes? For how long are they kept before being destroyed?
2   Are other types of relationship formed with clients after they have terminated counselling? What are the guidelines for this?
3   If a referral is made, what information is given to the new counsellor? Is there any contact made between the two counsellors?
4   How is the referral handled?
5   How is the counselling evaluated?

Answers to the above questions will depend on a number of factors: the counselling orientation will often dictate how arrangements are handled (e.g. the furnishing of the room); the freedom counsellors actually have (e.g. an agency may have one counsellor do an assessment before the client is allocated to a particular counsellor). However, what often happens is that these issues are not thought through before they happen. Obviously, training courses need to look in some detail at the administrative side of counselling: not to do so may affect the counselling relationship adversely.

The administrative aspects of counselling create a safe system where information flows throughout and at any given moment in the whole process there is safety for both participants. Engaging in employee counselling means continuing to manage the administrative side effectively.

The organizational side of counselling

Besides the personal and administrative dimensions of counselling, there is the organizational side. How does the context in which counselling occurs affect the actual work between counsellor and client? Organizations are involved in counselling in a number of ways.

The organizational aspect of counselling provision has to be considered carefully by counsellors. Whether they like it or not, the organization will play a significant part in the counselling provision offered to clients. Hawkins and Miller (1994: 269) warn counsellors of the tendency to see client problems 'in terms of individual pathology and interpersonal difficulty'. An in-house employee counsellor may see a client who has been referred by a manager because of his interpersonal difficulties at work, or an outplacement counsellor is seeing a redundant executive where information is being given to the outplacement counsellor by the client company. A doctor may want to know about an individual sent for counselling, or a concerned lecturer may want advice on how to handle a suicidal client he/she has referred to the counselling service. Individual clients may want the counsellor to take their side against the organization and be an advocate rather than a counsellor.

(1) Are there clear boundaries between the counsellor's responsibilities to the individual client and to the organization? It may be that an organization expects counsellors to inform them if clients bring certain kinds of information (e.g. an in-house counsellor in a banking establishment who is told about embezzlement; a counsellor hired by a diocese to work with a trainee for the priesthood where the diocese expects to know if there are serious reasons why the ordination should not proceed). Should counsellors work as if there were no organizational responsibilities or are there opportunities to work with *both* parties, individual client and organization?

(2) Will the organization (or members of the organization) be involved in any way in the counselling process of the client? Just as at times we recommend couples or family counselling, is there a place for setting up counselling with an individual and member(s) of the organization? Or is it healthy at times to involve a significant other from the organization in the counselling arrangement of the individual client? Some workplace counselling services see couples and families as part of their work.

A number of organizational questions need to be considered carefully before counselling begins so that they can be dealt with in a prepared way when they intrude into the counselling work:

1 What kind of organization is this and how does it understand counselling?
2 Where do the loyalties of the counsellor reside and to whom: company or client?
3 What happens when the values of the organization conflict with those of the counsellor, e.g. when the client is becoming more assertive and self-empowered as a result of counselling where the organization wanted someone who would do as he/she was told?
4 What are the politics, alliances and policies within the organization that make it difficult to conduct counselling?
5 When are the difficulties brought by clients due to poor management or bad policies within the organization (not all problems are internal, e.g. sexual harassment, racial prejudice, bullying), and how does the counsellor work with these? Should he/she take as a general principle the one recommended by Hawkins and Miller (1994: 269): 'One might then take as a working hypothesis

that the apparent pathology of the individual is a symptom of organizational illness.'

6   How can counsellors protect themselves against pathology within the organization so that the counselling relationship does not become contaminated by organizational problems?

There are very few counselling situations where an organizational context does not enter and influence the work being done, even in private practice. Individuals do not live in isolation, they belong to pairs, families, learning communities, work organizations. And these systems not only have an effect on their lives and are a part of their problems but often need to be involved in their treatment. Social support is seen as a crucial element in the efficacy of counselling (Mahoney and McCray Patterson, 1992), and this no doubt applies equally to organizations. The more support employees have in their workplace the more effective will be their counselling.

Re-entry of employees into the workplace

An organizational issue affecting workplace counselling, and one rarely dealt with, is that of helping individual employees who have been out of the workplace dealing with personal problems, on return to the workplace. By and large, individuals are left to find their own way back into the system they left. Their fellow workers are anxious about re-entry, how they deal with their colleague, whether they talk about what has happened, or do not mention it. And how does the individual employee re-enter the system they left to deal with mental illness? A format needs to be set up (formally) whereby the group is helped to deal with the individual's return, and where the individual is able formally to re-establish his/her place in the community. This can be done in several ways, and the counsellor is often the best person to do it.

(1) Meet with the individual client and assess what has happened. Establish why he/she was off work (alcoholism, eating disorder, stress and depression are but a few of the reasons for which employees may have been hospitalized, received psychiatric help or taken time off). The workplace counsellor ideally will have contact with the specialists who worked with the individual, know about medication and possible side-effects, and know on what basis the employee is coming back to work. Some employees return to work gradually rather than take up their full-time position. In many companies it will be important for the employee counsellor to work in close liaison with the occupational health department, particularly doctors since it is often they who monitor the return of employees and direct their working hours.

(2) With the client's permission, meet with the team/department to which he/she belongs. The counsellor may give explanations of why the employee has been on sick-leave, what the main issue was, and the development of the employee. This is an opportunity for the members of the team to ask questions, for information to be given, and advice and guidance received on how best to re-establish relationships; for example, that it is all right to refer to the reason why the employee was off work and to ask about progress.

(3) A formal meeting where the individual meets the department, with the counsellor present. At this meeting there is an opportunity to welcome the individual back, to talk openly about how he/she is, and to establish any guidelines for re-entry (e.g. working part-time, doing specific work).

It is essential to recognize individual preferences and the team's ability to deal with issues in this whole operation. Forcing individuals to go through a process that would stress them unreasonably, even for good intentions, is not helpful. It may be that a team or department is not in a position to deal effectively with the kind of process outlined above. Employee counsellors will judge the situation carefully before implementing procedures for re-entry of employees. The following examples illustrate what can happen with an employee who has been off work through illness.

Case example

Marjorie was an employee in this situation. Subject to a severe eating disorder, she was hospitalized for several weeks after which she was off work for about two months. When she returned to work no one mentioned her absence. It was almost as if she had had a long weekend off. On the other hand, she could see that people were treating her differently, like a delicate and fragile stem that could be broken easily. They overprotected her and actually failed to 'see' her and her situation.

Case example

Nick, on the other hand, had quite a different re-entry into his department. He had been hospitalized for overwork leading to severe stress and a suicide attempt when his marriage broke up. Before his return, the counsellor met with the whole human resources department, of which he was a member, talked to them about Nick and what had happened, and invited questions on how to work with him. On his return, the department met to welcome him, it was openly acknowledged that they knew the issues, and individuals asked how they could help. In the days immediately following his return, he met individually and informally with his colleagues who again took the initiative in offering their support and help.

In summary, while most training (and supervision) seems fairly good on the personal dimensions of counselling, there is room for improvement in helping trainees deal with the administrative and organizational sides of counselling. It is not sufficient to leave these alone until they arise: many difficulties within counselling arise precisely because they have not been foreseen. Time spent on rehearsing for the administrative and organizational dimensions of counselling is well spent and may spare counsellors and clients, as well as organizations, a lot of trouble.

The tasks of workplace counsellors
Carroll (1994) is clear in the conclusions to her research that employee counsellors fulfil a number of roles within organizations. Engaging with clients in the workplace means that counsellors often cross roles. Some of the key tasks expected from workplace counselling are:

- counselling
- welfare
- training
- organizational consultancy
- publicity
- facilitating
- organizational change agency
- management advice

This led Carroll (1995b: 23) to remark that:

> The employee counsellor has one of the most difficult counselling jobs, and has a thin line to tread between the organization and the individual. The organizational counsellor is, in addition, trainer, consultant, organizational agent of change, counselling manager, informant, advocate, advice-giver and diplomat. Maintaining all these roles with clear demarcation lines, acceptable boundaries and supportive relationships, calls for maturity and training.

Klarreich (1985) analysed his life as an in-house counsellor and found that 60 per cent of his time was spent on clinical work, 10 per cent on training, 10 per cent on education (lectures, presentations), 15 per cent on administration and evaluation, and 5 per cent on consultation and liaison. This not only demands a number of disparate skills but entails maintaining clear boundaries so that role conflict does not take place.

Without looking in detail at all the possible tasks of workplace counsellors, most of which demand particular skills rarely taught on counselling courses, a few points will be made about them in general. Though accepted that workplace counsellors often engage in various roles with employees, both individually and in groups, it needs to be stressed that boundaries remain essential to good counselling work. Different roles demand different relationships, and different follow-up and follow-through. Employee counsellors are often what Francek (1985) has called 'a broker of services'. In all instances counsellors need to ask:

- What is my relationship with this employee at this stage?
- How does the employee understand that relationship?
- What responsibilities do I have in this role as welfare officer, consultant, facilitator?
- Are employees aware of my responsibilities (e.g. sending in a report)?
- Is there conflict between this role and my counselling role with individuals and/or within the organization? For example, it might be inadvisable for the counsellor to write a report that indicts the organization for making unreasonable demands on an employee that have lead to a breakdown. On the other hand, not to do so may result in loss of integrity and damage client relationships.
- What might employee clients in the counselling service imagine if they saw me now? In other words, how would clients react to this particular role I am playing and how might they interpret talking to managers etc.?

Being aware of role conflicts, and possible misinterpretations by clients, will help employee counsellors rehearse for difficulties. Caution is always required when counsellors change or combine roles: even when they are clear about their responsibilities, clients can imagine all sorts of possibilities. A counsellor seen entering the personnel department can be interpreted by a client as looking up or putting information on his/her file. In many counselling services in the workplace, counselling managers remain free from seeing individual clients for counselling which allows them to negotiate with the organization and fulfil other roles without conflict, either real or imagined.

Engaging in counselling in the workplace remains a juggling act where counsellors need to keep a variety of tasks operational at the same time. Besides the roles they engage in, they need to be aware of the personal, administrative and organizational sides of their work.

Terminating workplace counselling

Terminating the counselling relationship has, quite rightly, been viewed as an essential part of the whole counselling process. It is likely that ending counselling with clients will bring up issues of termination in other areas of their lives: to some degree the same will happen to counsellors.

All people have to deal with endings as part of life: there are the built-in goodbyes that cannot be avoided, the endings forced on us by others, and the endings we initiate ourselves. Terminations can be dramatic (an abortion or a death); they can be intense (the end of a marriage); or they can revolve around everyday events that leave us dealing with loss (stopping smoking, losing one's health, letting go of youth, moving home). Goodbyes and endings are built into living.

The fact that endings are part of life does not mean that they are dealt with easily. Quite the opposite. Endings can be very difficult and bring up feelings of loss, grief, powerlessness, helplessness, guilt, rejection, abandonment etc. How we have coped with past terminations will be reflected in how we deal with termination in counselling.

All endings, all goodbyes, say something about death and how it is handled. Big deaths and little deaths are built into life. Counsellors seem to underestimate their importance to clients and as a result often underestimate how difficult the ending phase of counselling will be for them. Terminating counselling is a way of learning for clients about how they end relationships, a way of experimenting with endings, and a way for counsellors to model how endings take place.

Termination is not just about the ending phase of counselling: it is built into the very contract itself. Where a client is seen for one or two sessions, it may not be very formal. Where employees continue to work in the same company as the counsellor, it is always possible that they will return at a later date for further counselling. Still, termination needs to be considered even though it may be different from termination in other settings where counsellors have choices (in the workplace counsellors cannot refuse to see clients because they have worked with them previously).

Practicalities often determine termination in counselling: an employee is retiring or being made redundant, moving job or changing from one building to another. Other endings can be dramatic, perhaps the death of a counsellor or a client. When death ends a counselling relationship it is imperative that the remaining counsellor/client has the opportunity of dealing with this. Clients need another counsellor to help them work through issues that will have arisen for them. In some instances, termination can take place because the relationship breaks down: the counsellor cannot give what the client wants, the participants become competitive and end up disagreeing.

Case example
This happened between Emelia and Angela. Angela had always had problems dealing with strong women, a relic from her relationship with her mother. She came to see Emelia on an issue around her career, but within two sessions was competing with her, putting her down, challenging almost everything she said. Even though Emelia tried to work with the process and immediacy issues, Angela found it very difficult to hear her. Eventually, Emelia suggested that perhaps her male colleague might be of better help. After some sessions with a male counsellor, Angela was able to return and do some very valuable personal work with Emelia.

Termination can be seen through a number of issues:

---

1 Agreeing a termination date
2 Working towards termination
3 The process of termination
4 The final session
5 After termination

Agreeing a termination date
In many instances, workplace counsellors will agree a termination date at the beginning of counselling, perhaps six or eight sessions. This will be clear to both client and counsellor. The termination date may be flexible in that, as it approaches, more time is negotiated to help clients continue to work on their issues. Reminding clients about the number of sessions left can motivate them towards work and can help them rehearse for terminating counselling. Some counsellors work with open contracts, agreeing to see clients for as long as it takes and putting no conditions on the length of time involved. In such instances, it is important to clarify how termination

130 Workplace counselling

will occur: will the counsellor decide, will the client, will they negotiate when appropriate? Counselling can continue by default: both
parties are anxious about mentioning termination in case it hurts or
offends the other. Whatever the decision about how counselling
will be terminated, leaving sufficient time aside to deal with termination issues is essential. Termination in counselling should never take
place during the session in which the issue is raised (obviously this
does not apply where there is a single session or perhaps two
sessions). Some counsellors build 'termination contracts' into their
work; that is, should either party (counsellor or client) decide that
counselling will finish, then it is agreed that a certain number of
sessions (e.g. three or four) be continued before the contract is
terminated. This allows time to deal with unfinished business and to
terminate the relationship in a clear, negotiated way. Clients will
sometimes try to avoid the pain of ending by terminating abruptly,
or simply not coming back. Termination contracts attempt to forestall this.

Working towards termination
In longer-term counselling work, counsellors keep an eye towards
the time when clients might be ready to end counselling. In assessing
readiness for termination, a few pointers can help. Clients may be
ready to end if:

- initial problems or symptoms have reduced
- initial stress has dissipated
- coping has increased
- understanding and valuing of self and others is greater
- levels of relating to others and of loving and being loved have
  increased
- ability to plan and work productively is better
- the ability to play and enjoy life has increased

Clients sometimes give hints (act out) their readiness to finish
counselling by lateness for appointments or not coming to their
session (there may, of course, be other reasons for such behaviour).
Decrease in the intensity of the work, and even apathy on the part
of clients, can indicate that they are beginning to withdraw from
counselling. Because they cannot verbalize this, and often because of
their ambivalence in leaving, it may be that the counsellor needs to
put ending counselling into words. Taking time to arrange and
structure the ending will give it the importance it deserves and will
model for clients how seriously termination is being taken and how
necessary it is to formalize it.

The process of termination

There are various ways in which termination can take place: agreeing a date and ending on that date; creating longer spaces between counselling sessions with an agreed termination date; having a termination date and a follow-up three months or six months later to ascertain that problems have not returned. All of these are helpful ways of terminating, and deciding on which one is best with a particular client will take some thought, and probably some negotiation.

In the termination phase of counselling, time can be valuably spent on:

- reviewing the counselling time together and summarizing learning from the experience
- looking to the future and ways of consolidating what has been gained
- any further areas for consideration should the client move to other counselling
- a formal ending (how to set this up)

Methods of doing this could include:

- client prepares a progress report
- counsellor reviews notes/progress
- devil's advocate approach: client tries to convince counsellor why they should/or should not end counselling

In this phase, feelings that arise during the goodbye process will be explored, especially those of grief, loss and abandonment. It is also an opportunity for counsellors to consider their own feelings.

The final session

The final session ought to be structured so that formal goodbyes are said. Before that, because of particular issues in workplace counselling, it will be helpful to agree a number of strategies:

1 Client/counsellor will probably still meet since they often work in the same building: this needs to be discussed. How does the client wish to be treated by the counsellor should they meet in the corridor, in the company of others etc.? These issues may already have been discussed and agreements made early on in the counselling relationship.
2 What happens to the notes, how long will they be kept, and what, if anything, is included in the file (medical, personnel) of the client in respect of the counselling sessions?

Terminating counselling may not be a satisfactory conclusion for all participants. Clients may be unhappy at the end of counselling because their needs were not met: they may have wanted severance, or another person in the department dealt with, or a poor appraisal reconsidered. The counsellor may be unhappy because they were not allowed to intervene, or because they have been used by the client, or because they do not think the client should end the counselling relationship. The organization may be unhappy with the ending because no change is apparent, or because change has occurred that it did not want (e.g. a more assertive person, or the resignation of the client from the organization). These issues need to be acknowledged and worked through, in so far as they can.

The final session can include:

- agreeing any future contact
- resolving unfinished business
- an appreciation of the time together where both recount what they have valued about counselling and the counselling relationship
- a goodbye gesture, e.g. a handshake, a hug

After termination

What is more contentious than the possibility of meeting after counselling has ended is the possibility that counsellors/clients create a new form of relationship after the counselling one. This could be a professional relationship, a social one, or perhaps even a sexual one. While some of these relationships are mentioned in ethical codes, for example, the sexual relationship in the *Code of Ethics and Practice for Counsellors* (BAC, 1990a), guidelines regulating other forms are rarely specified.

Case example

Melanie was a client with Brenda for about four months while she was dealing with a particularly bitter divorce. They got on very well together and Melanie found counselling very supportive and helpful in her decision-making. About a month after ending counselling, Brenda was asked to be part of a small group helping the organization deal with transitions involving stress and a number of redundancies. She found that Melanie was also a member of the committee and occasionally after a meeting the group went together to the local pub for a drink.

If the relationship between counsellor and former client does continue, in whatever form it takes, it needs to be talked through carefully so that it is not a way of avoiding ending the counselling relationship. Sometimes a period of time for reflection and no contact can be helpful in creating space for all parties to consider the advisability of a different kind of relationship.

In brief, a number of strategies can be employed to help clients deal with ending workplace counselling (McRoy et al., 1986), including:

- building termination into the contract
- considering the influence of past experiences with separation/loss for counsellor as well as for client
- anticipating predictable client reactions to termination
- working with organizational factors which influence the content and process of the ending phase, e.g. redundancy, career changes, demands from the company
- encouraging clients actively to confront termination and to review both cognitive and emotional aspects of it
- formal endings and setting up a process for working with it

7

Evaluating Workplace Counselling

> There is an increasing demand for information on the effectiveness of Employee Assistance Programmes and counselling in the workplace. . . . Despite the enormity of the potential benefits of such services, there is a paucity of information about services in the UK and an even greater lack of research substantiating their effectiveness.
>
> C. Highley and C. Cooper, 'Evaluating EAPs'

Evaluating workplace counselling needs careful planning. Before beginning the process of evaluation certain questions are worth considering:

- why evaluate?
- for whose sake (for whom) is evaluation being done?
- when is the best time to evaluate?
- what exactly is being evaluated?
- how will evaluation take place?
- who will do the evaluation?
- where will evaluation be done?

Rather than making assumptions about counselling evaluation and its worth, being forced to answer such questions can help focus on what is being evaluated and the reasons for an evaluation. Answers will influence how evaluation takes place and how conclusions may be presented.

Evaluation is a key element in counselling provision. Not only is it a way of ensuring that clients are receiving services that are being monitored for their effectiveness, but it is also a way of convincing purchasers about the value of the service. Furthermore, evaluation, through in-depth analysis of what is happening, can be a worthwhile means of improving services. Elton-Wilson and Barkham (1994) have pointed out that most practitioners use evaluation to monitor their counselling work and make changes in what they do. Subjective means are one method: counsellors' own feelings of satisfaction, their interpretations of what has happened. Corney (1992) has shown that subjective evaluations of counselling in general health practice is very positive with counsellors, clients and doctors expressing overall satisfaction with what is offered. Furthermore, counsellors use moment-to-moment evaluation in their sessions with clients, continuously assessing their interventions and their effect on clients. There is a sense in which informal evaluation is part and parcel of continuing counselling work, and counselling practitioners engage in it almost unconsciously.

More objective methods are also used for evaluation purposes: feedback from supervisors, client reports and comments from managers and departments within an organization. Workplace counselling benefits from the same positive reactions and reports. Verbal reports of their effectiveness and satisfaction with their provision are generally the norm. However, there is relatively little formal evaluation of workplace counselling. Masi (1992) has estimated that less than 1 per cent of the 13,000 EAPs in the US have been evaluated, which seems a pity considering the values of formal evaluation.

There is still a reluctance on the part of many counsellors and counselling services to build in formal evaluation processes. Self-interest sometimes plays a part: many counsellors are anxious that evaluation will be negative and their jobs be in jeopardy. There is often worry about infringing confidentiality and allowing others access to information on clients and client groups, and sometimes there is the unknown quantity of how information from evaluation studies might be used. How data and evaluation studies are used is a central issue for counsellors.

Evaluation questions
The kinds of evaluation questions asked by workplace counsellors include:

● Does counselling do any good?
● What counselling works best in workplace settings?
● Why does counselling work?
● What evidence is there for the effectiveness of employee counselling?
● How does counselling give 'added value' to organizations?
● What impact does the organization have on counselling?
● Does counselling affect productivity for the better?
● What is the financial cost of providing counselling and is this cost-effective when compared with other interventions?

We cannot answer most of these questions with certainty, and in some areas there is very little research to help us; for example, on the impact certain organizations have on counselling services. Research into the value of counselling in general is about the only one of the above list on which there is clear evidence: it seems that, overall, counselling is effective and individuals engaging in counselling have a good chance of improving on a number of scales (Stiles et al., 1986; Sexton and Whiston, 1991; Elton-Wilson and Barkham, 1994). There is no reason why this evidence is not applicable to workplace counselling as well as counselling in other contexts. Having said this, specific research into the effectiveness of workplace counselling is 'embarrassingly thin' (Googins, 1985: 222) and is 'largely anecdotal and carried out almost entirely in the US' (Highley and Cooper, 1994). While these comments are made in respect of EAPs in particular, they are certainly applicable to counselling in organizations in general.

Evaluating counselling in organizational settings has tended to focus almost exclusively on work with individual clients. Some workplace counsellors have their own evaluation for clients (see Appendix 4 for an example of an evaluation form for individual clients). What is often missing is evaluation of the full counselling service and its impact on the organization; for example, evaluating the consultancy role of the counsellor. Klarreich (1985) has calculated that he spends 5 per cent of his time in consultation as part of his role as counsellor. This, too, should be evaluated: is it 'adding value' to the counselling service in the eyes of consumers and the company as a whole?

Reddy (1993a) has provided a range of questions to help focus evaluation:

1   Have we achieved what we set out to do?
2   Is it proving successful?
3   Are we getting value for money?
4   Can we measure the impact of the EAP in terms of quantifying changes?
5   Can we quantify a cost–benefit ratio?

It is worthwhile reminding ourselves, as Smith (1985) has done, that there are different levels of certainty, all of which are valuable: (a) *suggestive evidence* that indicates something is possibly true; (b) *preponderant evidence* that suggests it is probably true; and (c) *conclusive evidence* that shows it is undoubtedly true. It is not always possible in evaluation studies to have conclusive evidence, and the other two forms of certainty, while obviously less valuable, can still be used effectively to reach certain types of conclusions.

The usefulness of evaluation

Evaluation of workplace counselling has a number of advantages. Falvey (1987: 59) acknowledges that evaluation may be uncomfortable for some but points out its benefits:

No one particulary likes evaluation, and administrators are no exception. Yet evaluation is central to organizational growth. Without knowing the current status it is hard to set meaningful goals for the future. Effective administration includes collecting, analysing, and interpreting data by which to assess (1) service needs, (2) patterns of use, (3) program outcomes in bringing about desired change, and (4) the cost/benefit ratio of services offered.

Knowledge of service needs and patterns of use can be helpful in publicizing the service and in building in effective provision to meet emerging needs. It is also a good way of ensuring that the present services and their facilities are meeting the current needs of employees.

There is value in finding out how cost-effective, in financial terms, is workplace counselling. Wrich (1985) studied three US EAPs – General Motors, Control Data Corporation and United Airlines – which had statistical data to show their effectiveness in human and financial terms; for example, General Motors estimates that it makes 0.67 dollars for every dollar invested in the EAP. Employers, in particular, will be heartened by the financial returns on counselling services and eager to have data backing this up. It has been estimated that the US postal service saves two million dollars per annum through its EAP (Kim, 1988). Highley and Cooper (1994) have reported positive results from three American studies on the cost-effectiveness of EAPs: the McDonnell Douglas company which reported an estimated saving of 5.1 million dollars on using its EAP; the US Department of Health and Human Services which concluded that there was an approximate 7.1 dollar return per dollar invested in their EAP; and the Edison Company in Detroit which realized reduction in lost time, a reduction in health insurance claims, a 40 per cent improvement in suspensions and a similar improvement in the number of job-related accidents.

Egan (1994: 46–7) has suggested finding methods of costing psychological and social problems. His advice is, since personal misery and social disruption almost always detract from productivity, calculate the loss to the company of such misery in financial terms: for example, the loss of a key employee through sexual harassment; the hospitalization of a manager for clinical depression; the low morale that indicates that 10 employees are working at 80 per cent of their potential; the breakdown of a significant relationship that means a high-level manager is only 50 per cent productive for three months. Add to this the financial cost as low morale is spread, as customers meet less than excellent service, as opportunities are lost and the cost escalates out of all proportion. It is not impossible, but quite interesting, to cost financially the damage done by one obsessive-compulsive head of department within a university setting who knew nothing about management, who had a continual flair for antagonizing both his own staff and students. The turnover within his department was 30 per cent in one year (all good lecturers who could only take so much). Management knew what was happening but did nothing. It took the department about three years to recover after his retirement. A cost-benefit analysis to the company of psychological problems, of difficult employees, of individuals dealing with problems where they have no support from within the organization, is possible and beneficial.

Egan (1994: 50) also notes that prevention is financially more rewarding than cure. There is little point in saving money on a project that ends up costing more in personal disruption and morale. Furthermore, building in health and 'wellness' programmes can short-circuit later problems that become costly in human misery and finance to a company. Finally, according to Egan (1994: 51–2) lost opportunity costs should also be calculated: for example, the time a manager puts into dealing with a suicidal member of staff is time lost for other issues, the time dedicated to dealing with interpersonal conflict in a team or department because of poor management can be seen as lost opportunity, as can the industrial tribunal that takes precious time from other pursuits. We know that many industrial disputes are due to poor management.

There has been a move in Britain to review the economic evaluation of counselling services and this has been applied to counselling in health care (Tolley and Rowland, 1995). They suggest that the role of economic evaluation in counselling services has been overlooked for several reasons, not least of which is the impression that such evaluation is crude and non-rigorous. They set out to show, and use interesting examples to do so, how counselling can be evaluated financially.

In brief, evaluating counselling and counselling services in the workplace is an excellent means of ensuring that employee needs are being met, that the counselling service is fulfilling its aims and objectives; it can be used for forward planning and used to build in changes and modifications to counselling services. However, research into workplace counselling is relatively sparse. What has taken place is almost exclusively within EAP provision and these have been criticized for their lack of rigour (Klarreich et al., 1985).

Record keeping

Most workplace counsellors keep records of some sort. By records are meant accounts of information on the work of the counsellor(s); for example, work with individual clients, consultancy, training, publicity etc. Information on individual clients will be anonymous. Before beginning work with clients, it is helpful to ask what information is needed (a) for counselling assessment; (b) for referral; (c) for ongoing counselling work; and (d) for evaluation and reports. Records of such information may take several different formats. Here we are looking for information to help evaluate the service.

For those who need convincing, a number of reasons can be given why keeping records can help evaluation:

1   Records show who is using the service and who is not. Recording gender, job groups and age allows counsellors to review the service and who might be targeted for further publicity.
2   To review and articulate trends in the problems with which clients present. Are these work-related, professional, personal? Are they due to organizational stress? Is there any reason why four individuals have come from a particular department with this same problem?
3   Records can reveal problem areas that can be tackled through training, educational packages towards prevention, consultation within the organization. Many counsellors run courses on stress management and relaxation as a direct result of continually finding stress in their clients. Others involve themselves in communication skills, alcohol programmes, particular group sessions.
4   Records can be a way of moving the company towards particular policy statements. Counsellors can be instrumental in helping the organization to become aware of particular gaps in policies, e.g. equal opportunities, sexual harassment.
5   Records can be used as organizational audits. Most departments within organizations are required to audit their work, their budgets, personnel and quality, and there are strong reasons why counselling services should do the same.
6   Records on publicizing the service, on consultation to the organization, on training and education, and even records of record keeping, can be useful assets in evaluating other aspects of the counselling service.

An important part of record keeping is being able to manage the information so that it can be used towards evaluation. With modern computers this should not be a problem, and programmes can be used both to store and sift information towards required ends. However, the legal aspects of record keeping need to be noted, as well as client access rights and confidentiality issues, e.g. the typing of confidential notes by secretaries. Record keeping is nevertheless an essential facet of evaluation.

Evaluation

Evaluation is about assessment, making judgements, connections and drawing conclusions from information. It concludes about the worth of a venture, its purpose is to make judgements about the service, and it is a statement about accountability. Evaluating counselling within an organizational setting consists of assessing its effectiveness, its efficiency and its relevance within the organization. However, this is not always as easy as it sounds and various difficulties emerge in evaluating employee counselling.

(1) Questions as to the why, when and how of evaluation (Holosko, 1988). These questions are important and often determine the outcome of evaluation. The motivation for evaluation is crucial: if it is hinted that the reasons behind evaluating counselling is to show that it is not as cost-effective as other interventions, then it may influence how counsellors gather data. When evaluation takes place, and how it is done are equally important.

(2) Satisfaction is often equated with effectiveness. The fact that clients are 'happy' or 'satisfied' with the counselling service they receive sometimes gives rise to the conclusion that the service is effective, but they are not the same. What is meant by effectiveness in workplace counselling? Googins (1985) has noted some of the weaknesses in using absenteeism as a measure of effectiveness, pointing out that it may be unconnected to quality of work. In order to evaluate counselling, we need to be able to operationalize what is meant by 'effectiveness'. One way of doing this is to have goals for the counselling service against which measurements can be made. Durkin (1985: 246) has stated this well: 'The first step in developing an evaluation system is the identification of specific goals. Without goals, progress or success cannot be evaluated. Goals can be stated in broad or narrow terms, usually preceded by such phrases as: reduction of; improvement of; enhancement of; maintenance of. Wherever possible, goals should be stated in a way that they can be quantitatively measured and include specific time frames in which changes are to occur.' Care is needed, especially in the workplace, in equating counselling effectiveness with other behaviours: for example, less absenteeism, fewer sick days, the reduction of disability payments, improvement in job efficiency, reduction in the number of accidents, fewer grievances against employees or employers, or an

increase in cooperation. Showing the connection between these and counselling is quite difficult. Orlans (1991) asks how the positive aspects of health can be gauged after counselling: for example, the ability to love and care, a zest for life, purposefulness, generosity, autonomy, etc. Quantifying and measuring some behaviour can be very difficult.

(3) From whose perspective is effectiveness judged? It may be that what is considered effective by counsellor and client (the growing autonomy of the client, the choice of the client to resign from the company) may not be seen as helpful by employers.

(4) The use of control groups poses a difficulty within workplace counselling evaluation. Counsellors cannot refrain from offering counselling to some workers and then measure them against those who are already receiving counselling.

(5) To date, probably because counselling is tailor-made to many organizations, there are relatively few standard instruments for evaluating employee counselling. This raises the question of how reliable and valid are measures for gaining information for evaluation: questionnaires, interviews, observations?

(6) Evaluating organizational change as a result of counselling provision. Almost all evaluations of workplace counselling focus on individual work, and other roles remain untested. This results in little or no attempt to evaluate how counselling affects organizations overall. Part of the problem in evaluation studies is choosing which variables to monitor; obviously, monitoring organizational change due to counselling provision would be very difficult.

(7) Workplace counsellors are not always skilled in evaluating counselling services and, even when they are, evaluation is sometimes low on their priority list because of time constraints. Often, data for evaluation are poorly collected or organized and there may be a problem in allowing outsiders access to counselling services in order to evaluate.

Formative and summative evaluation

Evaluation can be either formative (taking place day by day through continuous feedback) or summative (formal and usually written up as a report). There is no reason why both of these methods of evaluation should not take place within counselling services in organizational settings. On a daily basis, counsellors will be receiving feedback (informal evaluation) on their work, from clients, from each other, from work colleagues, from line managers, from training and education, from supervisors. This is an important source of information and should be listened to carefully and evaluated by counsellors. As well as receiving feedback on its work, the counselling service will be continuously monitoring itself and implementing new ways of working as a result.

The more formal evaluation procedures will take place at stated times and will be more organized. In most organizations, there is an already existing appraisal system where counsellors will be assessed, probably annually, by line management. Inskipp and Proctor (1993: 13) have looked at appraisal for counsellors in organizations and recommended that such appraisal be done by a manager, or substitute, who is capable of (a) supporting the counsellor's work; (b) realistically appraising it; and (c) recognizing and appreciating the ethical dilemmas resulting from it. Falvey (1987: 40) has defined three major functions of performance appraisal systems that are applicable to workplace counsellors:

1   To provide feedback to individual staff on their performance in carrying out organizational goals.
2   To provide supervisors with a basis for identifying staff competencies, training requirements and problems in the work environment.
3   To provide cumulative data for management decisions regarding staffing needs, work assignments and salary or promotion considerations.

In most workplace settings, appraisal is part and parcel of life, often connected to pay and career prospects. In the case of workplace counsellors, it is important that their appraisal is performed by a manager who understands their work and is sympathetic to counselling. Good evaluation has a number of features.

Clear and agreed criteria for evaluation   These may be around the stated goals of the counselling service (about numbers to be seen, about reducing absenteeism, about reducing stress etc.). These can be used as guides to evaluate how effective the service has been. Clear criteria are the foundations of good evaluation. Klarreich (1985) has offered a number of characteristics of good counselling practice that could be used as evaluation criteria:

- counselling availability
- counselling accessibility
- counselling credibility
- counselling accountability
- meeting organizational needs

- counselling visibility
- counselling flexibility and adaptability

An agreed method for evaluation Methods of evaluation are diverse. There will be room for evaluation by clients, by counsellors themselves and by others within the organization. How will these individuals and/or groups evaluate? Will questionnaires be used, or interviews?

Who will evaluate? Since it is the responsibility of the organization to make the evaluation, it may choose to do it internally or to hire an outside and independent individual/group. There are certainly advantages in using outsiders. Roman and Blum (1985) have recommended using outsiders in the evaluation process for several reasons:

1 Appropriate outsiders can offer clear expertise in evaluation studies around data collection and analysis. One of the difficulties of evaluation studies in EAPs is that many of them, designed by EAP workers themselves, do not meet the criteria for design and measurement.
2 Outsiders increase the credibility of the evaluation. Since counsellors are heavily invested in the value of their service, there is always the risk that they interpret data in their own favour.
3 Outsiders, because they are not part of the organizational culture, can perceive dynamics at work that are hidden from participants and can interpret data from angles not available to employees.

Use of a variety of methods of evaluation Using a variety of evaluation methods helps clarify conclusions and removes the risk of bias. This can take place both in the instruments used and in the different types of research. Qualitative and quantitative measures are both valuable, and a combination of approaches can utilize the strengths of both.

Frequency with which evaluation takes place The more often measurements take place the better chance there is of understanding what is happening. Counselling effectiveness does not follow a linear pattern: sometimes clients get worse before they get better, sometimes they hit low points before beginning to move forward. The more frequently that progress is measured, the more opportunity there is of following that progress.

Methods of evaluation

A number of methods can be used to evaluate counselling in the workplace:

1   Statistical evaluation
2   Client evaluation
3   Counsellor evaluation
4   Organizational evaluation
5   Supervisor evaluation
6   Process evaluation
7   Outcome evaluation

Statistical evaluation
Statistics is one way of documenting information. Most workplace counsellors keep statistics and produce them in an annual report. This will include information on:

● how many employees have presented for counselling
● how many self-referred, how many were referred by others (and who has referred)
● age, gender, job group
● number of sessions attended
● presenting problem(s) and primary issues
● outcome from counsellor's perspective

Most annual reports from counselling services include such statistics and are a good judge of how well the service is being used and by whom. The data generated will depend on what information is requested from clients accessing the service. This differs widely depending on a number of factors: the particular orientation of counsellors, their background (medical, educational, etc.), their proposed use of the information, and their values around confidentiality. However, it would seem that certain basics are in order. Formats can be found in Durkin (1985).

Client evaluation
Usually clients fill in forms as a method of evaluation (see Appendix 4) after the termination of counselling. Such forms ask clients to evaluate the effectiveness of their counselling and are usually anonymous. Generally they contain questions on (a) satisfaction with how quickly they were seen; (b) how satisfied they are with the counsellor; and (c) how happy they are with the outcome of

counselling. Other questions relate to facilities (location, comfort, confidentiality, etc.) and to referral procedures.

Some programmes try to trace the process of counselling by asking clients to fill in a 'before' and 'after' questionnaire (Bayne, 1991, has used the Myers–Briggs Inventory to monitor client change). This allows the evaluator to ascertain what has happened and what progress has been made. Problems can arise here, though. Counsellors sometimes, and rightly, object to giving questionnaires when clients arrive for counselling in some distress. It seems, and can be, dismissive of their emotional state to face them with a questionnaire when their immediate need is for an understanding person.

It is also important to decide when evaluation takes place. Many counsellors ask clients to fill in an evaluation form after counselling is completed. Some send a further evaluation form three to six months after counselling has finished as a way of ascertaining whether or not change was maintained over time. However, there is a view that this is ethically questionable in that it resurrects issues for the client which had been left behind when counselling finished. Decisions need to be made about when to administer evaluation questionnaires to clients.

Counsellor evaluation

Counsellors have the opportunity to evaluate their own work after each counselling case. This may be done by means of self-administered questionnaires which help to determine:

- How well client and counsellor related to one another.
- Presenting problem and how it was worked with.
- Counsellor satisfaction with the counselling process.
- Evaluation of outcome.
- Were assessment and interventions appropriate with this client?
- What have I learnt from working with this person?
- Are there any ethical/professional issues emerging?
- What would I do differently now?
- Is there any further training I need in the light of this work?

Besides monitoring their own counselling work, workplace counsellors can use feedback from supervisors, colleagues, clients and managers as ways of evaluating their work and the work of the counselling service. This can take place informally at any time, or can be set up formally at specific times. Taking an audio tape of an actual counselling session to supervision can be one method of evaluation; a formal appraisal with a line manager can be another. Workplace counsellors need to be alert and open to the many ways in which formal and informal evaluation of their roles and the counselling service can take place.

Organizational evaluation

Roman and Blum (1985) have criticized what they call 'treatment-model evaluation' (evaluating individual clients), and suggest that EAPs have a much wider impact on the organization that ideally should be assessed. Highley and Cooper (1994) agree and recommend that both individual and organizational levels be evaluated. While individual client work will take up a substantial amount of counselling time, there will be other roles and responsibilities of counsellors that can have a huge influence on the organization and its functioning: helping with transition, managing stress through training, consultation with managers, facilitating managing difficult employees, helping construct effective policy statements are but a few of the extras. And, as Roman and Blum (1995: 220) have pointed out, there are the hidden benefits that defy measurement:

> These include the overall benefit of the employee's recovery to the community at large, the effects on his/her family, the effects on the morale of co-workers, and the unknown extension of the employee's productive career for the organization as a consequence of the intervention. Thus, a cost-benefit analysis is likely to underestimate program effectiveness.

Different ways in which the organization can evaluate the counselling service are:

1   Individual performance appraisals of counselling staff.
2   Cost-effectiveness of the service to the organization.
3   Identification of key people in the organization and assessment of their evaluation of the counselling service (e.g. Director of Personnel, Director of Human Resources, members of the occupational health department, health and safety individuals, departmental heads etc.).
4   Evaluation of whether the counselling service is meetings its goals, objectives and aims.

Supervisor evaluation

Clinical supervisors, especially those who are external to the organization, are closest of all outsiders to the client work of counsellors: their task is, with counsellors, to monitor counselling work and provide a forum where clients can be discussed honestly and where the personal and professional development of counsellors takes place (Carroll, 1995a). Most supervisors are used to writing supervisory reports. Here, too, it can be a valuable source of information and evaluation of a service. Evaluation is a continuing task within supervision (Carroll, 1995a) and used principally to ensure:

- the safety and welfare of clients
- the personal and professional development of counsellors
- that the organizational dimensions of counselling are monitored
- accountability at all levels
- that counsellors have clear feedback on their training and development
- quality control
- performance improvement

Process evaluation

Process evaluation is used to monitor the strengths and weaknesses of the counselling service itself and whether or not the service meets its own aims and objectives. As Kim (1988: 171) puts it: 'A program evaluation is a broad area of research activity devoted to collecting, analyzing, and interpreting vital information on the need, implementation, and impact of a given program for the purpose of some improvement and/or justification of the intervention efforts.' Such evaluation will ask for information on:

- Management commitment to the service.
- The administrative aspects of the service and how they work.
- A review of the organizational aspects of the programme, e.g. how well it is integrated into the organization.
- How well does it achieve it goals?
- How adequate is it? Does it really address employee problems? Is it reaching employees who need it?
- How efficient is it?
- What are the characteristics of clients using the service, e.g. age, gender, job group etc.

Process evaluation is also concerned with the specific process issues that make a difference in individual counselling. What helped the client change? These can be measured through questionnaires, interviews or a combination of both.

Outcome evaluation

Outcome evaluation is an attempt to access the results of employee counselling and sometimes to record these in terms of economics, performance indicators, change in absentee rates, and how the service has percolated within the organization. It requires much support from within the organization and access to personnel and departmental records.

Clear criteria are needed to establish the relationships between variables; for example, that counselling will help employees perform more effectively, will result in a reduction in absenteeism, etc. Evaluation before and after receiving counselling is a way of evaluating outcome and measuring what change has taken place, if any.

Conclusion

Fundamental to good evaluation in workplace counselling is clear agreement on *what* is being evaluated. This may differ from organization to organization. Time spent on clarifying the objectives of evaluation will be worthwhile. *Who* evaluates is a second consideration that could affect conclusions and the credibility of results. *How* evaluations are used could be seen as a vital part of the whole process. *Implementing* the conclusions of evaluations of workplace counselling – making decisions on the service as a result of conclusions drawn from evaluations – is a fundamental and final validation of what has taken place.

8

Ethical Issues in Workplace Counselling

> In all settings for human service practice, collisions in values
> amongst human service professionals, clients, employing organiz-
> ations and society are commonplace. . . . The fact that a host
> system's values may be inherently antithetical to human service
> values may heighten ethical dilemmas confronted by the prac-
> titioner.
>
> K.H. Briar and M. Vinet, 'Ethical issues concerning an EAP'

Training in ethical decision-making

Carroll (1994) entitled her research on workplace counsellors
'Building bridges' and saw one major aspect of the counsellor's role
as best summarized in the phrase 'sophisticated mediation'. Both
'building bridges' and 'sophisticated mediation' highlight the potential conflict between two worlds (counselling and business) and two
sets of responsibilities (to the individual client and to the organization). Standing at crossroads such as these inevitably raises ethical
issues and dilemmas for workplace counsellors. From my own experience of working with workplace counsellors, the issues that
cause most problems are always ethical. Counsellors in the workplace are constantly faced with ethical and professional dilemmas
unique to this setting, as well as the full range of ethical dilemmas
faced by counsellors in general. Oberer and Lee (1986) compare
workplace counselling with attempting to do family therapy with
one's own family. Some examples illustrate the ethical dilemmas.

Case example
A middle manager comes for counselling because his marriage is
breaking up and his wife intends leaving the city and moving
away. It will mean little contact with his children. He is
distraught and the counsellor picks up that he has suicidal and
violent thoughts. It is possible that the employee could be a
danger to others, especially in stressful situations. What does the
employee counsellor do? Has she any responsibility to the
organization as well as to the individual client?

Case example
In the course of counselling it emerges that a male client is drinking on the job and endangering the health and welfare of others. What does the counsellor do? Where are her responsibilities to the organization?

Case example
A client admits in a counselling session that she falsified information at an industrial tribunal that resulted in the dismissal of a senior manager. What does the counsellor do?

Case example
A manager phones the counselling service to tell the counsellor that a member of his department is about to be made redundant. Since she (the manager) knows that this member of her department is coming to the counsellor for personal counselling, she wonders if the counsellor will break the bad news to the client.

Case example
The workplace counsellor sees three individuals, all from the same department, and all complaining about the management style of the head of section. However, none of them is prepared to 'go public' with this information. What does the counsellor do?

Case example
A client who has just had a very poor appraisal that affects both his pay and his career prospects tells the counsellor that his manager (who did the appraisal) has 'had it in for him' for some time and has told him that even though he is doing very good work his appraisal will be poor because the manager does not want him in his department. What does the counsellor do?

Conflicting responsibilities create difficulties for the workplace counsellor and occasionally crystallize around loyalty to the individual client versus loyalty to the organization. Such issues, among a host of others, cause headaches to counsellors in workplace counselling and raise a number of issues for them:

1 When do they move outside counselling to involve themselves with the organization?
2 When do they see what is happening as an organizational issue and bring it into the organizational domain?
3 When do they break confidentiality with or without the permission of clients?
4 When do they 'tell on the organization' when unethical practices are taking place (e.g. health and safety rules)?

A recent edition of *Employee Counselling Today* (ECT) was devoted to confidentiality and ethics (vol. 4(4), 1992). While bringing out clearly the ethical dilemmas involved in workplace counselling, and using ethical codes, limited as they are, as a background to understanding ethical issues, there was little to help the busy practitioner make ethical decisions. Using ethical guidelines, as well as consultation with colleagues and supervisors, helps. The ECT Mini Survey (in the same edition), while recommending the need for policies for counselling in the workplace, has no hint of training for counsellors in ethical decision-making or what that training might look like.

Ethical issues

Counselling in the workplace not only contends with the full range of ethical issues emerging from counselling in general, but also must deal with a full set of ethical issues emerging from within the organization in which counselling takes place, and between the organization and the counsellor. Puder (1983: 96) suggests that the counsellor in such circumstances needs 'the rational and intuitive perceptiveness necessary for straddling the worlds of business and mental health'. To date, there are no ethical codes designed specifically for workplace counselling: the closest that come to dealing with such issues are the EACC Code of Professional Conduct for Certified Employee Assistance Professionals (USA), and the *UK Standards of Practice and Professional Guidelines for Employee Assistance Programmes* (EAPA, 1995).

Several ethical dilemmas arising from workplace counselling have been raised in the literature: confidentiality; the incompatibility between the organization's aims and the aims of counselling; the loyalty of the counsellor; and managing different roles with the same client. Even though these have been viewed in depth, and various aspects of the issues uncovered, there is little written on how the counsellor reaches an ethical decision. Few authors enable the practitioner to manage ethical issues and even fewer offer outlines for how ethical decisions can be implemented. Like ethical codes, the advice on how to reach decisions on ethical issues contains general principles rather than answers to particular situations. And, indeed, this is as it should be. Guidelines are meant to be general and their application to particular instances needs to be worked out rather than given. It is this 'working through', isolating the process of ethical decision-making, that is an important skill for counsellors.

Several difficulties in making ethical decisions in the workplace have been raised. Bishop and D'Rozario (1990) have pointed out that psychologists, and here we can include workplace counsellors, have largely an individualistic bias when assessing and working with clients. What is easily missed is the organizational dimension of this work. Rather than, too easily, making individuals responsible for their own problems, it is necessary to review the role of the organization in producing these same problems. Newton (1995) has used this same argument in reviewing the concept of stress in the workplace. He shows how easily we make individuals responsible for managing their stress at the same time as exonerating organizations from the blame of overloading or overworking employees. As a result, workplace counselling individualizes problems rather than attempts to see them in their collective context. Another ethical dilemma for workplace counsellors centres around their loyalties and when they might take the stance of an employee against the organization. This could happen in the event of a counsellor being convinced that an employee client was being blamed, and being punished, for what his/her boss did.

From a review of the literature on ethical issues in counselling, and from a survey of the various approaches to ethical decision-making, including the educational packages available, several areas emerge that seem basic to the field:

1 Making ethical decisions by 'intuition' (Kitchener, 1984) is not sufficient. Counsellors need to have a strategy for reaching decisions in counselling even though many of those decisions will be on an 'intuitive' basis.

2 Counsellors need access to a number of areas that will help them in the process of decision-making. These include supervision, colleagues with whom they can discuss situations, knowledge and access to codes of ethics, and various references from the literature that help in making ethical decisions.

3 Counsellors appreciate the use of case material as a way of struggling with the complexities of ethical issues in counselling. Their own cases, as well as examples from the work of others, can be used to great affect provided 'students do not overly concentrate on the clinical details of the case at the expense of its ethical dimension' (Fine and Ulrich, 1988: 546).

4 Ethical issues and dilemmas from organizational contexts in which counselling is used have particular aspects that need to be considered. Reviewing ethical decision-making within a purely individualistic approach, which psychologists and counsellors often use, does a disservice to the complexities of ethical problems within organizations. A further dimension to training in this area is required. This dimension needs to look at such areas as: conflicting values within counselling approaches and organizational philosophies/policies; assessing individuals for counselling within organizational settings: long-term and short-terms effects of ethical decisions within the organization; loyalties within the counsellor towards the client and the organization, e.g. who is the client?

Practical ethical decisions are a daily event for most counsellors: should I reach out and touch this client? Ought I to continue seeing this client or should I refer? Am I competent to deal with this issue? Is it time to end counselling in this instance? Many similar decisions are made, it seems, more by intuition than by design. Research appears to indicate that ethical decisions are made, not by reference to the books, or the codes of practice, but rather to 'unwritten, personal standards' (Patterson et al., 1989). Ethical issues are perhaps even more solidly in-built into counselling in the workplace, where organizational concerns are sometimes in conflict with individual well-being. The workplace counsellor plies his/her trade at the interface between individual and organization, while himself/ herself being a member of the organization. Boundary problems can become a nightmare, loyalties a major concern. Trying to reconcile organizational aims and objectives, especially those around success and profit-making, with concern for individuals and groups can be challenging. It seems unfair to allow the counsellor to face these either alone or without training in ethical decision-making. Providing the models to do so gives both confidence and competence.

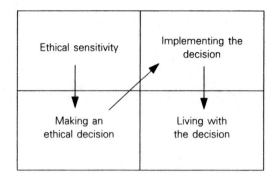

Figure 8.1 *Four components of ethical decision-making (from Rest, 1984: 20)*

Making ethical decisions in the workplace

Geist et al. (1973), in an article on rehabilitation counsellors, make the point that counsellors in organizations have little recourse when disagreements arise with the organization over loyalties – the organization tends to win. They illustrate the difficulty of imposing ethical standards on organizations and how easy it is for counsellors to get caught between care for the individual client and organizational demands that may, sometimes, not be therapeutic for clients.

Workplace counsellors need help in making ethical decisions that take into consideration both the individual client and the organization. Rest's (1984: 20) model of the four components involved in ethical decisions can be adapted by workplace counsellors to help them make sensitive decisions (see Figure 8.1).

Ethical sensitivity
The first component involves the ability to see and interpret behaviour and its effects on others. Pryor (1989) calls this 'ethical watchfulness' and recommends a number of ways of enhancing ethical sensitivity:

1 Being familiar with ethical codes and standards.
2 Making an effort to foresee ethically unclear possibilities before they actually occur.
3 Keeping an eye on the use of new techniques that may involve ethical dilemmas.
4 Examining the legal and organizational constraints of one's work in relation to one's ethical and professional allegiances.

5 Giving oneself time to think through ethically uncertain situations.

Ethical sensitivity implies a realization that virtually any action may have ethical implications. This highlights the need for careful forethought to prevent difficult situations arising for the counsellors. Some examples of this are:

1 Should the employee counsellor also see the spouse of a client who is talking about the difficulties involved in his marriage?
2 Will the employee counsellor talk to the manager of a client who wants the counsellor to intervene on his behalf?
3 Should the counsellor attend a disciplinary meeting with a client as an advocate against the organization?

Many people do not see the implications of their behaviour on others. Rest (1984) has summarized research in this area which indicates that some individuals have difficulty in interpreting even the simplest situation as ethical, others need dramatic signs before they become aware that their behaviour is seriously affecting another, while a further group is over-sensitive to the implications of every action. Even when situations are seen as ethical/moral, individuals do not always act. Bernard and Jara (1986) show that even when psychologists were aware that ethical issues were involved, they often did nothing, and Welfel and Lipsitz (1983: 320–32) present some relevant statistics:

1 In general, 5–10 per cent of practitioners appear substantially insensitive to the ethical dimensions of their work.
2 Violations of confidentiality and sexual intimacy have received the greatest attention in the literature.
3 Some 58 per cent of clinical psychologists believed that they were inadequately informed about ethical issues.

Besides the more obvious ethical violations, there are other ways in which counsellors and supervisors can exploit clients: excessive familiarity, non-clinical business matters, breaches of confidentiality, satisfaction of their own needs, impressing the client, asking favours of clients, being lax and being sadistic (Epstein and Simon, 1990: 451).

Creating ethical sensitivity means increasing awareness in counsellors that all situations are potentially ethical, and that the implications of behaviour can be far-reaching. There is certainly room for spontaneity in counselling but not for impulsivity. Carroll (1995a) has suggested a number of ways in which ethical sensitivity can be enhanced in counsellors:

- case reviews
- identifying ethical issues arising from counselling work
- reading ethical codes and related literature
- case vignettes (what would you do?)
- exploring value issues arising from counselling work
- clarifying and confronting one's own values
- creating awareness around the 'power' issues involved in counselling
- reviewing critical incidents within counselling
- evaluating ethical frameworks and theories
- ascertaining levels of moral development and how this affects ethical decision-making.

With a higher level of ethical sensitivity, workplace counsellors are more able to pick up signs that will alert them to possible hazards. That awareness, in turn, will lead them to decide what to do in the circumstances.

Making an ethical decision
This entails judging what is the best course of action in *these* circumstances for *this* individual (client) within *this* organization. All these factors – the individual client, the particular organization, the specific situation – are relevant. Here counsellors weigh up the merits of various courses of action and decide on one. It is here that care is needed not to be too individualistic in making moral judgements: what is good for the client could be unhelpful for others, or for the organization. For instance, to make the decision not to break confidentiality may benefit the individual client but could be disastrous for the organization (where someone was embezzling or involved in insider dealing). Carroll (1995a) has outlined a seven-stage methodology for ethical decision-making which is relevant to the workplace (see Box 8.1). While time will not allow this lengthy procedure to be followed in all instances of an ethical dilemma, knowing and understanding the stages can help counsellors 'short-circuit' the process when needed. However, even when a decision to act has been made and a particular course of action seen as the most appropriate, it does not follow automatically that counsellors will take the next step, translating the decision to act into behaviours.

Box 8.1 *Seven-stage methodology for ethical decision-making*

---

1 *Identify the ethical problem or dilemma*
- What are the parameters of the situation?
- What is the source of conflict for the client or for the counsellor?
- Is the conflict with another person, group of people, or family member, or with the organization?
- Is the conflict between the client and the counsellor?
- Does the conflict involve legal, moral, ethical, religious, cultural, gender or value issues?
- What are the counsellor's feelings about what is happening?
- How may the problem be clearly defined, especially where terms are emotionally charged?

2 *Identify the potential issues involved*
- What is the worst possible outcome?
- What could happen if nothing is done?
- What are the implications involved in this problem or dilemma?
- What are the rights, responsibilities and welfare of all affected parties?

3 *Review the relevant ethical guidelines*
- Do guidelines, principles or laws exist that are relevant to the dilemmas and may provide a possible solution?
- Are the counsellor's values, ethics or morals in conflict with the relevant principles or guidelines?
- Is the counsellor aware of the effect of values and does he or she have a rationale for the behaviour?
- Are there relevant codes, sections, chapters of books etc. pertinent to this issue?
- What further information is needed to help resolve the issue?

4 *Obtain consultation*
- Bring the situation to supervision.
- Talk with colleagues, where appropriate.
- Consult line managers, if appropriate.
- Talk to a lawyer (or an expert from another profession), again if appropriate.

continued overleaf

Box 8.1   *(continued)*

---

5   *Consider possible and probable courses of action*
- What are the alternatives (brainstorming without evaluating is helpful)?

6   *Enumerate the consequences of various decisions*
- What are the implications for the client?
- What are the implications for others?
- What are the implications for the counsellor?

7   *Decide on what appears to be the best course of action*
- Could you recommend this action to other counsellors in similar circumstances?
- Would I condone this behaviour in another counsellor?
- Can I defend this behaviour if it were made public?
- Would I treat other clients in the same situation differently?

Implementing the decision

Implementing an ethical decision is not always easy. It can conflict with other interests, e.g. career, friendship, loyalty. A counsellor who made the decision to back a client who was bringing action in a case of sexual harassment was subjected to long and demanding telephone conversations from the manager in question who was insisting that the charges were selfishly motivated. Other managers asked the counsellor to think of dropping her support in the light of the organization's need to keep this manager. It took a lot of courage to implement the decision. Putting the ethical decision into practice can result in a lot of hard work, demanding substantial time, and put loyalties to the test.

Carroll (1995a) has suggested steps to be taken when a moral decision has been made and needs to be implemented:

1   What steps need to be taken to implement the decision?
2   Which people are involved and who needs to be told what?
3   What restraints are there *not* to implement the ethical decision (e.g. politics of the situation, protection of a client, rationalization etc.)?
4   What support is needed (by the counsellor, by the client, by others) to implement and to live with the results.

It is relatively easy to underestimate the strength needed at times to implement ethical decisions, especially in the light of influence from colleagues, friends and, sometimes, parties with their own vested interests. Business settings are notorious for putting up with bad situations and doing nothing even when it is known what should be done.

Perhaps one of the reasons for not implementing ethical decisions is the knowledge that once implemented they have to be accepted and lived with as a part of organizational life.

Living with the decision

Unlike other decisions, an ethical decision can never be shown to be the correct and only course of action. Living with such a decision is about never knowing what was the right course of action to take. Even after a client has been hospitalized, on the recommendation and action of the workplace counsellor, the doubts are not alleviated. Counsellors are still left with thoughts that they may have acted prematurely, especially if the client reacts negatively to their decision. Carroll (1995a) has defined some of the issues involved:

1 Dealing with anxiety around the final decision.
2 Letting go of the situation and the dilemma.
3 Accepting the limitations involved.
4 Learning from the experience.
5 Using personal and professional support to live with the consequences of the decision.

In summary, there are no easy ways to make ethical decisions in the workplace. Counsellors will want to use supervision, colleagues, ethical codes and networks as methods of discussion and rehearsing for ethical demands of working in this setting. What is essential, and recommended by most authors, is the need to have clear and documented agreements on a number of areas:

1 Clarification of potentially conflictual relationships.
2 An understanding of the implications and limits of confidentiality in the workplace.
3 A clear formula by which employee counsellors are required to share information about clients with the organization.
4 The need to let clients know the limits of confidentiality if there are limits.

Ethical responsibilities for and to clients

Workplace counsellors provide the same ethical responsibilities to and for clients as do counsellors in other settings (e.g. the BAC *Code of Ethics and Practice for Counsellors*, 1990a). Counsellors are recommended to acquaint themselves with these general ethical guidelines and to have read some of the dilemmas and issues emerging. Workplace counsellors are responsible for:

- setting up a safe environment for clients
- ensuring privacy
- safeguarding notes
- managing the counselling process
- negotiating confidentiality with clients
- ensuring clients understand what counselling means
- how they work with clients in other contexts (e.g. committees, canteen, sports facilities, etc.) so that confidentiality is safe
- clarity on what information, if any, counsellors would relay back to the organization with or without the consent of the client

Confidentiality is a key issue in counselling with clients in workplace settings. Many clients do not use workplace counselling services because of their fear that word may get back to the organization, or notes made on their records, or it might affect their career prospects. Salt et al. (1992: 11) recommend clarity on the meaning of confidentiality in the workplace: 'Confidentiality as a concept is an all-or-nothing phenomenon. Something is either confidential or it is not. There is no room for shades of confidentiality. A clear policy stating *who needs to know what and why* is fundamental to providing an organisation with rules for maintaining confidentiality.' This policy needs to be carefully negotiated with clients. Even when confidentiality is clearly agreed, the counsellor can be put in a compromising situation by clients who exploit the counselling relationship for their own ends. Clients are not adverse to telling management that 'their counsellor told them' to take time off, that there was nothing wrong with them, that management style is to blame etc. Clients are not bound by confidentiality as are counsellors. In outlining the importance of confidentiality, Bond (1993) points out times when it can be broken:

- when clients give permission
- when information is already in the public domain
- when the public interest in preserving confidentiality is outweighed by the public interest in disclosure, e.g. when harm could result to the client or others
- for supervision/consultation purposes

Bond also indicates how important is the contract between organization and counsellor in respect of confidentiality. He quotes the Law Commission (1981: 8) which is worth reproducing here:

A doctor or a psychologist employed in industry is faced with the demand by his employer for the disclosure of medical records relating to other employees of the firm who have frankly discussed their personal problems with him on a confidential basis and without any express or implied understanding that the information would be made available to the employer. Assuming that no question of the public interest is involved (as it might be, for instance, if the health or safety of other employees was at stake), we think that the doctor or psychologist must preserve the confidences of those who confide in him. Of course, if he accepts the confidence only on the express or employed understanding that, pursuant to his contractual duty, he may disclose the information to the employer, this would constitute a limitation on the scope of the obligation of confidence to which he is subject.

This raises several issues that need to be absolutely clear for workplace counsellors:

1   What is agreed with the employing organization in respect of client confidentiality? Are there contractual areas where counsellors must reveal information passed on to them by clients, with or without their (client's) permission?
2   Are potential clients aware of the limits governing confidentiality?
3   In contracting for counselling, counsellors will acquaint clients of the limits of confidentiality in this setting (i.e. counsellors will not offer a higher degree of confidentiality than that permitted by their contract).

A further issue of responsibility to clients is that of notes. Who should have access to these, both the official file and the personal notes of the counsellor? The *UK Standards of Practice and Professional Guidelines for Employee Assistance Programmes* (EAPA, 1995) makes several suggestions under the heading of keeping records: handle the destruction of individual client records in a confidential way; ensure the security of client files; be clear about who has access to these files; in so far as possible prevent their files being used in arbitration, employee litigations and disputes between the individual and the organization. Lee and Rosen (1984) offer three hints on protecting client privacy: minimize intrusiveness by controlling the amount of information gathered; maximize fairness in record keeping; and create legitimate expectations of the confidentiality of records, especially from organizations.

Workplace counsellors have a responsibility to employees about how they assess their 'problems'. Difficult and problematic employees are often so labelled because of their lack of conformity to the role expectations of the organization. Fairness to clients demands that employee counsellors bear in mind that the culture of the organization may be at variance with the client, and creating a problem between them. This awareness can save clients from being labelled as 'problems' when what is at issue is a mismatch between individual and organization. In other instances, employees can be viewed as problems when the organization is at fault, as in cases of sexual harassment or managers who are bullies.

Ethical responsibilities for and to the organization

Workplace counsellors are employed by organizations and as such have responsibilities to those organizations. Clarity around the organization's demands is needed and clear contracts need to be drawn up so that roles and responsibilities are not in doubt. These include:

- maintaining the service
- agreeing to organizational policies
- a policy about the role of counselling in the organization
- when to involve the organization in counselling work
- feedback and statistics (reports)
- evaluating the service

However, the workplace counsellor also has an ethical responsibility to help the organization review and change workplace practices and policies that are antagonistic to human welfare. These can range across physical conditions, mental wellness, stress levels, equal opportunities, sexual harassment, management practices, and a host of other areas. In a sense, employee counsellors are the 'conscience' of the organization, monitoring how people are treated and cared for and moving fast to build in safeguards where possible. Helping organizations to change to more ethically sound principles and practices for their employees is a key responsibility for workplace counsellors, and yet not a responsibility for which they are trained. How far are workplace counsellors responsible for the social and communal concerns of employees that arise from working within a particular organization? Some codes of practice would see this as a legitimate concern for the counselling practitioner. Others tend to side with the organization. Patterson (1971) quotes sources who, when faced with a problem between the organization and the individual, usually give preference to the organization. These conclusions are in the context of a school setting where there may be some differences.

Lee and Rosen (1984) have outlined suggestions for maintaining ethical responsibility to the organization:

- develop an economical model to justify the counselling work
- negotiate a contract that specifies the interests of counsellors, consumers and organization as well as the rights and responsibilities of each
- outline a framework for defining the problems appropriate for the counselling service
- develop guidelines for record keeping
- create and maintain professional relationships
- ascertain accreditation standards for programmes in industry

Little has been written on the ethical responsibilities of workplace counsellors for and to the organization that employs them. Some authors see wide roles that the counsellor can legitimately play within the organization; others suggest narrowing tasks to those which deal directly with individual employees coming for counselling. What is clear, however, is that counsellors and, indeed, organizations ought to have an understanding of what those ethical responsibilities are before tasks are allocated.

Employee counsellors' ethical responsibilities for and to themselves

All counsellors, not just counsellors in the workplace, need to care for themselves. This is not just good advice but enters into the realm of an ethical responsibility; there are far too many examples of burn-out within the helping professions. This is partly due to good people working too hard, not recognizing the signs of stress in themselves even though they are good at recognizing them in others, and eventually having to rest because they 'break down' or become ill, physically and/or mentally. Inskipp and Proctor (1993: 34) put this well: 'It is your ethical responsibility to your clients, and your human right to yourself, to nurture and maintain your physical, emotional, intellectual and spiritual well-being.'

Within organizational situations there are further elements to be considered; including how the culture and management of the organization may affect counsellors. There is some research to show that counsellors working in organizational/institutional settings suffer greater levels of stress than those working in private practice (Hellman and Morrison, 1987; Farber, 1990). Burn-out may be as much the result of organizational stress as it is the result of individuals not caring for themselves.

In an enlightening chapter, Brady et al. (1995) have reviewed the literature on stress among counsellors, and present seven steps of stress. Obviously, these stresses apply equally to counsellors in the workplace.

- patient (client) behaviours
- working conditions
- emotional depletion
- physical isolation
- psychic isolation
- therapeutic relationships
- personal disruptions

Some of these factors will be more applicable to individual counsellors than others. And, of course, as House (1995: 87) remarks in the context of counselling in a medical setting, 'setting-specific stress will be experienced to the extent that the characteristics of the setting resonate unhelpfully or pathologically with the counsellor's personality dynamics.' Looking after self 'physically, emotionally, intellectually and spiritually' means having in place a number of support systems that will defray overstress and burn-out:

- managing the organization
- negotiating terms and conditions
- managing time
- managing self
- supervision
- networking
- continuing training
- personal and social support

Managing the organization
Much has been written about stress in the workplace in the past few years and it has become a commonplace to see stress as an everyday factor in modern organizational life rather than an exception. Many of the problems arriving at the door of the workplace counsellor will revolve around stress in the workplace. Not only does the employee counsellor have to deal with these problems and provide a place of 'containment' for them, but he/she will have to deal with his/her own stress and the stress emerging from working within particular organizations. The organization can stress counsellors in many ways.

Direct management style The managerial style of the line manager of counsellors can be a very powerful source of stress. I know of one instance in which the line manager was not very sympathetic to counselling provision, seeing it as a luxury that pampered the weak when what they really needed was, as he put it, a 'good kick up the backside'. Consequently, the counsellor was continually fighting for recognition. After several months she realized that she was battling to prove that counselling was helpful and spending more time trying to justify what she was doing than working with clients. It was not just the beliefs of the manager but his 'macho-style' of management that eventually led to her resignation. It was only when she compared her new job (with a manager who not only saw the importance of what she did, but encouraged her creativity in the role) with her old job that she realized how stressed she had been.

Looking after themselves and ensuring that they are working well sometimes means that counsellors in organizations have to 'manage their managers'. This can be educational. Not all organizational managers understand counselling, what it means, the boundaries involved, the stresses it puts on counsellors, and the emotional and psychological commitments necessary. Educating them to this can be time well spent and can result in an understanding that is supportive rather than a misrepresentation which can be stressful.

Organizational culture We know enough about organizational culture (see Chapter 4) to realize how influential it is on counselling provision, and how stressful that culture can be to counsellors. Within achievement cultures the counsellor will feel the stress of having to be an 'achiever', to show the effectiveness of counselling in the organization, to be alongside other achievers in a sometimes competitive and cut-throat market. Being able to manage the stresses of organizational culture will be extremely important if counsellors are not to collude with the very pathology of the organization.

Bureaucratic demands Rarely are counsellors allowed to get on with counselling work alone. There are quite a number of time-consuming and emotionally draining requests from the organization. Brady et al. (1995: 6) put it well:

> virtually all healing contexts are dominated by a sense of damage, despair, and disease. And that's only the clients. Throw in bureaucratic nonsense, colleague misbehaviour, inadequate resources, onerous paperwork and assorted other organisational and peer problems and one begins to recognise the potential damage of working conditions in the helping professions.

There can be further commitments and demands from the organiz-ation: attending committees, managing budgets, helping devise policies, travel to other sites, sitting in on appraisals and interviews. Being alert to all these demands, knowing when to, and being able to, say 'no', as well as organizing self, are key issues in managing the organization.

Emergencies   Organizations are notorious for creating crisis-times: the report that should have been written by yesterday, the employee who has 'broken down' and must be seen immediately, the sexual harassment accusation which cannot be delayed, the fire-alarm that keeps going off, and a host of other areas that refuse to allow counsellors to get on with their everyday duties. A workplace coun-sellor remarked that everyday life is dealing with chaos and that the opportunity of having a well-organized day that goes according to plan is a myth. Egan (1993a) has pointed out that modern managers need to be able to handle chaos as the order of the day. The same applies to workplace counsellors.

Negotiating terms and conditions

From the very beginning of working as a counsellor in an organiz-ation it is essential for counsellors to negotiate their tasks, roles and conditions of work. It is easy for boundaries to become unclear, and unless contracts are drawn up that allow counsellors to clarify their place in the organization, they will be in no position to negotiate when further demands are made. There is some research to show that role ambiguity and role conflict result in fatigue and emotional depletion (Kelloway and Barling, 1991).

Managing time

Crucial to the busy employee counsellor, and I have yet to come across one who is idle, is his or her way of managing time. Without doubt, and within a few months of being employed, there will be huge demands on time. Managers will want them to see troubled employees, work with difficult members of staff, involve them in team development, and advise them on how to work with their people. The training department will want them to put on training in counselling and related areas, human resources will try to involve them in organizational change and development, and every em-ployee with a grievance will attempt to enlist their help as an advocate against the organization. And this is not to look at the administrative side of their work: keeping statistics, publicizing the service, fielding the telephone calls, talking to outside individuals and groups who want to know about employee counselling, or are writing dissertations on counselling in the workplace and want access to information. Nor does it take into consideration the time spent in networking, in supervision, in continuing training and education. The demands are immense and, since most organizations are involved in some form of organizational change today, this will mean further individual demands from stressed clients.

A number of factors can help here:

- prioritizing activities will be essential
- maintaining a reasonable caseload
- time for emergencies
- time for administration
- time for reflecting on what is being done and what could be done
- assertiveness
- stress management techniques
- flexibility
- self-knowledge

Knowing, recognizing and applying to self the signs of stress is equally important. The old Chinese proverb 'Sometimes the fish are the last to know about the sea' is very applicable here. Employee counsellors often do not recognize their own stress as effectively as they recognize it in others.

Managing self
Looking after oneself is crucial in counselling work, not only physically but emotionally and psychologically. Some factors here are:

1 How am I dealing with stress? Am I drinking alcohol above levels that are healthy (14 units a week for a woman, 21 for a man)?
2 How am I sleeping? Am I constantly tired? Sleep is often one of the first elements in life to be affected when stress becomes overwhelming. Too much sleep, too little sleep, early morning waking can all be signs of stress.
3 Am I exercising regularly? In the late 1960s, when R. Carkhuff was influential in counselling research and training, it was said that his first question to those who would train with him concerned their physical fitness. Apparently, he would not allow individuals on his course until they had reached an acceptable level of physical fitness, working on the principle that we are not fragmented individuals and our physical well-being affects our personal and working lives. In a particular instance (it is again

reported), he asked one participant to run several laps of a short field to show that he was ready for counselling training.
4   How rushed do I feel?
5   How do I fare on a stress inventory?
6   How am I emotionally, interpersonally?

Supervision
Several authors have attested to supervision as one way of helping contain some of the anxieties and emotions that arise in counselling work (Hawkins and Shohet, 1989; Inskipp and Proctor, 1993; Carroll, 1995a). It is invaluable to workplace counsellors, offering a forum to think through what is happening to them as well as what is happening to their clients. It provides support to deal with the difficulties of workplace counselling, an opportunity to review particular clients and work with them, and a place to monitor the connections between the workplace and counselling provision. Chapter 10 contains an account of supervision for employee counsellors.

Networking
Besides supervision, making and maintaining contact with other employee counsellors is a very valuable way of creating a forum for individuals who may have the same issues for discussion, for hearing how others in similar circumstances are dealing with their problems, and for sharing ideas and strategies for managing stress. Talking is undoubtedly one of the main ways in which people deal with stress (Hope, 1985) and networking is a great forum for conversation. Realizing that other counsellors face similar difficulties can itself be a source of hope besides providing a safe environment in which to look at possible ways ahead.

Continuing training
Time needs to be left aside in a busy schedule for continuing training and education in counselling and the dimensions of workplace counselling. Training needs can be discussed within supervision and within networking where others can share training they have done and its effects on their work. Often training (and lunch) are the first elements to go when activities increase. This is a pity.
    Not only is time on training time-out from a hectic schedule, but it is also the way to gain new skills, build up confidence, and be creative with new ways of working. All these can bring enthusiasm and creativity to work. We know that one way in which stress affects people is to stunt their enthusiasm and creativity: they go onto 'remote control' and do not have the mental or physical energy to think about new ways of doing old things.

Personal and social support

Paramount in people's well-being is the social support system they have. In his book *Counseling and Social Support*, Pearson (1990) is very clear about the connections between social support and effectiveness as a human being. 'As we have seen', he writes, 'social support is a process basic to the development of humanness itself. Its presence or absence bears heavily on the development and maintenance of personal effectiveness. Therefore, we should expect to find support-related issues and events surfacing in almost any area of human endeavour' (1990: 201).

While personal support systems will differ from person to person, what is necessary is that employee counsellors know and be able to set up, within their personal lives, the support they need. Hawkins and Shohet (1989: 17) suggest a method for 'mapping your support system' that could be very helpful for employee counsellors. They apply it particularly to workplace support, but it can be easily widened to include personal support. I am adapting their process slightly to gear it more specifically towards personal support systems.

Briefly, they suggest using a large piece of paper to draw a map of your support system. In the centre draw a symbol to represent yourself and around it draw or represent all the elements of your support system (using symbols, diagrams, words, pictures etc.). These will include individuals, teams, learning, courses, personal and professional relationships, places you go, meetings you attend, holidays – anything and everything in your life that sustains, supports, energizes, nurtures, enthuses, excites and challenges you positively. Next, show the connections between each representation and yourself: strong/weak, close/far away. Follow this by showing how you use that support system or not as the case may be, what blocks you from using it more. Draw in areas of support you would like but do not have at the moment. Hawkins and Shohet (1989) suggest sharing this with another person and looking in some detail at the following questions:

- Is this the kind of support you want?
- Is it enough? What sort of support is missing? How could you go about getting such support?
- What support is really positive for you to the extent that you must ensure that you nurture and maintain it?
- What blocks could you do something about reducing?

An action plan on building the support systems needed can be outlined from this discussion.

Workplace counsellors also use their own personal counselling as a source of support and self-assessment. Orme (1994) has argued that personal counselling may be more necessary for workplace counsellors than for counsellors in general because of the extra roles and responsibilities entailed in the job.

In summary, employee counsellors have a responsibility to care for themselves so that they can be effective within an organization and with their clients. Obviously, this entails monitoring closely what is happening to them and being able to take steps to offset dangers to their personal and professional lives.

The organization's ethical responsibilities for counselling provision

In setting up counselling within its ambit, organizations have a responsibility to make it work effectively. Organizations have the responsibility of serving counsellors as they work with clients. Some of these responsibilities involve:

- providing administrative support
- providing secretarial support
- providing professional leadership and management
- listening to statistics and reports
- offering realistic budgets
- supporting counsellors as they publicize the service
- working out policies on counselling and confidentiality
- allowing counselling to influence corporate culture
- supporting counsellors' continuing development, training and support (especially in supervision)
- support from top levels of management
- working out clear contracts that cover confidentiality and what it means; the roles and responsibilities of counsellors

Counsellors will want to consider whether they should work with organizations who refuse some or all of the above. Major problems emerge when organizations do not take their responsibilities to counselling and counsellors seriously, either because they do not understand what is involved, or have not thought through the implications enough, or simply do not resource the service sufficiently.

Conclusion

Ethical decision-making is a daily event for workplace counsellors. Great sensitivity, not to mention diplomacy, is needed to cope with what is potentially a minefield of problems. Counsellors need ethical antennae, as well as support, to help make key decisions that affect individual and organizational lives, and strength to live with the implications of those decisions. The sooner employee counsellors have a code of ethics for workplace counselling the better it will be for them: guidelines are not the final answer but they are valuable signposts along the way.

9

Training for Workplace Counsellors

As the organization increasingly shapes the quality and conditions of clinical practice, clinicians have to develop organizational skills.

> A. Gitterman and I. Miller, 'The influence of the organization on clinical practice'

At present, workplace counselling is in search of a model for its training and while it waits it draws upon the generic training model for its inspiration.

> E. Pickard, 'Designing training for counsellors at work'

Methods of training workplace counsellors

It has only been in recent years that specific training for workplace counsellors has been translated into educational packages. Before that counsellors adapted their own counselling training to employee counselling.

Case example

Gloria is an example of such a counsellor. Initially a teacher, Gloria started her counselling training in her early thirties and for several years combined her counselling/pastoral role with teaching in a secondary school. She then did an MSc in counselling psychology, one aspect of which was to work in a GP surgery as a part-time counsellor. Soon after finishing her degree she joined a counselling team in a university setting and, two years later, applied for the job of employee counsellor with a large multi-national company. At the beginning she found it difficult to coordinate all aspects of the job. Although she was the first full-time counsellor in the organization, she had presumed that the company and individuals within it would understand her role. Unfortunately, they did not. She was affiliated to the personnel department and several of her colleagues asked her, jokingly of course, why she saw only four or five clients a day while they were able to shift up to 20.

Managers referred employees for all sorts of reasons and then wanted to know what was happening. Employees were often unsure of why they were sent to her and several wanted to enlist her help in organizing grievances against the company. After two months and a lot of work with her supervisor, she devised a new 'game-plan' that cut down on her number of clients and increased her education of the organization. She visited managers, departments, teams, small groups, and explained about counselling, what it entailed, its boundaries, her relationship with clients and with other colleagues. Soon she felt that the organization had a working knowledge of who she was and what she did. Sometimes she was called in to advise managers on working with their employees, on how to recognize signs of distress, and how to refer to the counselling service. When asked, she squirms at the embarrassment of those early days. She tells the story of a workplace counsellor she knew who left the job after four months because she was not able to cope with the organizational demands. Gloria is now committed to prior training of employee counsellors especially to help them work with the organization.

Gerstein and Shullman (1992) have summarized the training in counselling psychology related to work in industry in the US, and have given outlines of two courses entitled 'Occupational counselling psychology' and 'A seminar in counselling psychology in business and organizational settings'. While the second of these is more about the applied skills, the first covers a range of topics:

- the history of counselling psychology in business and organizational settings
- the vocational behaviour of adults (career, work)
- vocational assessment strategies with adults
- career development of organizations
- models and technologies of consultation and programme evaluation
- workplace wellness and safety programmes
- EAPs
- research issues and questions of interest
- trade publications important to the business community

The training outline shows some of the areas in which counselling psychologists are expected to have skills and knowledge, and presumably some of the roles they are expected to take on if they are employed as counselling psychologists in organizations.

In Britain, at present, is the first generation of employee counsellors, the pioneers who have had to learn workplace counselling from a background of generic training (Carroll, 1994). Such counsellors have often come from welfare departments where they had to combine a number of roles with employees, one of which was counselling. There was little specific training for employee counsellors or counsellors working in organizational settings. Pickard (forthcoming) has reviewed training for workplace counsellors and designated three stages in its development:

Stage 1:   counselling in organizations where counsellors trained as counsellors and applied their work to organizational settings.

Stage 2:   counselling for organizations which combined counselling provision and organizational needs, e.g. through the use of an EAP.

Stage 3:   organizational counselling, which is an attempt to provide an overall philosophy of employee care where counselling is 'integrated both conceptually and theoretically into organizational philosophy and practice' . . . This distinction provides a framework for considering training for workplace counsellors: knowing their roles and responsibilities is a foundation for a suitable curriculum. We are attempting to coordinate what we know, at this stage, into workable training packages for potential workplace counsellors.

The following is offered as a synthesis of thinking within the field and a model for discussion rather than a rigid process that must be followed slavishly. Like all models, it is helpful as a rough map providing significant points; it is unhelpful if it eliminates the intuitive, the spontaneous, the interpersonal, and the flexible. Training, in the final analysis, is about learning, and that is a personal, emotional experience as well as an intellectual journey. There are three ways in which training in workplace counselling takes place.

(1) One way is through specific courses set up to train employee counsellors. Previous counselling experience can be used as the basis for specialist training in workplace counselling. A course that seems to do this is the Diploma in Counselling at Work at the University of Bristol. It requires applicants to have had 'some training in counselling' before beginning the course. There are also courses for individuals who have had no previous training in counselling. The Diploma in Counselling at Work from Training Development Associates (TDA) and Roehampton Institute, as well

as the Certificate in Counselling at Work run by the University of Birmingham, are examples of courses which demand no previous experience from participants, although it is expected that they have been working with people in some capacity. Most, in fact, come from a business background like personnel, human resources, welfare or consultancy.

(2) A second method by which counsellors gain training in workplace counselling is to set up and manage their own training portfolio. With a background of generic counselling training, they add short focused training packages to their existing counselling experience. These can be one, two, three or five-day courses. A random review of *Counselling at Work*, the Journal of the Association for Counselling at Work, reveals a number of such courses. 'Workplace welfare and its legal aspects', 'An introduction to employee assistance programmes' and 'Exploring the context of employee counselling' are just a few examples of short programmes devised specifically for workplace counsellors.

(3) A third way in which counsellors gain training in employee counselling is by doing it. They join an already existing counselling service in a company and learn the trade by apprenticeship.

Case example
Michael was already an occupational psychologist who returned to do a master's degree in counselling. Because of his background in business, he was eager to work as a counsellor in a workplace setting. He contacted the counselling service of a large private company and worked there for a year under the direction of the senior counsellor and under supervision of the team supervisor.

In evaluating the above three methods of training, it is clear that the third method is valuable as a part of continuing training. It is the method used by most employee counsellors who had no training available to them when they started. However, with training for employee counsellors becoming more available it is no longer necessary, and the weakness of this method is that there is no organized theoretical input and no formal training as such. The learning is totally experiential and emerges specifically from client work. It is based on an 'apprenticeship' understanding of learning. It is certainly recommended, but as part of a larger training package, rather than standing on its own as a full training in employee counselling.

The second method has a number of disadvantages. It is all too easy to choose training that is liked rather than what is needed. Because most short courses take all-comers and do not monitor applications, and because most have no in-built assessment or evaluation, it is possible that participants have no method of knowing whether or not they are suitable for this kind of work. Buyers in the short-course market can dip into various dimensions of interest and application in workplace counselling. But what is missing is a systematic training that integrates pieces of learning into overall models. Devotees of short courses alone can end up with a lot of information and skills but without the coordination and integration of what they have learned. Again, this is valuable training, but to be recommended after a full initial training has taken place. In this way, it has a context that gives it meaning and allows it to make sense in an overall picture.

Obviously, formal training in workplace counselling is the preferred route. I believe there are problems for individuals coming to training as employee counsellors who already have existing training in counselling. Generic counselling training does not always fit a person for workplace counselling. In fact, some facets may actually be unhelpful in making a transition as a counsellor into the workplace. Generally, counselling training is good at looking in depth at boundaries, at specific counselling roles, at confidentiality, what I call the personal and interpersonal dimensions of counselling. And, unless it is done with couples, families, or involves systems and systemic training, there is a tendency to concentrate solely on the individual client. The administrative and organizational dimensions of counselling work are not well taught on many training courses in counselling. Contexts are not high on counselling training agendas. Connor (1994), in her book *Training the Counsellor: An Integrative Model*, has a short section entitled 'Understanding family and social systems, organizations and contexts'. But, besides saying how important it is to understand these (it concentrates almost exclusively on the social background from which clients emerge), it gives no hints or ideas on how to help trainees develop knowledge and the skills to work with the context. It has almost nothing on working at the interface between the individual and these systems. A recent publication specifically on counselling in the workplace (Summerfield and van Oudtshoorn, 1995) concentrates on training in counselling skills and provides outlines of skills training workshops. It also isolates the counselling skills needed to work with career counselling, mentoring and outplacement counselling. But, again, it does not seem to offer an integrated approach to professional counselling in the workplace. Understanding the multiple dynamics that go to make up the workplace counsellor's job is not sufficient of itself and help is needed to implement such skills and knowledge. Chiefly, it is this ability to work with multiple roles, and the skill of maintaining clear boundaries with clients who are work colleagues in the same organization, that needs special training. Negotiating with an organization entails understanding something of organizational culture. Hence, the three main areas necessary for workplace counsellors are:

1 Managerial training to help workplace counsellors set up, understand and administer a counselling system within an organization.
2 Consultancy skills whereby they are able to involve themselves in organizational change through their counselling work.
3 Counselling training through which they are able to assess, maintain and terminate a workplace relationship that is professional counselling.

My preference is for a course that, from the very outset, thinks systemically, organizationally and individually. Training for employee counselling is not a training about counselling individuals, but about counselling individuals *within a workplace context*. That context is going to colour what happens in the counselling room, how counselling is understood, how assessment takes place, how confidentiality is agreed, where notes are kept, and a host of other issues pertinent to this setting. The type of course required is not about adapting counselling to working with employees, but offering workplace counselling as an understood intervention in its own right. Counselling can be seen as an integrated part of employee care as well as a force for organizational development and change.

In looking at any professional counselling training, heed must be given to what the British Association for Counselling calls the 'eight basic elements of training' in their *Recognition of Counsellor Training Courses* (1990b). These are broad headings and need adaptation to training for workplace counsellors. They are presented below as outlined in Dryden et al. (1995: 13–15). A professional counsellor training course:

1 Has a detailed admissions policy and selection procedure.
2 Provides opportunities for self-development.
3 Stipulates that students should have opportunity for substantial and regular client work.
4 Ensures that students receive regular supervision during the course.

5 Provides structured opportunity for skills training.
6 Provides a thorough grounding in counselling theory with special reference to the course's core theoretical model.
7 Provides opportunities for professional development.
8 Designs and implements proper assessment and evaluation procedures.

While this chapter will not review these eight elements as applied to workplace counselling, it will take some essential aspects of them.

Before looking in more detail at curricula for workplace counselling, there are a few areas that need further consideration. Primary among these is selection for training in employee counselling. To date this has been a problem. On the first training I organized in workplace counselling I was given my trainees. There was no organized selection procedure, no criteria by which participants could measure themselves, or be measured by others. Obviously, such criteria are connected to what are seen as the features of the job: what is expected from individuals who would be employee counsellors. The Diploma in Counselling at Work (University of Bristol) tries to capture some of these characteristics, 'namely warmth of personality, flexibility of thinking, the capacity for sensitive response to a wide range of people and issues and the ability to argue critically and evaluate ideas and outcomes'. The following is offered to start a discussion on this issue rather than being seen as a definitive list of criteria. Individuals who put themselves forward for training as employee counsellors, and who may eventually end up as in-house workplace counsellors, need to satisfy the following criteria given in Box 9.1. Selection of candidates for counselling in the workplace needs to be done not by just scrutinizing an application form, but by interview, where a number of the criteria can be checked, and where the interpersonal aspects of the interview can be used as a form of interpersonal assessment. It is always helpful to have two interviewers who can discuss their own reactions.

The dynamics of counselling training

There is a tendency in considering training for counsellors and allied professions to concentrate almost exclusively on the *curriculum*, that is, what is needed by trainees to become professional at their work. And without doubt this is a key element in training, probably the most important area. Page and Wosket (1994), in their outline of supervision training, focus entirely on the 'course' and the learning of the trainee; and Connor (1994) does the same in her book *Training the Counsellor: An Integrative Model*. However, often forgotten, is

Box 9.1 *Essential and desirable criteria for employee counselling trainees*

Essential	Desirable
Self-awareness (insight into one's personality, interpersonal style, blocks to relating etc.)	Have been in personal counselling/personal psychotherapy for some time
Ability and willingness to work with one's own issues	Have a background showing interpersonal abilities and work with people
Able to maintain clear boundaries and understand the dynamics of professional relationships	Have experience in and understanding of organizational issues, culture, politics
Flexibility	A basic understanding of what counselling means and how it differs from other forms of intervention
Openness and ability to learn theory (counselling, organizational)	
Ability to look after self (assertive, decision-making skills)	Have experience of helping people in distress
Negotiating skills	Have worked with people in crisis
Ability to learn skills (counselling, teamwork)	
Training and consultancy skills	
Ability to evaluate counselling, counselling service, keep statistics of the service	

the *context* in which counselling training takes place. Important as the curriculum is, and the dynamics of the training relationships, they need to be integrated with the context into an overall dynamic of training. Figure 9.1 outlines five factors in such a training. These five factors are integrated into an overall training. Each will be considered in more detail.

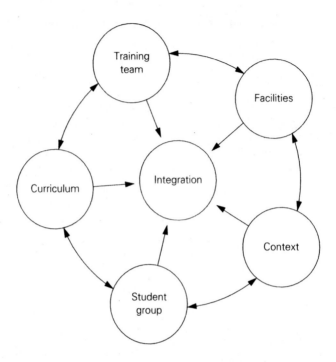

Figure 9.1   *Five factors in workplace counsellor training*

The training team

Connor (1994) specifies the qualities of good trainers. However, rarely, if ever, is the counselling training team considered as a significant factor in student training. We know enough about groups and teams to understand that the dynamics within the training team will come through to the student group. How the trainers work together, how they deal with their own dynamics, how they organize their teaching, what information they share in respect of individual students, are all major team issues in the training of the student group. Students are adept, sometimes quite unconsciously, at picking up and using divisions within the teaching team and will pitch staff members against each other. Several areas need to be considered here:

• What qualities do we need in the staff team?
• What strengths (personnel, expertise) are we missing from the team?

- What issues arise for full-time members of staff? For part-time staff?
- How often does the full team meet?
- Is there a leader, a director, who manages the team as well as the programme?
- Is there a forum for dealing with team dynamics?
- Who facilitates that process?
- What is the team doing that is affecting the students adversely?

Creating the kind of training team that models how teams work is itself a creative learning environment which teaches by modelling.

Facilities

One of the major criticisms of students on training courses concerns the poor facilities offered by a programme. Facilities for non-traditional students (who tend to be older, often have part-time or full-time jobs) are often not considered and, if considered, are often low on the priority list. Simple issues, such as car parking, library facilities adapted to particular student groups, eating arrangements etc., can all lack appropriate care. I know of one college which runs a counselling training course in the evenings. Unfortunately, the college library has closed by the time the students arrive and the canteen serves its final food at 5.30 pm – just too late for them. No wonder they feel marginalized.

Counselling training today cannot work effectively without good video equipment and people who are trained to use it. Training students to use video, to edit their own video work, and to know the basics of video technology, is time well spent. Sufficient teaching space is vital, as is the ability to manage that space. One college has good teaching facilities but they are all geared to lecturing, with upright chairs and tables set out in formal rows. The rooms cannot be adapted easily to small group work or large group work. The teaching facilities do not encourage counselling training.

Which journals are taken by the programme, where they are, and how they are managed are crucial for students returning to formal education after an absence of some time. Library facilities and technology have changed out of all proportion over the past 10 years. Literature reviews are now offered on such systems as Psych. Litt. Understanding how to use facilities, how to study, how to manage learning time are all skills easily attained. Too many counselling students are left to their own devices rather than helped to use facilities effectively.

Context

As organizational counselling stresses the context in which counselling takes place, so the context in which training occurs is essential to the effectiveness of a programme. Is the training in an educational establishment, a medical setting, a private and profit-making organization, a company? Contexts influence what happens within them. Whatever the context it is important:

- that it supports the programme, not just verbally, but in fact
- that it understands the programme and its particular needs
- that it builds in quality control and validation
- that it monitors reports clearly and fairly
- that the programme team is aware how the context and its culture/ecology can affect learning outcomes

Politics within the organization will percolate to the training group either overtly or covertly. The organization in which training takes place (the educational establishment) will itself be a training arena for learning about how organizations impact on work and training. Why not use it as a focus for that learning? Many institutes of higher education, where certificates and diplomas in counselling at work are obtained, are themselves going through major reorganizations not unlike those in the private sector.

The student group

The student group needs consideration. Balance within the group affects learning and support for individuals. People from different cultural backgrounds will benefit from the support of others from similar backgrounds racially or regarding sexual orientation. I know of one black trainee on a course where the rest of the students were white. While there was no hint of personal racism, she felt that no one understood the particular issues she was working with as a black trainee counsellor. Gender is important and many courses currently find it difficult to have a match of men and women. The only male student on a counselling training course of 18 found the experiential group very difficult: he was the only focus through which the women could work out some of their issues with men (even the group facilitator was a woman). For effective work on gender issues, it is important to have both men and women in the one group, but sufficient of each to make sure that some of the load is shared. Age, race, disability, gender and sexual orientation are all factors in choosing a student group that will best facilitate learning.

The curriculum

Carroll (1994) asked 12 in-house counsellors in the private sector, none of whom had received specific training in workplace counselling, to design a course for themselves as employee counsellors. Besides the skills of counselling and how to use supervision, they suggested specialist areas:

> Organisational psychology was most frequently mentioned as the area most useful to counsellors. Participants believed that a general awareness and understanding of the powerful dynamics within organisations was essential. Knowledge of the particular culture and policies of the company for which they worked was an important element but it was felt this could be picked up once in post. . . . Other specialist work-place issues mentioned were stress management, dealing with job loss and managing change, responding to trauma, performance appraisal, disciplinary issues, and alcohol dependency. Training in couples and systems therapy was suggested because they provide a helpful model for when organisational interventions are appropriate, and in particular mediation situations between individuals and the organisation. Implicit in much that was said involved guidance in setting up, developing, and monitoring an in-house counselling service which included identifying needs, engaging management support, establishing boundaries, writing policies, and pinpointing location and suitable counsellors. This includes the skills of training and presentation-giving, particularly when marketing the service. No one mentioned training in collecting and presenting statistics even though there is no standard formula for collating such information. (Carroll, 1994: 48–9)

Fisher's research (1995) also tried to isolate some of the characteristics of workplace counsellors that could help define training for them. Having an understanding of the conflicts clients experience with their work life – in work relationships, work policies, procedures or practices – was mentioned as essential. Lewis and Lewis (1986: 22) list six areas needed by employee counsellors to supplement their counselling training: 'program development and management . . . short-term counselling/assessment . . . resource utilization/networking . . . organizational consultation . . . education and training . . . public relations and marketing'.

However, caution is needed in reviewing all the demanding roles required of contemporary workplace counsellors. There is a tendency to make the workplace counsellor a jack of all organizational trades. They are asked to be professional counsellors, organizational consultants, trainers, welfare officers, personnel officers, internal or external change agents, with expertise in individual work, group dynamics and human resources management. The all-inclusiveness of their tasks could be interpreted as a lack of clarity on the particular aims of workplace counselling. The need to become acceptable to industry could drive counsellors into roles not appropriate to their profession.

Using ideas from the above and my own experience of organizing and teaching a two-year Diploma in Counselling course, a prospective design for a curriculum for training workplace counsellors is offered, based on five important areas:

---

1 Knowledge base
2 Skills training
3 Personal development
4 Supervision of client work in a workplace setting
5 Ethical/professional issues in employee counselling

Knowledge base
In this section of the course, the following areas of knowledge and understanding would be considered:

1 Counselling theories and their application to the workplace, in particular:
 (a) Brief therapy
 (b) EAPs: history and theory
2 Understanding the counselling process:
 (a) Assessment for workplace counselling
 (b) Setting up, maintaining and terminating a counselling relationship in the workplace
 (c) The stages of counselling
 (d) Managing the counselling process
 (e) Organizing counselling
3 Personality and developmental theory, psychological problems, work-related problems
4 Organizations and how they affect counselling provision: this section would review a number of organization types and their characteristics, in particular how different workplace cultures affect counselling (see Chapter 4).
5 How to introduce counselling to organizations: this section would understand counselling in relation to total employee care and relate it to other relationships in the workplace, e.g. mentoring, appraisal. It would encourage students to look at systems of employee care as well as systems of counselling provision
6 How to evaluate counselling in organizations
7 Ethical decision-making in workplace counselling

Skills training

To develop a range of skills to facilitate working with individuals and groups in an organization, including the skills of:

- individual counselling in the workplace
- negotiating with an organization
- ethical and professional decision-making
- using supervision effectively
- training and running short training courses
- welfare and social work
- consultation and advising within the organization
- team-building and conflict resolution
- publicizing and representing the counselling service, including public speaking/presentations
- evaluating and keeping statistics
- writing documents, policies, statements
- maintaining boundaries amid multiple roles

Personal development

There are various ways in which personal development can be integrated into counselling courses. Some programmes demand that trainees be in their own personal counselling as a way of understanding and working through some of the areas that could block their work as counsellors. The Diploma in Counselling at Work at the University of Bristol includes this in its requirements. Orme (1994) has argued that the complexity of workplace counselling is all the more reason for making personal counselling a requirement for trainees.

Other courses include an experiential group as part of training and as a method of furthering personal growth. The following is an explanation of the background to and rationale for an experiential group from one programme (MSc in Psychological Counselling and Psychotherapy, Roehampton Institute London):

Objectives The experiential group provides a setting which is complementary to each student's own personal counselling, while directly relating to the theoretical and practical aspects of the course. The theory, skills training and supervised counselling practice, together with work and home life, stir up unresolved conflicts, feelings and responses from different times in each person's life. In the developing relationships of the group, these are explored, individual strengths recognized and new ones learned, while dysfunctional responses can be seen for what they are and discarded.

The setting   This is a model for good counselling practice, with clear, consistent boundaries of time and place. A quiet room, properly furnished, with each person able to see everyone else in the room from the circle of chairs round a small table, with a clock visible to all. The group is conducted by a professionally trained and experienced facilitator of groups.

The method   The group lasts for 1¼ hours. It starts and finishes on time. There is no fixed agenda; the group grows according to the contributions of the members guided by the conductor's under-standing of group and individual processes. The anxiety caused by the relative lack of structure gives each person the opportunity to experience their own and other people's methods of coping, i.e. their defence mechanisms. Where these are dysfunctional they will cause conflict in the group and, in the developing relationship of the group, will eventually be modified. Coping with conflict and toler-ance of anxiety is an important quality for counsellors.

The progressive stages of whole group development echo the stages of individual psychological development. So, for example, in the early stages of the group, early developmental difficulties, where they exist, will emerge for each person. These difficulties, which may be expressed as symptoms or in behaviour, need to be felt, expressed, translated and understood and thus modified if they are not to interfere with the counselling of people with similar difficulties. Issues from the course and daily life become the material of the group, each person will respond idiosyncra-tically to the group topic, and in the atmosphere of tolerance and relative freedom which is facilitated by the conductor and develops in the group, better understandings are reached for each individual on such issues as dependence, authority, loss, sexuality, race and so on.

The mature working group develops a cyclical motion so that individual issues can be worked and reworked. This evolutionary process which eschews exercises and techniques provides a safe setting, protecting students (who have to meet for the rest of the day) from being plunged into material which is too difficult to handle. One of the values of the group is the real experience of the importance of boundaries.

This is one model – and it needs to be pointed out that it is psycho-dynamic in orientation – of how personal development can be part of a training group. Other approaches are also useful, using different counselling orientations and different methods. One counselling course in the north of England uses personal journals as a way of facilitating self-exploration, self-awareness and monitoring change. Another course expects students to involve themselves in co-counselling. What is essential in training workplace counsellors is that there be designated methods by which personal development takes place.

Supervision of client work in a workplace setting
Supervised client work is a central part of training for workplace counselling. Because of the factors involved, it would obviously be helpful if trainees had experience of client work in organizational settings. This allows them to learn about the dynamics involved and discuss them in supervision.

Supervision, besides dealing with client work and organizational issues, will also help trainees set up what they need to care for themselves. It is hoped that by the end of the course participants will be able to set up:

- effective supervision
- personal support both in work and outside work
- a networking system to support them
- ways of managing their stress
- methods to control case-loads

Chapter 10 looks specifically at supervision for counsellors in organizational settings.

Ethical/professional issues in employee counselling
Many times throughout this book reference has been made to the difficulties of maintaining clear boundaries among the multiple roles of employee counselling. Training for workplace counsellors needs to help them devise strategies for:

- making ethical decisions affecting their work
- working and relating to other professionals in the field
- understanding business ethics and how they impinge on work-place counselling
- maintaining clear boundaries with clients and organizations.

Practically, this means working out policies to cover all eventualities. Organizations work best with policies.

Chapter 8 has a fuller account of ethical issues in the workplace and the kind of areas that could be used within training. It also contains case examples that can be used specifically for training purposes. The areas covered would be:

- setting up and managing boundaries within the organization
- managing conflict, role conflict, role confusion, role overload
- managing flexible and multiple roles with clients

Assessment

Assessment in training is important. Both the informal feedback that is a continuing part of the course, from self, from peers on the course, and from tutors and the director of the course, from experiential group leaders, from personal counsellors. Formal evaluation will also take place through written assignments, skills assessment, supervisory reports, written case examples. There are many ways of doing this, but what is important is that assurance is built-in that the individuals graduating from the course have attained certain levels on all aspects of the course. The following is a suggested format for the use of various methods of assessment:

- written assignments
- viva examinations on client work
- video skills training assessment
- class presentations
- projects
- case study write-ups

Self, peer and tutor assessment is continuous. A process for feedback in training is given in Box 9.2.

The learning community

Ideally, it is helpful if the training group can continue throughout the course of the programme to give a greater chance for support and challenge. One of the drawbacks of modular programmes is that, while they are well suited to the individual and his/her particular pace, they are weak on being able to set up a learning community. The learning community allows people to test themselves in an organizational setting.

Some questions for those looking for training in workplace counselling:

1 Do I want a particular counselling orientation to inform my counselling work?
2 Does the course help me understand the interface between the individual employee, the organization and the counsellor?

Box 9.2 *A process for feedback in counselling training*

---

1 Monitor the relationship to ensure that it can sustain feedback and to judge what feedback is suitable for this stage of the relationship. If the relationship is not sound and secure then positive feedback may be interpreted as 'being nice' and negative feedback seen as punitive.
2 Connect feedback to agreed learning needs and objectives. In this way it can be seen as more objective rather than the prejudices or bias of outsiders.
3 Review your own motivation in giving this feedback at this stage. If you were totally free what would you like to say?
4 Deliver feedback in a way that is constructive, characterized by being:
   ● clear
   ● specific (and behavioural)
   ● objective
   ● owned (take responsibility for the feedback)
   ● balanced between positive and negative
   ● focused on inconsistencies and incongruities
   ● regular (not just a one-off)
5 Allow discussion of feedback. It is helpful to encourage receivers to restate the feedback and share their reactions and feelings to it. This clarifies that it is understood. It also allows both parties to look at any blocks to feedback, e.g. counselling orientation, cultural issues, overloading by the amount of feedback.
6 Discuss how the feedback can be used to create more effective work. Does the trainee need to work on some issues, e.g. skills, theoretical base, particular arrangements with clients? How can these be implemented with clients?
7 Look at ways in which feedback can be reciprocal between all parties.

---

3 Does the course clearly define the purpose of counselling in the workplace?
4 Does the course define the multiple roles involved in employee counselling and help me learn the skills of various roles?

Conclusion

Training to be a workplace counsellor demands knowledge and competencies beyond those of generic counsellors. We are presently in a strong position to gather the accumulated wisdom and package it as training in this area. However, what seems the overarching element in training for workplace counselling is that part of the training that helps counsellors integrate their working into a managerial, consultancy and counselling frame of mind that enables them to work with the organization as well as the individual.

10

Supervising Workplace Counsellors

> Supervisors and supervisees are subject to bringing environmental norms and stressors into their relationship and ultimately to transmitting these attitudes to the counselling situation; thus, it seems important for them to understand their roles and behaviours in the context of organizational conditions.
>
> E.L. Holloway, *Clinical Supervision*

> One of the great values of having supervision, because you need it in an organization like this, is to have the opportunity to analyse what's going on in the organization.
>
> H. Fisher, 'Plastering over the Cracks?'

Naomi is a professional counselling psychologist who, among other commitments, works with her diocese to see professional religious people for personal counselling. Some of these are referred by the diocese itself and occasionally Naomi has to meet with her client and representatives of the diocese. She explains how supervision helps her in her work:

Supervision is where:
(1) The needs of the client and the organization are analysed both separately and as they interrelate. As I 'bring' the individual client to supervision, I am almost always bringing the organization as well, sometimes explicitly, sometimes implicitly.
(2) The developmental needs of the organization are articulated and clarified. Strategies for facilitating the development of counselling systems within the diocese are worked out, rehearsed, refined, shaped into policies and my relationship with management is monitored. I take a draft report to supervision which is discussed and refined. Sometimes I role-play verbal reports I have to give to management. In particular, to role play the other side of the chief executive/senior manager has helped me in my search to understand their feelings and problems.
(3) I have the opportunity to evaluate and be evaluated on the practicalities of facilitating organizational development in areas relevant to counselling.

It is clear from Naomi's account of her supervision that working at the interface between individual clients and the organization from which they come (the diocese) is a crucial aspect of her work and her supervision. However, using counselling supervision in this way does not always fit easily with supervisors. Supervisors, like counsellors in general, have been trained primarily to work with individuals and the main focus of their work is the person in front of them. Historically, counsellors have worked with the internal world of the client and, like supervisors, tend to understate the relevance and impact of the environment. Even now, how much supervisors take into consideration the contexts in which supervisees live and work is variable. Some supervisors (Carroll, 1995a) see their role as working solely with supervisees and would never dream of involving themselves in the organizational context in which counsellors work. However, supervisors are becoming increasingly aware that contextual and situational issues affect counselling work, and supervision needs to be seen as a forum in which workplace dynamics can, and indeed ought, to be considered. Supervisees, too, are realizing how important it is to use supervision to deal with organizational aspects of their counselling work. I asked four counsellors who work in organizational settings to recount their experiences of supervision. Their comments will be used throughout this chapter. Carole, employee counsellor with the British Council writes (private communication):

> Supervision is important for case work, as it is for counsellors working in any context, but I also find it very useful for talking through particular organizational issues such as constant change, restructuring and redundancies, and the way they impact on case work. I also use supervision for talking through my position in the organization and issues that might arise from that, such as boundaries, feeding into policy decisions and my various roles.

Despite the fact that the organizational aspects of counselling work are finding their way into supervision, there is not much written to guide supervisors or supervisees in how to use supervision effectively as a process in workplace counselling. Not to be aware of the underlying organizational dynamics that infiltrate counselling and supervision relationships is to be in danger of colluding with the unhealthy side of the organization. This can result in supervisors and supervisees replaying and replicating the very problems brought by their clients rather than becoming aware of them, understanding them and breaking their hold on individuals and the organization. Margaret, who works in a counselling service in higher education, outlines the values of supervision for her (private communication):

> Supervision provides a safe, impartial space to deal with issues with colleagues, the organization at large, and the workload with clients, even the supervision of placement counsellors. It is somewhere to take and discuss interpersonal issues about which I may not feel safe enough, for any of a variety of reasons, to bring up in regular staff meetings. We also use it as a sounding board for policies we may be considering changing or

political stands we may feel we need to take within the Institute, so we have someone else's feedback on the impact and the implications of what we may be contemplating. Supervision provides the support and the 'other place' which then frees me up to work conscientiously and clearly with the students who come to the service. I also have a better idea of what I am willing to do or not do, and what my colleagues can justifiably expect of me, and me of them. The organizational aspects of our job as counsellors within the service are more important than our individual client issues in our work supervision . . . I didn't realize this!

As can be seen from the above, supervision is used to cover a variety of areas: client work, teamwork, organizational issues, expectations, workload and even supervision of supervision.

A very brief introduction to supervision will be offered here before reviewing different supervisory relationships as they pertain to workplace counselling. The particular tasks involved in supervision in this context will be considered, as will a method for helping supervisees who are employee counsellors prepare for supervision.

What is supervision?

The word 'supervision' has many meanings. In organizational contexts it sometimes means 'to oversee', often entailing authority, line management and appraisal. Supervision as seen from within counselling is something different. Although there are no agreed definitions of counselling supervision, by and large it can be viewed as an arrangement between two qualified personnel where one offers to help the other reflect on his/her counselling work and the contexts surrounding that work. Without reviewing all aspects of supervision, it can be seen as a formal relationship between professionals where they meet, either as a dyad, or with other supervisees, to review and reflect on the counselling work of the counsellor(s). The two main purposes of this relationship are the professional development of the supervisee and the welfare of the client.

Elsewhere I have looked in detail at the full range of options within supervision (Carroll, 1995a). Here I will reproduce some of the assumptions I see as underlying counselling supervision in general before applying it to workplace counselling. These assumptions include the following:

1 Supervision is an essential requirement for working counsellors, both trainees and qualified, and no longer an optional extra.
2 Supervision is a formal, professional relationship between supervisees and supervisors.
3 The purposes of supervision are the professional development of supervisees and the welfare of clients.

4   Supervision is not counselling or psychotherapy.
5   Supervision is primarily an educational process focused on the learning of supervisees.
6   Good counsellors do not necessarily make good supervisors.
7   Supervisors require training in supervision. Supervisors who work with workplace counsellors need to know about and understand organizational dynamics.
8   Supervisors enable supervisees find *their* way of being counsellors.
9   Evaluation (formal and informal) is a crucial part of supervision.
10   Contracting and negotiating in supervision is essential.
11   The roles and responsibilities of supervisors and supervisees ought to be clear to all participants in supervision. This is particularly important if there is an organizational context to the counselling work.
12   Bad/poor supervision exists.
13   There are several forms of supervision (individual, group, peer, team); all have strengths and weaknesses.
14   The relationship in supervision is made up of a number of roles, not just one, and good supervisors are able to provide a multiplicity of roles with supervisees.
15   Issues of gender, race/culture and power play large parts in supervision and need to be addressed.
16   Ideally, supervisors should have a forum where they can discuss their supervision.
17   Supervisors and supervisees ought to be aware of the *Code of Ethics and Practice for Supervisors* (BAC, Association for Counsellor Education and Supervision, 1995).
18   Supervisees have a right to expect help in taking on the role of supervisee, and be assisted in preparing for supervision.
19   Supervision works best when both parties in supervision are allowed the choice to work together and supervisees are not always best served by being assigned to a supervisor, either individually or in groups.
20   The learning process in supervision emerges from the counselling work of supervisees. Supervision is not about formal teaching, skills training in counselling, learning ethical codes, dealing with personal issues, that are unconnected to the work being done with clients.

While these 20 assumptions about counselling supervision are general, there are applications of supervision needed when applied to particular contexts. The workplace is one such environment.

Figure 10.1 *Counsellor and supervisor are both employees of the same organization*

Supervisory relationships in workplace counselling

A number of possible relationships emerges when supervisors work with supervisees who are employee counsellors. If the supervisor is employed by the organization then the set of relationships looks like Figure 10.1. There are undoubtedly some advantages in supervisor and supervisee belonging to the same organization. First of all, it is probable that they will both understand the culture of the organization for which they both work. This common knowledge will help them understand problems that emerge from the organization. Their awareness of the 'shadow' side of their workplace will be an added advantage when they come to looking at possible changes that might take place. Secondly, it is possible for supervisors to intervene more directly and perhaps effectively when they belong to the same organization as their supervisee(s). They will, it is hoped, know which individuals and groups to approach, may well have the credibility within the organization to make a difference, and will understand the politics sufficiently to know when and how to intervene.

There are also disadvantages. Supervisors may know the clients brought to supervision by counsellors and there is more likelihood of their having prior relationships with potential clients than would happen if the supervisor were not an employee of the organization. And both supervisor and supervisee, by being part of the organization, may be too close to the organizational dynamics to be able to have an objective viewpoint. Caught up, like other employees, in the

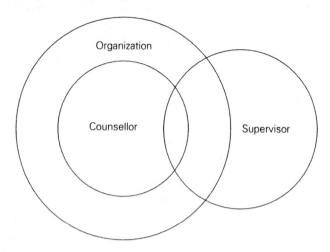

Figure 10.2   *The supervisor is paid by the organization but is not an employee*

organizational culture, it may be difficult for them to question what is taken for granted, to confront values that may be detrimental to individuals, and to be able to see the organization from outside.

The seriousness of these disadvantages seem to me to indicate that workplace counselling supervision is best done by someone who is not an employee of the organization. They may still be paid by the organization but their only role within it is that of supervisor. This allows them the distance they need to be objective, removes them from the conscious and unconscious dynamics of the organization, and gives them freedom to question and challenge organizational structures, policies and practices.

This leads us to the second supervisory relationship within a workplace setting, where the supervisor is not part of the organization but is paid by it to supervise their counsellor(s). Figure 10.2 shows the relationships involved between organization, workplace counsellor and supervisor. Of course, there is a disadvantage in the supervisor not being part of the organizational climate and understanding the dynamics of organizational life from within the organization. But it seems to be outweighed by the advantage they have of being outside 'looking in'. It is still important that such supervisors understand 'how things are done around here' but with the vantage point of objectivity their understanding can be translated into helpful supervisory strategies to facilitate counsellors working more effectively. Cathy, employee counsellor with Shell International, emphasized this aspect of supervision (private communication):

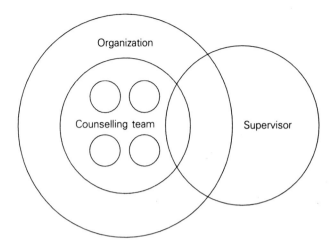

Figure 10.3 *Team supervision*

> Supervision helps the organizational aspect because it takes place with
> someone outside of the whole setup who can objectively reflect back and
> help me identify patterns, trends, unseen issues, parallels. Also it helps me
> deal with my own feelings of anger, sadness, demotivation as well as
> excitement. I use it to explore tactics and practise/rehearse responses.

In this supervisory relationship, where the supervisor is external to
the organization, he/she is often not as powerful in intervening in the
workplace should that be necessary. Organizations are always wary
of outsiders telling them what they should do, especially if they sense
that those outsiders do not understand the politics and climate of the
group. On the other hand, distance and freedom give these supervisors increased objectivity.

In some instances, where there is a team of counsellors, it is
possible for group supervision to take place. Having an outside
supervisor who works with the counselling team can be very valuable
in helping to understand not just the group dynamics, but also the
organizational issues that are infiltrating the team and affecting
counselling. Figure 10.3 visualizes the dynamics of this situation.

Margaret, quoted earlier, highlights some of these issues:

> We have supervision as a team. Organizational issues seem to take
> priority over client work. If we are not functioning as a team with issues
> out in the open, then client work will suffer. These issues have figured
> largely around two areas: changes in the team composition itself and the
> role of the counselling service within the Institute.

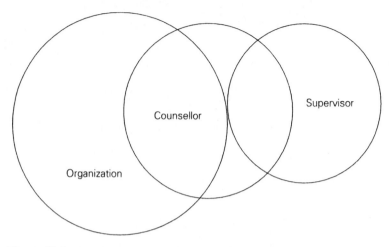

Figure 10.4   *Private supervision for an employee counsellor*

When the supervisor is not paid by the organization but is paid privately by the supervisee slightly different dynamics are at play. Figure 10.4 shows the relationships involved. Like the other supervisory relationships, this brings other issues. Since the supervisor is employed by the counsellor rather than by the organization for which the counsellor works, the organization has little say in the contract and has no right to request reports or feedback from the supervisor. It makes it more difficult for supervisors to intervene directly in the organization should that be necessary.

Most workplace counsellors do not have to pay for their own supervision, though most seem to be free to choose their supervisors. This situation may pertain where an EAP is using counsellors who have their own private supervision. Mostly, EAPs provide a case supervisor who is available for consultation by counsellors.

Whatever the supervision arrangements (the four above or others), a number of factors comes through forcefully. What is essential is that the roles of and relationships between all parties have been negotiated and are clear, preferably written. Some areas covered in these discussions will be the following:

- Responsibilities and the limits of these responsibilities.
- When would a supervisor report the organization without permission of the supervisee?
- What areas should supervision involve?
- When will a supervisor visit the organization, meet with whom, say what?

- Will reports/feedback be given to the organization on any part of the supervision arrangements?

The roles and responsibilities of organization, supervisor and supervisee(s) need to be clarified from the very beginning.

Supervision for workplace counsellors

Supervision of workplace counsellors can have a number of foci. Besides client work, there are other areas on which supervision can concentrate. Cathy, the employee counsellor at Shell, outlines her experience of using supervision:

> To prepare for supervision I note down, not only clients I've seen, but also any organizational issues or ethical dilemmas which may have arisen around the Internal Counselling Service and/or our External EAP. Over time and with gaining experience, I have noticed I need to bring fewer clients and find I use supervision increasingly to deal with wider organizational difficulties such as boundaries, juggling the various roles I offer as the sole in-house counsellor. This includes reviewing the standard and delivery of the service.

Using supervision to support workplace counsellors is essential. In what can be a very demanding, stressful job, workplace counsellors need to have a forum where they can be sustained as they work with their clients and within the organization. Proctor (1986) has called this the 'restorative' aspect of supervision which offers a space where counsellors can ask for the help they need, look at the personal dimensions of their work and its demands on themselves, and in a professional relationship find validation for the work they do. Part of that restorative function is the containment of the supervisee. It is very easy for the whole area of organizational work to become 'uncontained': counsellors may be working too hard, seeing unreasonable numbers of clients with a wide range of problems. The demands on counsellors from individuals and groups within the organization can become overwhelming. Supervisors monitor the effects on workplace counsellors of working within the organization.

Supervision is also about monitoring the quality of the service offered. There is a sense in which supervision is the 'quality control' dimension of professional work. It ensures that clients are getting a quality service, that that service is being evaluated continually, and that counsellors are working at their best. In the context of the workplace this means involvement with the subtle interface between the counsellor, the client, the organization and the supervisor. Issues will be acted out in supervision that are part of organizational dynamics. Effective supervision will understand how the pathology within the organization can affect both counselling and supervisory relationships. Understanding how this particular organization marshalls its defence against anxiety will help supervisors and supervisees understand individual client work. Obholzer (1987: 203) suggests that 'in looking at institutional processes it is obviously very helpful to have some inkling of what the underlying anxieties inherent in the work of the institution are.' In taking this stance, supervision will highlight the unhealthy issues in organizations that give rise to individual problems.

Effective supervision will provide a range of interventions and strategies to help counsellors in the workplace, changing task as is needed by supervisee learning. Good supervisors know when to teach and when to allow learning to emerge: they understand how their supervisees learn effectively. They are also good consultants, problem-solving when required, working with supervisees to understand client dynamics, the counselling relationship, and suitable counselling interventions. Helping supervisees deal with their own reactions and feelings towards both individual clients and the organization will remain a constant focus of supervision. Supervisors will do this without allowing the process to become individual counselling rather than supervision. The whole range of ethical/professional issues will be a further area of concern for supervision. The particular nuances of ethical dilemmas in the workplace need special attention within supervision. Feedback and evaluation will be continuous in supervision as will monitoring the administrative and organizational aspects of workplace counselling.

There are five areas of particular interest to the supervisor who is working with counsellors in organizational settings. I have dealt with these in more detail elsewhere (Carroll, 1995a) but here would like to combine them with the roles and responsibilities of counsellors in the workplace as a basis for understanding the emphasis of supervision. The five areas are the following:

1 Enabling supervisees to live and work within organizations.
2 Helping supervisees control the flow of information within the organization.
3 Helping supervisees manage the counselling service.
4 Working with supervisees at the interface between individual and organization.
5 Ensuring supervisees look after themselves as a result of working within an organizational setting.

(1) *Enabling supervisees to live and work within organizations*: the workplace demands a number of roles from employee counsellors that often involve professional boundaries. Being involved in a number of roles with the same people can create role confusion and 'leakage' from one relationship to another; for example, doing stress management with employees seen for individual counselling, being on a committee with former clients, meeting clients in corridors or in the dining-room. Living and working within an organization requires constant vigilance lest professional counselling work suffers because of boundary issues. Carroll (1995b: 24) paints several scenarios:

> The client you saw yesterday afternoon is in the same meal queue as you for dinner: you suddenly realize that a 'bit of gossip' from a work-colleague over coffee involves a client you have been seeing for the past two months, and the charming and articulate manager regaling you with interesting stories is the very person your recent client is complaining about as making life impossible in the office. Managers ring to find out how the employee they sent you for counselling is getting along. The employee-client wants you to write a letter so that his medical release can be supported. What is clear to the counsellor in private practice becomes muddied in the organizational context.

Supervision is a forum that helps supervisees monitor the boundaries of their work, make decisions about which roles fit with which, and enables and empowers workplace counsellors to argue for the appropriate roles they adopt within the organization. An outplacement counsellor with Cavendish Partners reflects on how supervision helps here (private communication):

> Working in multiple roles as an outplacement counsellor requires the awareness of moving into counselling mode, and out of it after its need has ended, while adhering to the standards and codes of counselling. The organizational setting provides for additional and ongoing support which is professional and ethical because it is supervised. Supervision helps maintain boundaries and good working relationships with clients. The shared experiences with other counsellors in regular supervision at Cavendish Partners enhances the whole process.

Living and working within the organization involves holding a number of relationships and roles in creative tension. Using supervision as a place to reflect on the boundaries between these roles seems sensible. Leakage from one relationship to another can occur too easily, and imperceptibly, in organizational settings.

(2) *Helping supervisees control the flow of information within the organization*: this is a two-way process: what information is given out by the counsellor, and what information is received back by him/her. Organizations, quite rightly, expect workplace counsellors to feed back into the system. Statistics, particular problems from

employees, what institutional issues are affecting employees, all these can be the basis of annual reports from the counselling service. Counsellors may need assistance from supervision in designing and writing reports.

On the other hand, workplace counsellors need to control information as it comes to them. There are times when they are compromised by what is said; for example, a manager who refers a client and begins to give confidential information to the counsellor. Counsellors may well have to take information outside the counselling room, as in the case of a client who wants to bring action against a boss who has been involved in sexual harassment. Controlling the flow of information can be a major task for counsellors in the workplace. Supervisors can be of help here.

(3) *Helping supervisees manage the counselling service*: workplace counsellors set up a counselling service, a system, that needs to be managed carefully. Most workplace counsellors are counselling managers who need to administer counselling provision. This requires policies, statements and a structure that cares for clients as well as processing the counselling work. What seem like simple issues can become major headaches if not handled properly: the location of the counselling room, secretarial support and what secretaries are aware of, who has access to counselling notes, and a host of other issues.

Supervision will help workplace counsellors make decisions about setting up and maintaining the counselling service. As new problems emerge they will be tackled not just as individual problems but as part of a counselling system. Supervision may have to spend time with workplace counsellors in helping them work out systems of counselling: how to set up a counselling service, how to monitor and evaluate it, and how to help counsellors work out policies and statements on different aspects of counselling, e.g. publicity, information for clients, keeping notes and statistics.

(4) *Working with supervisees at the interface between individual and organization*: supervisors are interested in the organizational culture in which their supervisees work and want to monitor the effects of that culture on individual client work. Culture will affect counsellors and the counselling service in different ways. Supervisors who understand the organizational culture within which their supervisees work will know how best to support and challenge them.

(5) *Ensuring supervisees look after themselves as a result of working within an organizational setting*: because of demands from individual clients, and often from the organization, workplace counsellors all too easily overworked. Effective supervisors keep an eye on the welfare of workplace counsellors challenging when they feel they are not caring for themselves sufficiently. The section in

Chapter 8 on ethical responsibilities for looking after themselves can be used by supervisors and counsellors as a checklist for monitoring self-care.

Parallel process in workplace counselling

One particular dynamic that works within all counselling and supervision, and has particular application within workplace counselling, is the concept of *parallel process* (see Chapter 2). I have written of this more extensively elsewhere (Carroll, 1995a) and will only summarize some of the issues here. Parallel process (other terms used are 'reflective or reflection process', 'mirroring', 'parallel re-enactment') describes how aspects of the counselling relationship are expressed in the supervisory relationship. Figure 10.5 shows how issues move between the various subsystems within workplace counselling.

Several reasons have been offered to explain why parallel process takes place, the majority of which are psychodynamic. First, it is possible that supervisees identify with the defensive behaviour of clients and then represent that defensiveness in supervision. This is a form of communication with the supervisor. Being unconscious, and not being able to verbalize the issues, supervisees act them out, in much the same way as repressed memories are subject to repetition according to Freud. So supervisors get a real-life drama of what is happening in the counselling relationship.

Case example
One of my supervisees suggested at the beginning of supervision that she would like to read her notes about a client. She had never done this before, which is often an indicator that parallel process is at work. As she read, I interrupted to ask a question. She seemed angry at my interruption and quickly answered my question and returned to reading her notes. I interjected a second time, intentionally, and there was a marked note of anger in her annoyance at being stopped again. This time I stopped her reading and asked her to look at what was happening. Soon we realized that what she was doing to me, controlling the supervision session, was exactly what her client was doing to her. Unconsciously, she was presenting the client in the very way she was reporting her work with him.

In a second explanation, projective identification is used to understand what happens. The client projects feelings into the supervisee

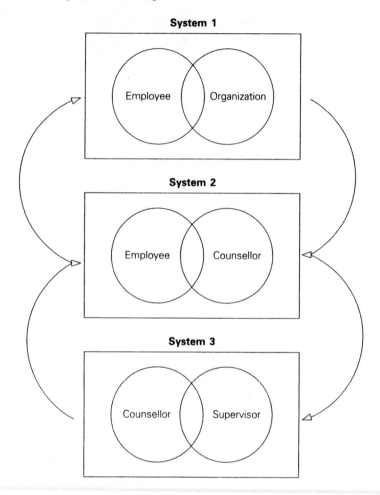

Figure 10.5   *Parallel process in workplace counselling*

who in turn projects them into the supervisor, a sort of handing the problem down the line. What cannot be dealt with in counselling is passed on, acted out, in supervision. In one small group supervision which I led I suddenly became aware that three of us were attacking the client of the fourth member of the group, who was defending the client who was making inappropriate demands on him. In looking at the process we could see that the anger of the client was projected onto the counsellor who was shifting it into the members of the group. We were acting out the anger that neither the individual supervisee nor the client would express. Others explain parallel process as reflecting the impasse between counsellor and client (Mueller and Kell, 1972), or as representing that part of the supervisee's learning that is similar to the client's problem (Ekstein and Wallerstein, 1972).

In workplace counselling there is, as it were, a double parallel process. Clients will often act out their relationship with the organization with the workplace counsellor. Alert counsellors will realize that they are witnessing how the organization has affected the individual client. In turn, it is possible that, if they are not aware, workplace counsellors will act out that relationship with their supervisors.

What is the purpose of parallel process? Again, several reasons are offered. Some view it as a process of communication when words cannot be used: supervisees are telling supervisors what actually happened in their relationship with clients in action rather than words. It could also be a way of learning: if the supervisee does to the supervisor what has been done to them, then they can learn, it is hoped, how to deal with the situation. A third explanation is that it is about concealing rather than communication (Bromberg, 1982): supervisees get anxious about working with certain clients and try to hide this anxiety, which then is revealed by acting out the whole process. A fourth factor sees personality similarities as a basis for parallel process. Doehrman (1976) has reviewed the unequal relationship between the two sets of participants, client/counsellor and counsellor/supervisor, as a possible reason for mirroring, especially when issues of authority and power emerge.

However it happens, and whatever explanations are offered for its occurrence, it does appear that paralleling in supervision takes place. Furthermore, there seems to be some benefit in looking at various explanations of why it happens, and counselling theories, other than the psychodynamic, have been slow to offer alternatives. The best use of parallel process is to help supervisees understand what is happening within their counselling relationships. Supervisors can monitor their own relationships with supervisees and use that information to help supervisees be aware of the dynamics within counselling. There seem to be several factors worth remembering in using parallel process in supervision:

(1) *Parallel process is most effective, educationally, with more advanced supervisees*: for beginning counsellors it can be either confusing or meaningless, and sometimes interpreted as punitive. In Doehrman's (1976) research the least experienced supervisee was the only one who did not appreciate parallel process.

(2) *Parallel process is not just unidirectional*: it works back through the system to the client. What happens in supervision will

also be represented in the counselling relationship. In a rather dramatic example, Doehrman (1976) points out that a cancelled session by the supervisor resulted in a cancelled session by the counsellor. Supervisees constantly remark that when they have dealt with something in supervision it seems to loosen up the counselling relationship. This, of course, is a good transfer of learning, and does not always require unconscious reference as a way of understanding what is happening.

(3) *There is a danger in seeing no parallel process in supervision*: just as there is a danger in seeing everything that happens in supervision as parallel process. Neither is very helpful. An awareness of its possibility, with a clear way of explaining it to supervisees to help their awareness and learning, can be useful. It is equally helpful to alert supervisees to parallel process and ask them to monitor how they may be presenting their clients in supervision through this process. After an initial obsession with the concept, they usually settle down to being excellent observers of their own processes.

(4) *The conduits for parallel process are supervisees*: they are members of both systems (though with different roles) and carry one system into the other. They stand at the interface between counselling and supervision. Because of their centrality in all systems, there is a great deal of potential learning for them. It is possible to use parallel process to understand the dynamics of what is happening to the client, or the relationship between client and counsellor. Both these are represented by the supervisee within supervision. However, potential learning can go further and help supervisees understand their own dynamics, how these dynamics affect their work and result in their identification with clients. Parallel process can be a source of help for supervisors as they monitor what is happening to them in their relationship with supervisees, noticing when they act unusually or when they get drawn into the dynamics of the client/counsellor relationship.

There is a tendency to believe that parallel process disappears as soon as it reaches awareness. This would be a dangerous conclusion to draw. Individuals seem to be stuck within parallel process even when they have adverted to it. Awareness and acknowledgement are not sufficient alone to break parallel process. Working effectively with parallel process entails being able to explain it clearly and tentatively. Timing is obviously important. To attempt an interpretation of parallel process while supervisees are still struggling with strong emotions connected to the experience may simply increase resistance and/or denial. In such instances, trainees may feel they are being misunderstood or judged (Williams, 1987). Checking continually with supervisees is important if they are to learn effectively from the experience of parallel process. One way of effectively working with parallel process is role play. Role playing clients by supervisees can be an effective method of accessing and learning from parallel process and takes the emphasis for explanations from supervisors.

In conclusion, though there are several explanations, mostly psychodynamic, of parallel process, we still know relatively little about it other than its occurrence. Caution must be advised in working with it so that it enhances rather than hinders learning for supervisees. And, of course, the motivation of supervisors in using it is important. It could too easily contribute to the narcissism of supervisors and make them all-important interpreters of the unconscious than being a means to the further training of supervisees and to the increased welfare of clients. What is important is not to underestimate the importance of the organization and its impact in both counselling and supervisory relationships. It will be present, consciously and unconsciously, in both rooms.

Helping workplace counsellors prepare for supervision

Naomi, already quoted on how she uses supervision in her work, tells how she prepares for supervision:

> My preparation for supervision begins as I leave supervision. I am already formulating goals for working with individual clients and with the organization. Ethical issues have a priority on my agenda. In working with organizations these seem to arise much more frequently. I am aware that there is no ethical code covering this area of counselling work. I also anticipate supervision by preparing anything I have to write for the organization – reports, policies, statements. I also bring any communications with the organization for monitoring and evaluation. My own professional development is always on the agenda, but it often gets squeezed out because of time. With the greater multiplicity of variables in organizational counselling, preparation for supervision has increasingly to be about reflection and openness about myself, including my values and vulnerabilities.

One way to help supervision be more effective is to train counsellors in how to set it up, negotiate contracts, and prepare for supervision. Inskipp and Proctor (1993) have written very clearly about these issues, and I will adapt their framework for use in workplace counselling. Perhaps the most important preparatory skill in helping supervisees make effective use of supervision is the skill of reflexivity. Reflexivity has been described as 'focused contemplation' (Newfeldt et al., 1996: 3) where the events of counselling are followed by reflection both personally and in supervision to lead to new counselling behaviours. Reflexivity is a decision-making process whereby counselling events are dissected so that understanding what happened can be the basis of personal and professional development. Taking and maintaining a stance of critical enquiry on one's counselling work enables supervisees to learn about their work. Newfeldt et al. (1996: 3–9) asked five experts to illustrate the issues of reflexivity and the following were some statements which emerged from their interviews. Interviewees used statements such as 'a search towards a more profound understanding of something', 'it is directed to the therapist's own actions, emotions, and thoughts in the counselling session', 'things are happening, things are popping up, you're getting signals, you're trying to figure out the meaning of them as you're interacting there', 'I think fairly strongly that . . . maintaining that position of not knowing is an extremely important aspect of the process.' From the above study four dimensions emerged that characterize a reflective stance: (a) intention (reviewing the purpose of the event); (b) active enquiry; (c) openness; and (d) vulnerability (taking a humble approach). These four can result in 'giving meaning' to what happened and using them to learn and create new ways of working as a counsellor. Newfeldt et al. (1996: 8) summarize the process:

> The reflective process itself is a search for understanding of the phenomena of the counselling session, with attention to therapist actions, emotions, and thoughts, as well as to the interaction between the therapist and client. The intent to understand what has occurred, active inquiry, openness to that understanding, and vulnerability and risk-taking rather than defensive self-protection characterise the stance of the reflective supervisee. . . . Supervisees use theory, their prior personal and professional experience, and the experience of themselves in the counselling session as sources of understanding. . . . To complete the sequence, reflectivity in supervision leads to changes in perception, changes in counselling practice, and an increased capacity to make meaning of their experiences.

In helping supervisees create a reflective position to their workplace counselling, supervisors are helping them to learn how to learn first of all. Knowing and watching their own processes of learning can be an initial help in creating an environment of learning and an understanding of personal dynamics within that process. Allowing awareness to surface without defensiveness can be difficult for beginning supervisees who are afraid of 'getting it wrong'. Inskipp and Proctor (1993) have talked about developing a 'fair witness' to counselling work. Four elements appear here of benefit to supervisees:

- learning how to learn
- creating awareness of what is happening

- openness to 'fair witness'
- developing the 'helicopter ability', i.e. the skill of seeing the problems of clients in wider and wider contexts

The following is one method (adapted from Inskipp and Proctor, 1993) to help workplace counsellors prepare for supervision:

Step 1:   Gathering information
Step 2:   Reviewing the information
Step 3:   Making decisions

Gathering information
At this stage supervisees reflect on their work and gather information pertinent to critical enquiry. This is best helped if the supervisee has a personal notebook for reflections. These will be different from client notes but will emerge from client work. These reflections will be awareness arising from individual client work or counselling work in general, or from the contexts in which the counselling emerged. An example of this is taken from the notebook of one counsellor:

> I keep wondering why I feel so frustrated working with this client. I keep wanting to intervene and tell him what to do. I can see it happen. He looks so powerless and pitiful and I feel solutions rising within me. I really have to force myself to keep quiet and not solve his problems. I know exactly what he should do, and I want to tell him.

These notes are good material for supervision. Some supervisees review their notes on individual clients as a preparation for supervision sessions. One counsellor talks about reviewing all clients:

> I prepare for supervision by going through my diary to identify clients seen since my last supervision session. I then asterisk clients I wish to discuss and put them in order of priority. I review why I am concerned to bring this client at this time. I briefly review who I am *not* bringing and ask myself why.

Information can be gathered on other roles within the organization, how the organization is affecting the counselling service, and reviewing policies, publicity and the management of the counselling service. The 'gathering information' stage is intended to be open and free-floating. Its objective is to collect a broad range of data from which the content of supervision will be chosen. For this reason it is best to keep it as wide as possible.

Reviewing the information
When information has been gleaned from a number of areas, supervisees take a stance of enquiry, of contemplation, before it. It is

allowed to affect, to come through in its own way, to impact, to speak its messages. Supervisees monitor their feelings and reactions to this information, review what can be faced, what not.

It may be that a particular client and an individual session surfaces. The counsellor can prepare by asking questions using an interpersonal process recall (IPR) style of questioning. Cashwell (1994: 8) summarizes some questions:

- What do you wish you had said to him/her?
- How do you think he/she would have reacted if you had said that?
- What would have been the risk in saying what you wanted to say?
- If you had the chance now, how might you tell him/her what you are thinking and feeling?
- Were there any other thoughts going through your mind?
- How did you want the other person to perceive you?
- Were those feelings located somewhere physically in your body?
- Were you aware of any feelings? Does that feeling have any special meaning for you?
- What did you want him/her to tell you?
- What do you think he/she wanted from you?
- Did he/she remind you of anyone in your life?

Information can be reviewed under headings:

- individual clients
- patterns/themes emerging from client work in general
- organizational issues
- the counselling service
- policies and procedures
- team/colleague relationships and their impact
- training and development of the counsellor

Making decisions

As a result of their interpretations, counsellors may want to make decisions that they can bring to supervision. Here is an extract from a black counsellor from South Africa who trained in counselling in Britain and is now reflecting on applying that practice to her work in a black township:

It has become absolutely impossible for me to adhere to the boundaries as defined in psychodynamic counselling. I have given up sticking to the precise time. With Mrs. . . I suggested 10.00 a.m. and she arrived between 8.30 and 9.00 a.m. I am not going to be able to persuade her to observe the exact time – she is uneducated, very keen to come and transport is a real problem. It is part of the Zulu culture to greet cordially and to enquire after one's health and that of the family. I cannot interfere with this. It is customary in our culture to offer someone something to eat . . . I therefore offer tea and a sandwich and I feel it is right for me to do this. This does not reduce the professional relationship to friendship. . . . I feel that these are all important issues as counselling must fit into the African culture if it is to be readily accessible and acceptable.

While this is a rather extreme example of a counsellor trained in one culture applying counselling work in another culture, it is a good example of the kinds of decisions counsellors may be faced with in their work. It is also a fine agenda for supervision.

From their material and reflection on it, supervisees will decide what they intend to bring to the next supervision session. It is always good to ask: what am I looking for from this supervision session, and from my supervisor and colleagues if there is team supervision? This may determine the method of presenting in supervision (Carroll, 1995a).

Conclusion

Supervision is one of the most important support mechanisms for the workplace counsellor. Not only does it provide a place for reflection on work but it offers support in what is a very demanding job. Besides support, it is a forum for monitoring the quality of the work in general and in particular. Supervision is for the welfare of clients as well as the development of the supervisee. And the welfare of clients is tied in closely to what is happening to the counsellor, and how workplace counsellors are affected by working within the organization.

Epilogue

Writing this book has been both enjoyable and daunting. I have enjoyed reading the literature and discovering resources relevant to the topic. I have found it daunting because there is so little written for the professional counsellor who wishes to be employed in the workplace. Distinctions are constantly made between those who want to use counselling skills as part of their existing job, those who use counselling among other roles with people in organizations, and those who opt to be professional counsellors in the workplace. While these distinctions may be worthwhile in theory, they seldom work quite as well in practice. They indicate, along with other workplace musings on counselling, that this area of counselling work is very much in its infancy. My hope is that this book has gathered what is current and suggested models and frameworks that can now be built upon.

I had hoped to include a section on cross-cultural/multicultural aspects of workplace counselling in the book. I am very aware how important are individual differences in counselling work, whether these are around race, gender, sexual orientation, disability or age. I realize how little the workplace has considered these issues and how, in the future, they will play a major part in organizations. Several times I began but never quite finished the section to my satisfaction. Its absence from the book is not about its unimportance but more about my inabilities.

I have no doubt that workplace counselling will increase within the foreseeable future, both within organizations and as external provision. That increase will require more counsellors trained to work at the interface between individual employees and organizations, more counselling supervisors to provide external support and evaluation and more research on counselling in the workplace. It was heartening to come across four masters dissertations on workplace counselling which have been written in the past two years. With these, and the increase in training courses, workplace counselling will definitely be a recognized professional vocation for counsellors. And not before its time: for too long the counselling profession has had little impact on the place that takes up the time and energy of so many individuals – the workplace.

APPENDICES

1 An Example of a Counselling Contract with an Organization

Contract for the provision of personal support sessions to tutors on the Sex Offenders Treatment Programme (HM Prison Service)

1 *The purchaser of the service is:*
(hereafter referred to as 'the Purchaser').
The provider of the service is:
(hereafter referred to as 'the Provider').

2 *Services to be provided:*
- 3 sessions of personal support counselling of 50 minutes each for each individual tutor for each SOTP programme
- to be normally provided at the place of work
- these services will be confidential to the counsellor/tutor
- an annual report outlining problem areas dealt with, particularly those that seem to be arising from delivering the SOTP. This report will not mention names but give generic problem areas
- set up referral to specialist resources when appropriate
- contact the Treatment Manager when a tutor has not fulfilled his/her allocated number of sessions
- duty to inform: counsellors will inform the Treatment Manager should they become aware that a tutor has been involved in a case of sexual deviancy (legal definition) or if a tutor was likely to be of harm to self or others

3 *Quality standards:*
The counsellor(s) delivering the personal support will be:
- BAC accredited counsellors, UKCP registered psychotherapists, or a Chartered Counselling Psychologist (BPS) or equivalent
- in ongoing professional supervision with a supervisor trained in supervision
- a member of a professional counselling body (e.g. BAC) who adheres to a prescribed code of ethics and practice

- aware of the SOTP and have a working knowledge of cognitive/behavioural group work
- have knowledge of working with individuals from an organization context
- have experience of short-term, brief counselling

4   *Commencement date*:
This contract is effective from . . . . . . for the period of . . . . . .

5   *The price*:
Each personal support session is priced at . . . . . . Payment will be paid by monthly instalments invoiced by the Provider.

6   *Review*:
The service will be reviewed every . . . . . . months or at a frequency agreed between the parties to this agreement.

7   *Service failure, dispute, disagreement and arbitration*:
Any dispute, disagreement or failure to deliver the service, or any difference in the interpretation of this agreement shall be referred to an independent arbitrator to be agreed between the parties should they fail to reach an agreement together.

8   Neither party will disclose to any third party information acquired during the period of the agreement without prior consent.

9   *Assignment and subcontracting*:
Neither party shall assign or subcontract the whole or any part of this contract without written consent obtained in advance.

10   *Termination*:
This agreement can only be terminated within the . . . . contract by giving two months notice or in accordance with section 7 above.

11   *Renewal*:
The service specification offered and the price agreed will be re-negotiated annually.
    If the Purchaser or Provider does not intend to renew the service then notice must be given in writing two months before the end of the current agreement.

12   Signed on behalf of the Purchaser
    . . . . Date
    Signed on behalf of the Provider
    . . . . Date

(My thanks to Veronica Ford and Ruth Mann for permission to use the above format.)

2   Two Examples of a Counselling Policy

Employee counselling service policy statement

The employee counselling service seeks to contribute to organizational aims by providing an independent, confidential workplace counselling service and other support systems to the staff of . . . ., in a systematic and readily available manner to agreed professional standards.

Principles and values

1   The term 'counselling' in this context incudes work with groups, pairs or individuals referred to as clients. The objective of particular counselling relationships may vary according to client needs. Counselling may be concerned with developmental issues, addressing and resolving specific problems, making decisions, coping with crisis, developing personal insight, working through feelings of inner conflict and improving relationships with others, whether at work or at home.

2   The counsellor's role is impartially to facilitate the client's work in ways that respect client values and personal resources.

3   The counselling service is independent of line management. Its function is to empower the individual users to seek their own solutions and not to mediate or advocate on behalf of management.

4   The counselling service seeks to balance organizational aims and objectives with those of clients by assisting managers in the identification and amelioration of stressors (i.e. causes of stress) in the workplace which impact on the performance and morale of staff.

5   The counselling service reflects the organization's recognition that a physically and mentally healthy employee is an asset and that the availability of appropriate counselling services is beneficial to both employee and employer.

6   Personal and work-related problems affect job performance, employee health, quality of life and ultimately quality of service. Employees who are experiencing problems may be unable to function safely, efficiently or effectively and are therefore a legitimate concern for the organization.

7 To reinforce independence from line management, access to the counselling service is through SELF-REFERRAL ONLY. Successful counselling depends upon trust, self-motivation and commitment. It is therefore not effective with clients who are referred by a third party. However, managers need to be aware of the range of services and RECOMMEND how they can help staff experiencing difficulties. Self-referral also helps prevent a client perception that counselling services are integral to disciplinary, grievance and absence monitoring procedures as a management function.

Management of client information

The counselling service records are strictly confidential and are not noted on any official or personal file. To monitor client usage and to evaluate the service, certain details of clients will be required, e.g. location, occupation, age.

To protect individuals from identification, client case records are unnamed and coded. The master-list is maintained ONLY by the counselling manager.

Information about individual service users is NOT available to management of staff. However, in its role of preventing and identifying causes of stress, the counselling service will provide feedback to the organization in the form of a quarterly narrative report without identifying or compromising clients.

Ethical considerations

The counselling service adheres to the British Association for Counselling *Code of Ethics and Practice for Counsellors* (1990a) which outlines the boundaries of confidentiality and the management of client information (copies of the *Code* are available on request).

Exceptions to confidentiality and the release of client information are outlined in the *Code*. They include circumstances where the counsellor has good grounds for believing that the client will cause serious physical harm to themselves or others. Counsellors could be instructed by court order to release information. Additionally, the Prevention of Terrorism Act dictates that it is a crime for anyone to withhold information about terrorist activities.

In brief

The counselling service has two aims:

1 To provide a confidential counselling service to individual or groups of employees distracted from the effective performance of their duties by a range of personal concerns, including but not

limited to: emotional stress, relationships, family, alcohol, drugs, financial, legal or work-related stress, welfare rights, organizational change, and career issues.

2 To assist the organization in the identification and amelioration of workplace stressors which adversely affect job performance through the provision of consultancy, training and group support.

(My thanks to Helen Fisher, North Staffordshire Combined Health-care Counselling Service, for providing me with the format above which was originally constructed from a variety of sources.)

Employee counselling service mission statement

Prevention is generally seen to be preferable to cure so consequently the staff counselling service outlined in this document will offer staff and the organization, at every level, opportunities to participate in preventing psychological ill health. The counselling service will, in addition, provide a responsive, free, confidential, high-quality counselling facility for employees and their immediate families whose behaviour may be attributed to psychological ill health. Finally, the service will develop a practical resource facility which will offer either direct or indirect advice and guidance on a number of issues.

Service objectives
Preventive component

1 To offer all departments, at every level in the organization, a consultancy and group facilitation service. The purpose may be as diverse as team building or the prevention or amelioration of stress.

2 The counselling service also offers skills training to individuals or groups with the purpose of enhancing functioning and performance in the workplace.

3 The counselling service will participate with colleagues from others services and disciplines, in offering to employees at every level, educative seminars on a range of topics with the purpose of promoting psychological health.

Reactive component

1 To provide a counselling service which offers initial assessment and appropriate treatment interventions for employees and their families.

2 To provide, where assessment reveals the need, referral-on to other mental health professionals. In these instances, counsellors

will follow-up those referred both to ensure continuity of care and provide a link with the employee's organization.

3 To conform to the *Code of Ethics and Practice for Counsellors* (1990a) of the British Association for Counselling.

4 To provide a counselling service irrespective of the race, age, gender, disability or sexual orientation of the client.

Advice and guidance component

1 To develop a resource directory, with the purpose of encouraging self-help, which may be of help to employees and their families who seek practical advice and guidance on a range of issues and problems.

2 To provide managers and supervisors with advice and guidance concerning handling or referral of troubled employees.

3 To promote the take-up of the service and its appropriate use by managers, supervisors and employees.

(My thanks to David Broadbent, Staff Counselling Psychology Service, St James's University Hospital, Leeds, for providing the above.)

3 An In-take and Progress Form

General information   Where seen: _____

Date: _____   Date of 1st session: _____

Pseudonym: _____   Age: _____
(Please keep the full name, address and
telephone no. in a confidential place)   Sex: _____

Marital status: _____

Children (no.) _____   Ages: _____

Ethnic group: _____   Religion: _____

Referred by: _____

Address: _____

_____

_____   Tel no. _____

Date of referral: _____

Reason for referral:

Other current professional help:

GP (name and address): _____

Medication (if any): _____

Name and address of counsellor: _____

Name and address of supervisor: _____

Where seen: _____

Assessment   Date: _____

(to be completed not later than 4th session)

Pseudonym of client: _____

Name of counsellor: _____

Presenting problem:

Family history/family tree:

Assessment/formulation by the counsellor:

Contract

● Frequency and duration of sessions:

● Place:

● Fees:

● Problem areas/issues to work on:

● Goals/aims:

Rapport (give brief description of how you experienced the client and his/her response to you)

Progress form

(to be completed at 3-monthly intervals)

Name of counsellor:_____   Date: _____

Date of lst session: _____

Pseudonym of client: _____

Present situation/response to counselling

Attendance

Is the client punctual?   Yes ___   No ___

Does the client attend regularly?   Yes ___   No ___

If no, give number of missed sessions and reasons:

Problem areas/issues worked on:

Goals (achieved, changed: specify)

Rapport (give brief description):

If counselling ended:

Date of last session: _____

Outcome:

Has relevant information been sent to referrer?

4 An Evaluation Form for Individual Clients

Evaluation questionnaire

We would greatly appreciate your help in evaluating the counselling service by filling in this questionnaire. All replies are confidential and results will be presented only as general statements. Please tick or circle the answer.

Questions around counselling in general:

1 When visiting the counsellor for the first time were you:
keen
reluctant
mixed
other? (please specify) . . . .

2 How did you feel about subsequent sessions:
keen
reluctant
mixed
other? (please specify) . . . .

3 Did using the service help?
yes
made no difference
made things worse

4 Would you have liked:
more sessions
fewer sessions
just right?

On a scale of 1–10 (where 1 is very poor and 10 excellent) can you answer the following questions:

How would you rate the quality of the service you received?

Did what you receive meet your expectations?

How satisfied are you with the service you received?

Optional questions:

Male
Female
Age

Questions about the counsellor:

On a scale of 1–10 (1 = very untrue, 5 = not sure, 10 = very true) answer the following:

I felt I could trust my counsellor to be open and honest with me

I did not have a lot of faith in the counsellor

The counsellor understood my problems

My counsellor helped me understand my issues more clearly

My counsellor and I established a good working relationship

My counsellor did not seem to help me much

I thought my counsellor was too challenging

My counsellor seemed uncomfortable when I talked about certain things

My counsellor helped me develop skills to deal more creatively with the group

My counsellor was friendly and at ease

My counsellor was concerned for me

My counsellor helped me handle issues better as a result of being with him/her

I am very pleased I had the opportunity to be with this counsellor

Questions on how counselling has had an influence on your life:

Please circle the number which best reflects your opinion using the scale below:

5 = a very positive effect
4 = some positive effect
3 = no effect
2 = a slightly negative effective
1 = a very negative effect

What effect do you think being in personal support counselling has had on the following areas of your life:

relationship with colleagues
relationship with line manager
relationship with others
your self-confidence
your job performance
your enjoyment of life
your decision-making ability

Please let us know any further comments you have on the counselling scheme:

_____

_____

_____

_____

_____

_____

Thank you for you help.

(My thanks to Cathy Carroll, David Broadbent and Ruth Mann for their assistance with the above.)

5 An Assessment Format

1 Before seeing the client:
   (a) make sure the setting is as you want it!
   (b) referral considerations:
   - Is it a self-referral or referred by others?
   - If 'other referred', has the client been involved in the decision? How does he/she feel about the referral? About the referrer: passed on, abandoned?
   - What information has the client been given?
   - What information has the referrer given me?
   - Is there a letter of referral?
   - Is it necessary to contact the referrer for additional information?

2 Seeing the client:
   (a) Introduction: introduce self, indicate seating arrangements
   (b) State length and purpose of meeting
   (c) Share the information you have (from referrer, from the client)
   (d) Start with open-ended questions such as:
   - Tell me what brought you here?
   - How do you think I can help?

(Listen for client's unspoken hopes and fears, e.g. 'Is something wrong with me?', 'Am I mad?')

During the session, note both the content and form/style of the 'dance between you'. Give the client the change to lead, but prompt for personal meaning and/or feelings. Watch for themes that emerge during the session.

3 After the assessment interview, evaluate what took place between you with questions such as:
   (a) What are my feelings about the client?
   (b) Could I work with this person and the problems he/she has?
   (c) What were the client's feelings?
   (d) Did we have a working alliance?

The CAT (Cognitive Analytic Therapy) assessment approach

The following headings have been identified as helping formalize assessment and providing a map for the counsellor:

C   Complaint
H   History
R   Reformulation
A   Aim
P   Plan

Complaint

Is the presenting problem offered as a 'passport' or 'ticket' or the genuine difficulty (e.g. physical symptoms): how did it evolve, any previous episodes? Note the implicit problems not volunteered, e.g. low self-esteem, pervasive guilt etc. Try these out on the client when appropriate. Identify why the client has come at this time, 'Why now?'

Some questions that might help:

● when did it all start?
● what else was happening at the time?
● has it occurred before, when?
● what triggers it off?
● what does it feel like?
● who else knows about it? (testing for available support system)
● any previous experience of counselling?

History

During history-taking it is important, besides gathering facts, to monitor how the story is told, e.g. jokey, matter of fact, despairing, cynical, angry, detached, too fast (not wanting to be heard), too slow (you are on tenterhooks).

Is the client's stance in life visible from posture. Listen for what is missing (e.g. no mention of either or one parent, or a particular period of life).

What is the main theme: 'I am too weak', 'I have to go it alone', 'nobody understands', 'the world owes me a living', etc.

In reviewing life-history, start with what is most immediate for the client but try to get a sense of:

● *adult life*: occupation, living circumstances, current and past relationships, intimate, social and work contexts, physical disability or illness. Ask if anything important has been left out.
● *childhood*: family structure, disruptions, role models, rivalries, cruelties, abuses, major separations, family rules, beliefs. What

did it feel like to be this person as a child? What sense did he/she make of the situation? What were his/her survival procedures?
- *adolescence*: separation from family, how was the transition into adult life negotiated (what support was available?), school–peer relationships and achievements, sexual relationships and experiences and problems, sexual orientation? Can enquire about drugs, alcohol, crime, eating disorders, any other important areas.
- *any history of psychiatric illness*, e.g. major depression, deliberate self-harm, psychotic episodes, any medication? How does the client understand his/her problems?
- *other areas* such as medical history, separation and loss, death, adoption, religion, beliefs, hopes and aspirations.

Reformulation

Feedback the main facts you have heard to ensure that the client knows you were listening. The essence of the reformulation in the context of assessment is a brief linking of the client's presenting problems with his/her coping strategies in early life. An example of such a reformulation would be: 'It sounds to me as though, with a drunken father who used to come home and violently abuse you and your mother, the best way of coping was by keeping your head down, your mouth shut and staying out of sight. And nowadays when you do this you get ignored and overlooked and end up feeling as if you are of no importance.' The content is:

- this is what you bring
- this is how I understand it
- this is how we understand it together

Aim

Clarify what the client hopes from counselling and what you think you can offer. Clarify vague aims like 'I want to be happy.' It may be necessary to find a compromise between the client's (sometimes unrealistic) hopes and what can be achieved realistically in 16–24 sessions. This is what you and I do about it.

Plan

If it is not suitable for you to work with this client explain why and arrange to refer appropriately. Alternatively, if in doubt, offer one or two more trial/assessment sessions.

Work out contact details (number of sessions or open-ended), client availability, when to start, where, finance, etc. Briefly describe the CAT structure and its collaborative nature.

Check about sex/race of counsellor.
Check about emergencies, e.g. suicide (give details of Samaritans).
Is there anything the client wants to ask?

(My thanks to Valerie Coumont and the Association of Cognitive Analytic Therapists, for permission to use this brief outline of the CAT assessment approach.)

6   Information for Clients

What is counselling?

Life is complex – most of the problems we experience have many facets to them. This sometimes means finding solutions on a practical as well as an emotional level. For some problems there are no solutions – but it can help to gain understanding and therefore acceptance. Counselling is a process that helps you to explore and understand the situation and therefore be able to choose the solution that meets your needs.

Who can counselling help?

Counselling can help with a wide range of work or emotional problems including people who are experiencing difficulties in relationships whether at work or at home. People who want to come to terms with loss or with change. People who are feeling anxious or depressed and are seeking insight into the causes and for ways to cope.

What to expect from us?

- An initial assessment to find out whether short-term counselling of up to eight sessions is what you need, or whether you would benefit from referral to other kinds of help.
- An experienced counsellor qualified to recognized standards who adheres to the British Association of Counselling *Codes of Ethics and Practice for Counsellors* (1990a).
- Impartiality: we are not here to make judgements about you or your situation. Nor is our role to mediate or advocate to a third party.
- Confidentiality: no one will know you are using the service unless you tell them. Client information is strictly between the counsellor and client. The only exception is if someone else's personal safety is at risk.
- Client records are kept to act as an *aide-mémoire* to counsellors. Records are allocated a number only: your name or means of identification will not appear on them.

230 Workplace counselling

- Counsellors receive professional support and supervision from outside the counselling service to maintain the quality of their work and for the protection of the client.
- We will give you an appointment as quickly as possible. Your appointment will last for 50 minutes.

What we expect from you:

- To attend on time for your appointment(s). If you cannot attend, to telephone and cancel so someone else may have your appointment time.
- In order to evaluate and improve the service, we may ask you to complete a questionnaire about the help you received. To do this we will ask for a contact name and address which will be kept separately from your records by the counselling manager.

If you have any questions about the counselling service or wish to complain please contact:

(My thanks to Helen Fisher for permission to use this format.)

7 A Counselling Agreement with a Client

In undertaking to meet with you I am committing myself to meeting at the time(s) we have agreed and providing a safe setting within which you can explore your issues and difficulties and, if appropriate, move towards change. I will endeavour to facilitate you in this process.

In undertaking to see me for counselling you are committing yourself to seeing me regularly at the agreed time and endeavouring to make use of the time we have together.

Confidentiality
The counselling service is confidential but with the following exceptions:

1 I receive regular supervision of my work and your sessions may be discussed. Reasonable efforts are made to maintain your anonymity. Supervision takes place with persons not employed by our company/organization.
2 If you give me information which leads me to believe that someone is in danger of serious harm then, after giving the matter careful consideration, I may take steps to minimize this danger. Any action would usually be discussed with you first.
3 Situations may arise in which I am required by law to communicate certain information to the relevant authorities (e.g. concerning my knowledge of acts of terrorism).

Cancellations
If you wish to cancel or change the time of a session, please let me know well in advance. Another appointment will be offered unless you request an end to the counselling. I would appreciate the opportunity to have a final session with you if this is the case.

Late or missed sessions
If you do not arrive on time and have not cancelled by the beginning of the session, I will assume you are coming. If you miss the session without notification we will offer you another appointment, but it may not be as soon as you would wish.

Duration and termination
Once I agree to see you my commitment to you is open-ended. I will
see you for as long as you wish and we agree counselling is useful.
You may, of course, finish seeing me at any time. I ask that you give
me a minimum of one session notice of your decision to stop. It is
generally better to plan the ending in advance but this final session
allows for a degree of closure.

Records
Any written notes are kept secure and anonymous. Notes are
usually destroyed 24 months after your last session.

Policy documents
These cover areas of complaints procedures, client information and
our codes of ethics. They will be made available on request.

I have read and understood this agreement.

Name   Signature   Date

(My thanks to David Broadbent for permission to use this format.)

References

American Psychiatric Association (1987) *Diagnostic and Statistical Manual of Mental Diseases.* Washington, DC: American Psychiatric Association.

Anastasi, A. (1982) *Psychological Testing.* New York: Macmillan.

Antoniou, C. (1995) Private paper, School of Psychology and Counselling, Roehampton Institute London.

Bakalinsky, R. (1980) 'People versus profits: social work in industry', *Social Work,* November: 471–5.

Balgopal, P.R. and Patchner, M.A. (1988) 'Evaluating employee assistance programs: obstacles, issues and strategies', *The Clinical Supervisor,* 3(3/4): 95–105.

Bateson, G. (1979) *Mind and Nature: A Necessary Unity.* London: Fontana.

Bayne, R. (1991) 'Psychological type, the MBTI and counselling', *Employee Counselling Today,* 3(1): 9–12.

Bernard, J. and Jara, C.S. (1986) 'The failure of clinical psychology graduate students to apply understood ethical principles', *Professional Psychology: Research and Practice,* 17(4): 313–15.

Bion, W.R. (1961) *Experiences in Groups.* London: Tavistock Publications.

Bishop, B. and D'Rozario, P. (1990) 'A matter of ethics? A comment on Pryor "Conflicting responsiblities" (1989)', *Australian Psychologist,* 25(2): 215–19.

Bond, T. (1992) 'Confidentiality: counselling, ethics and the law', *Employee Counselling Today,* 4(4): 4–9.

Bond, T. (1993) *Standards and Ethics for Counselling in Action.* London: Sage.

Brack, G., Jones, E.S., Smith, R.M., White, J. and Brack, C.J. (1993) 'A primer on consultation theory: building a flexible wisdom', *Journal of Counseling and Development,* 71(6): 619–28.

Brady, J.L., Healy, F.C., Norcross, J.C. and Guy, J.D. (1995) 'Stress in counsellors: an integrative research review', in W. Dryden (ed.), *The Stresses of Counselling in Action.* London: Sage. pp. 1–27.

Briar, K.H. and Vinet, M. (1985) 'Ethical issues concerning an EAP: who is the client?', in S.H. Klarreich, J.L. Francek and C.E. Moore (eds), *The Human Resources Management Handbook: Principles and Practice of Employee Assistance Program.* New York: Praeger. pp. 342–59.

British Association for Counselling (1990a) *Code of Ethics and Practice for Counsellors.* Rugby: British Association for Counselling.

British Association for Counselling (1990b) *The Recognition of Counsellor Training Courses,* 2nd edn. Rugby: British Association for Counselling.

British Association for Counselling (1995) *Code of Ethics and Practice for Supervisors,* 2nd edn. Rugby: British Association for Counselling.

Bromberg, P.M. (1982) 'The supervisory process and parallel process in psychoanalysis', *Contemporary Psychoanalysis,* 18: 92–111.

Buckingham, L. (1992) 'A headache that won't go away', *Guardian,* 31 October, p. 38.

Bull, A. (1994) 'How effective is counselling in the workplace?', *Evaluation of Counselling: Selected References*. Rugby: BAC Publication.

Bull, A. (1995) *Counselling Skills and Counselling at Work: A Guide for Purchasers and Providers*. Rugby: British Association for Counselling.

Carroll, C. (1994) 'Building bridges: a study of employee counsellors in the private sector', unpublished MSc dissertation, City University, London.

Carroll, M. (1995a) *Counselling Supervision: Theory, Skills and Practice*. London: Cassell.

Carroll, M. (1995b) 'The counsellor in organizational settings: some reflections', *Employee Counselling Today*, 7(1): 23–32.

Carroll, M. and Holloway, E. (1993) 'Redundancy counselling: is it really counselling?', *Employee Counselling Today*, 5(4): 14–20.

Carroll, M. and Pickard, E. (1993) 'Psychology and counselling', in B. Thorne and W. Dryden (eds), *Counselling: Interdisciplinary Perspectives*. Milton Keynes: Open University Press. pp. 107–28.

Carter, I. (1977) 'Social work in industry: a history and a viewpoint', *Social Thought*, 3: 7–17.

Cartwright, S. and Cooper, C. (1994) *No Hassle: Taking the Stress out of Work*. London: Century Business Books.

Cashwell, C.S. (1994) 'Interpersonal process recall', in L.D. Borders (ed.), *Supervision: Exploring the Effective Components*. ERIC/CASS Digest Series. North Carolina: Greenborough. pp. 7–8.

Clarkson, P. (1990) 'The scope of stress counselling in organisations', *Employee Counselling Today*, 2(4): 3–6.

Clarkson, P. (1994) 'Code of ethics for the office', *Counselling*, 5(4): 282–3.

Clarkson, P. (1995) *The Therapeutic Relationship*. London: Whurr.

Cocks, G. (1985) *Psychotherapy in the Third Reich*. New York: Oxford University Press.

Cole, D.W. (1988) 'Evaluating organizations through an Employee Assistance Program using an organizational developmental model', *Employee Assistance Quarterly*, 3(3/4): 107–18.

Connor, M. (1994) *Training the Counsellor: An Integrative Model*. London: Routledge.

Cooke, R.A. and Rousseau, D.M. (n.d.) 'Behavioural norms and expectations: a quantitative approach to the assessment of organizational culture', supplied by Verax.

Cooper, C.L. and Cartwright, S. (1994) 'Healthy mind, healthy organization – a proactive approach to occupational stress', *Human Relations*, 47(4): 455–71.

Cooper, C.L., Sadri, G., Allison, T. and Reynolds, P. (1990) 'Stress counselling in the Post Office', *Counselling Psychology Quarterly*, 3(1): 3–11.

Cooper, C.L., Sloane, S.J. and Williams, S. (1988) *Occupational Stress Indicator: Management Guide*. Windsor: NFER-Nelson.

Corneil, D.W. (1985) 'Social policy issues and EAPs', in S.H. Klarreich, J.L. Francek and C.E. Moore (eds), *The Human Resources Management Handbook: Principles and Practice of Employee Assistance Program*. New York: Praeger. pp. 335–41.

Corney, R. (1992) *Evaluating Counsellors in Counselling in General Practice*. London: Royal College of General Practitioners, Clinical Series.

Crandall, R. and Allen, R.D. (1982) 'The organisational context of helping relationships', in T.A. Will (ed.), *Basic Processes in Helping Relationships*. London: Academic Press. pp. 431–52.

Critchley, B. and Casey, D. (1989) 'Organizations get stuck too', *Leadership and Organization Development Journal*, 10(4): 3–12.

Crouch, A. (1992) 'The competent counsellor: an open-ended competency framework designed to enhance counsellor training', Paper delivered to the BPS Counselling Psychology Conference, Birmingham, May 1992.

Cunningham, G. (1994) *Effective Employee Assistance Programs: A Guide for EAP Counselors and Managers*. Thousand Oaks, CA: Sage.

Deverall, M. (forthcoming) 'Assessing organizations for counselling', in M. Carroll and M. Walton (eds), *The Handbook of Counselling in Organizations*. London: Sage.

Dickson, W.J. (1945) 'The Hawthorne plan of personnel counselling', *The Journal of Orthopsychiatry*, 15: 343–7.

Doehrman, M.J. (1976) 'Parallel processes in supervision and psychotherapy', *Bulletin of the Menninger Clinic*, 40(1): 1–104.

Drum, D.J. (1987) 'Counseling psychologist or Hefflelump?', *The Counseling Psychologist*, 15: 280–6.

Dryden, W. (1990) 'Counselling under apartheid: an interview with Andrew Swart', *British Journal of Guidance and Counselling*, 18(3): 298–320.

Dryden W., Horton, I. and Mearns, D. (1995) *Issues in Professional Counsellor Training*. London: Cassell.

Durkin, W.G. (1985) 'Evaluation of EAP programming', in S.H. Klarreich, J.L. Francek and C.E. Moore (eds), *The Human Resources Management Handbook: Principles and Practice of Employee Assistance Program*. New York: Praeger. pp. 243–59.

Egan, G. (1993a) 'The shadow side', *Management Today*, September: 33–8.

Egan, G. (1993b) *Adding Value: A Systematic Guide to Business-driven Management and Leadership*. San Francisco: Jossey-Bass.

Egan, G. (1994) *Working the Shadow-side: A Guide to Positive Behind the Scenes Management*. San Francisco: Jossey-Bass.

Egan, G. and Cowan, M. (1979) *People in Systems*. Monteray, CA: Brooks/Cole.

Ekstein R. and Wallerstein R.S. (1972) *The Teaching and Learning of Psychotherapy*. New York: International.

Elton-Wilson, J. and Barkham, M. (1994) 'A practitioner–scientist approach to psychotherapy process and outcome research', in P. Clarkson and M. Pokorny (eds), *The Handbook of Psychotherapy*. London: Routledge. pp. 49–72.

Employee Assistance Programmes Association (1995) *UK Standards of Practice and Professional Guidelines for Employee Assistance Programmes*. London: EAP Association.

Employee Counselling Today (1992), 4(4).

Epstein, R.S. and Simon, R.I. (1990) 'The exploitation index: an early warning indicator of boundary violations in psychotherapy', *Bulletin of the Menninger Clinic*, 54(4): 450–65.

Falvey, J. (1987) *Handbook of Administrative Supervision*. Virginia: ACES Publication.

Farber, B.A. (1990) 'Burnout in psychotherapists: incidence, types, and trends', *Psychotherapy in Private Practice*, 8: 35–44.

Fine, M. and Ulrich, L. (1988) 'Integrating psychology and philosophy in teaching a graduate course in ethics', *Professional Psychology: Research and Practice*, 19: 542–6.

Fineman, S. (1993) 'Organizations as emotional arenas', in S. Fineman (ed.), *Emotions in Organizations*. London: Sage. pp. 9–35.

236   *Workplace counselling*

Fisher, H. (1995) 'Plastering over the cracks?: Employee counselling in the NHS', unpublished MA dissertation, University of Keele.

Folkman, S. and Lazarus, R.S. (1980) 'An analysis of coping in a middle-aged community sample', *Journal of Health and Social Behaviour*, 21: 219–39.

Francek, J.L. (1985) 'The role of the occupational social worker in EAPs', in S.H. Klarreich, J.L. Francek and C.E. Moore (eds), *The Human Resources Management Handbook: Principles and Practice of Employee Assistance Program*. New York: Praeger. pp. 144–54.

Frankl, V. (1959) *Man's Search for Meaning*. New York: Kangaroo.

Franks, J.D. (1993) *Persuasion and Healing: Comparative Study of Psychotherapy*, 3rd edn. London: Johns Hopkins University Press.

Geist, G.O., Curin, S., Prestridge, R. and Schelb, G. (1973) 'Ethics and the counselor–agency relationship', *Rehabilitation Counseling Bulletin*, 17: 15–21.

Gelso, C.J. and Carter, J. (1985) 'The relationship in counselling and psychotherapy', *The Counseling Psychologist*, 13(2): 155–243.

Gerstein, L.W. and Shullman, S.L. (1992) 'Counseling psychology and the workplace: the emergence of organizational counseling psychology', in R. Brown and R.W. Lent (eds), *The Handbook of Counseling Psychology*, 2nd edn. New York: Wiley. pp. 581–625.

Gitterman, A. and Miller, I. (1989) 'The influence of the organization on clinical practice', *Clinical Social Work Journal*, 17(2): 151–64.

Googins, B. (1985) 'Can change be documented? Measuring the impact of EAPs', in S.H. Klarreich, J.L. Francek and C.E. Moore (eds), *The Human Resources Management Handbook: Principles and Practice of Employee Assistance Program*. New York: Praeger. pp. 221–31.

Gordon, J. and Dryden, W. (1989) 'Counselling employees: the rational-emotive approach', *Employee Counselling Today*, 1(4): 14–20.

Gray, K. (1984a) 'Counsellor interventions in organisations', in W. Dryden and A.G. Watts (eds), *Guidance and Counselling in Britain: A 20-year Perspective*. Cambridge: Hobson. pp. 163–77.

Gray, K. (1984b) 'Postscript', in W. Dryden and A.G. Watts (eds), *Guidance and Counselling in Britain: A 20-year Perspective*. Cambridge: Hobson. pp. 178–80.

Halton, W. (1994) 'Some unconscious aspects of organizational life: contributions from psychoanalysis', in A. Obholzer and V.Z. Roberts (eds), *The Unconscious at Work: Individual and Organizational Stress in the Human Services*. London: Routledge. pp. 11–18.

Hampden-Turner, C. (1994) *Corporate Culture*. London: Piatkus.

Harrison, R. (1972) 'Understanding your organization's character', *Harvard Business Review*, 50(23): 119–28.

Harrison, R. and Stokes, H. (n.d.) *Diagnosing Organisational Culture*. Horsham, West Sussex: Roffey Park Management College.

Hawkins, P. (forthcoming) *The Heart of the Learning Organization*. London: Sage.

Hawkins, P. and Miller, E. (1994) 'Psychotherapy in and with organizations', in P. Clarkson and M. Pokorny (eds), *The Handbook of Psychotherapy*. London: Routledge. pp. 267–85.

Hawkins, P. and Shohet, R. (1989) *Supervision in the Helping Professions*. Milton Keynes: Open University Press.

Hay, J. (1989) 'Transactional analysis as a counselling medium in a management development programme', *Employee Counselling Today*, 1(4): 21–8.

Hay, J. (1992) *Transactional Analysis for Trainers*. Maidenhead: McGraw-Hill.

Health and Safety Executive (1995) *Stress at Work: A Guide for Employers*. London: Health and Safety Executive.

Heller, J. (1966) *Something Happened*. London: Black Swan.

Hellman, I.D. and Morrison, T.L. (1987) 'Practice setting and type of caseload as factors in psychotherapist stress', *Psychotherapy*, 24: 427–33.

Highley, C. and Cooper, C. (1994) 'Evaluating EAPs', *Personnel Review*, 23(7): 46–59.

Highley, C. and Cooper, C. (n.d.) *An Assessment of UK EAPs and Workplace Counselling Programmes*. London: Health and Safety Executive.

Hillman, J. (1983) *Interviews*. New York: Harper & Row.

Hirschhorn, L. and Barnett. C.K. (eds) (1992) *The Psychodynamics of Organizations*. Philadelphia: Temple University Press.

Hitchings, P. (1994) 'Psychotherapy and sexual orientation', in P. Clarkson and M. Pokorny (eds), *The Handbook of Psychotherapy*. London: Routledge. pp. 119–32.

Hochschild, A.R. (1983) *The Managed Heart*. Berkeley, CA: University of California Press.

Hochschild, A.R. (1993) 'Preface', in S. Fineman (ed.), *Emotions in Organizations*. London: Sage.

Holloway, E.L. (1995) *Clinical Supervision: A Systems Approach*. Thousand Oaks, CA: Sage.

Holosko, M.J. (1988) 'Prerequisites for EAP evaluation: a case for more thoughtful evaluation planning', *The Clinical Supervisor*, 3(3/4): 59–67.

Hood, A.B. and Johnson, R.W. (1991) *Assessment in Counseling: A Guide to the Use of Psychological Assessment Procedures*. Alexandria, VA: American Association for Counseling and Development.

Hope, D. (1985) 'Counsellor stress and burnout', unpublished MA thesis, University of Reading.

Hopson, B. (1977) 'Techniques and methods of counselling', in T. Watts (ed.), *Counselling at Work*. Plymouth: Bedford Square Press. pp. 25–30.

Hoskinson, L. (1994) 'EAPs: Internal versus external service structures. The key differences and potential synergies', Paper presented at the European EAP Conference, Augsburg, Germany, October.

Hoskinson, L. and Reddy, M. (1989) *Counselling Services in UK Organizations: An ICAS Report*. Milton Keynes: ICAS.

House, R. (1995) 'The stresses of working in a general practice setting', in W. Dryden (ed.), *The Stresses of Counselling in Action*. London: Sage. pp. 87–107.

Income Data Services Ltd (1992) *Performance Management*. IDS Study 518. London: IDS.

Inskipp, F. and Proctor, B. (1993) *Making the Most of Supervision*. Twickenham: Cascade Publications.

Institute of Personnel Management (1992) *Statement on Counselling in the Workplace*. London: IPM.

Jones, O.F. (1985) 'The rationale and critical issues of EAP development', in S.H. Klarreich, J.L. Francek and C.E. Moore (eds), *The Human Resources Management Handbook: Principles and Practice of Employee Assistance Program*. New York: Praeger. pp. 7–12.

Kelloway, E.K. and Barling, J. (1991) 'Job characteristics, role stress and mental health', *Journal of Occupational Psychology*, 64: 291–304.

Kets de Vries, F.R. and Miller, D. (1984) *The Neurotic Organization*. San Francisco: Jossey-Bass.

Kim, D.S. (1988) 'Assessing employee assistance programs: evaluating typology and models', *The Clinical Supervisor*, 3(3/4): 169–87.

Kitchener, K.S. (1984) 'Intuition, critical evaluation and ethical principles: the foundation for ethical decisions in counseling psychology', *The Counseling Psychologist*, 12(3): 43–55.

Klarreich, S.H. (1985) 'Stress: an intrapersonal approach', in S.H. Klarreich, J.L. Francek and C.E. Moore (eds), *The Human Resources Management Handbook: Principles and Practice of Employee Assistance Program.* New York: Praeger. pp. 304–18.

Klarreich, S.H., Francek, J.L. and Moore, C.E. (1985) *The Human Resources Management Handbook: Principles and Practice of Employee Assistance Programs.* New York: Praeger.

Labour Research Department (1994) *Stress at Work: a Trade Union Response.* London: Labour Research Department.

Lakin, M. (1991) *Coping with Ethical Dilemmas in Psychotherapy.* New York: Pergamon Press.

Lane, D. (1990) 'Counselling psychology in organisations', *The Psychologist*, 12: 540–4.

Law Commission (1981) *Breach of Confidence.* Cmnd 8388. London: HMSO.

Lee, S.S. and Rosen, E.A. (1984) 'Employee counselling services: ethical dilemmas', *Personnel and Guidance Journal*, January, 276–80.

Lewis, J. and Lewis, M. (1986) *Counseling Programs for Employees in the Workplace.* Monteray, CA: Brooks/Cole.

Lodge, D. (1988) *Nice Work.* London: Penguin.

McCaughan, N. and Palmer, B. (1994) *Systems Thinking for Harassed Managers.* London: Karnac Books.

McLean, A., Ellis, W., Lipsitch, I. and Moss, L. (1985) 'Contemporary occupational psychiatry', in S.H. Klarreich, J.L. Francek and C.E. Moore (eds), *The Human Resources Management Handbook: Principles and Practice of Employee Assistance Program.* New York: Praeger. pp. 129–43.

McLeod, J. (1993) *The Organisational Context of Counselling.* Keele: Centre for Counselling Studies, Keele University.

McRoy, R.G., Freeman, E.M. and Logan, S. (1986) 'Strategies for teaching students about termination', *The Clinical Supervisor*, 4(4): 45–56.

Magnus, S.M. (1995) 'Taking the agony', *Guardian*, 1 July, p. 2.

Mahoney, M.J. and McCray Patterson, K. (1992) 'Changing theories of change: recent developments in counselling', in S.D. Brown and R.W. Lent (eds), *Handbook of Counseling Psychology*, 2nd edn. New York: Wiley. pp. 665–89.

Malan, D. (1976) *The Frontier of Brief Psychotherapy.* New York: Plenum.

Martin, P.A. (1994) 'The effects of counselling training on public sector managers', unpublished MSc dissertation, University of Surrey/Roehampton Institute London.

Masi, D.A. (ed.) (1992) *The AMA Handbook for Developing Employee Assistance and Counseling Programs.* Amacom: American Management Association.

Maynard, J.B. and Farmer, J.L. (1985) 'Strategies of implementing an EAP', in S.H. Klarreich, J.L. Francek and C.E. Moore (eds), *The Human Resources Management Handbook: Principles and Practice of Employee Assistance Program.* New York: Praeger. pp. 31–42.

Mearns, D. (1995) *Developing Person-centred Counselling.* London: Sage.

Megranahan, M. (1989a) *Counselling: A Practical Guide for Managers.* London: Institute for Personnel Management.

Megranahan, M. (1989b) 'Counselling in the workplace', in W. Dryden, D. Charles-Edwards, and R. Woolfe (eds), *Handbook of Counselling in Britain*. London: Tavistock/Routledge.

Menzies, L. (1960) 'Social systems as a defence against anxiety: an empirical study of the nursing service of a general hospital', in E. Trist and H. Murray (eds), *The Social Engagement of Social Science, Vol. 1: The Socio-psychological Perspective*. London: Free Association Books, 1990.

Morris, G.B. (1993) 'A rational-emotive paradigm for organizations', *Journal of Rational Emotive and Cognitive Behaviour Therapy*, 11(1): 33–49.

Mueller, W.J. and Kell, B.L. (1972) *Coping with Conflict: Supervising Counsellors and Psychotherapists*. New York: Appleton-Century-Crofts.

Nahrwold, S.C. (1983) 'Why programs fail', in James Manuso (ed.), *Occupational Clinical Psychology*. New York: Praeger. pp. 105–15.

Nelson-Jones, R. (1995) *The Theory and Practice of Counselling*, 2nd edn. London: Cassell.

Newfeldt, S.A., Karno, M.P. and Nelson, M.L. (1996) 'Experts conceptualization of supervisee reflexivity', *Journal of Counseling Psychology*, 43(1): 3–9.

Newton, T. (1995) *Managing Stress: Emotion and Power at Work*. London: Sage.

Nixon, J. and Carroll, M. (1994) 'Can a line-manager also be a counsellor?', *Employee Counselling Today*, 6(1): 10–15.

Oberer, D. and Lee, S. (1986) 'The counselling psychologist in business and industry: ethical concerns', *Journal of Business and Psychology*, 1(2): 148–62.

Obholzer, A. (1987) 'Institutional dynamics and resistance to change', *Psychoanalytic Psychotherapy*, 2(3): 201–5.

Obholzer, A. and Roberts, V.Z. (eds) (1994) *The Unconscious at Work: Individual and Organizational Stress in the Human Services*. London: Routledge.

Offermann, L.R. and Gowing, M.K. (1990) 'Organisations of the future: changes and challenges', *American Psychologist*, 45(2): 95–109.

O'Leary, L. (1993) 'Mental health at work', *Occupational Health Review*, September/October: 1993.

O'Leary, L. (1994) 'Fitness at work – is it worth it?', *Occupational Health Review*, March/April: 14–16.

Opus (1995) *Organizational Stress in the National Health Service*. London: NHS Publication.

Orlans, V. (1986) 'Counselling services', *Organizational Personnel Review*, 15(5): 19–23.

Orlans, V. (1991) 'Evaluating the benefits of employee assistance programs', paper for the first EAP Conference, London, April.

Orlans, V. (1992) 'Counselling in the workplace: Part 1: Counsellor perspectives and training', *EAP International*, 1(1): 19–21.

Orlans, V. and Shipley, P. (1983) *A Survey of Stress Management and Prevention Facilities in a Sample of UK Organizations*. London: Stress Research and Control Centre, Birkbeck College, University of London.

Orme, G. (1994) 'The role of personal therapy in the training of workplace counsellors', unpublished diploma in Counselling at Work, TDA.

Osipow, S.H. (1982) 'Counseling psychology: applications in the world of work', *The Counseling Psychologist*, 10(3): 19–25.

Page, S. and Wosket, V. (1994) *Supervising the Counsellor: A Cyclical Model*. London: Routledge.

Patterson, C.H. (1971) 'Are ethics different in different settings?', *Personnel and Guidance Journal*, 50: 254–9.

Patterson, J.B., Buckley, J. and Smull, M. (1989) 'Ethics in supported employment', *Journal of Applied Rehabilitation Counseling*, 20(3): 12–20.

Pearson, R.E. (1990) *Counseling and Social Support*. Newbury Park, CA: Sage.

Perry, J. (1993) *Counselling for Women*. Milton Keynes: Open University Press.

Pfeffer, J. (1994) *Competitive Advantage through People*. Boston: Harvard Business Press.

Pheysey, D.C. (1993) *Organizational Culture*. London: Routledge.

Pickard, E. (1993) 'Designing training for counsellors at work', *Counselling at Work*, Autumn: 7–8.

Pickard, E. (forthcoming) 'Developing training for organizational counselling', in M. Carroll and M. Walton (eds), *The Handbook of Counselling in Organizations*. London: Sage.

Presnall, L.F. (1985) 'Foreword: historical perspective of EAPs', in S.H. Klarreich, J.L. Francek and C.E. Moore (eds), *The Human Resources Management Handbook: Principles and Practice of Employee Assistance Program*. New York: Praeger. pp. ix–xvi.

Proctor, B. (1986) 'Supervision: a co-operative exercise in accountability', in M. Marken and M. Payne (eds), *Enabling and Ensuring: Supervision in Practice*. Leicester: National Youth Bureau. pp. 21–34.

Pryor, R.G.L. (1989) 'Conflicting responsibilities: a case study of an ethical dilemma for psychologists working in organisations', *Australian Psychologist*, 24: 293–305.

Puder, M. (1983) 'Credibility, confidentiality, and ethical issues in employee counselling programming', in James Manuso (ed.), *Occupational Clinical Psychology*. New York: Praeger. pp. 95–103.

Putnam, L.L. and Mumby, D.K. (1993) 'Organizations, emotions and the myth of rationality', in S. Fineman (ed.), *Emotions in Organizations*. London: Sage. pp. 36–57.

Randall, R., Southgate, J. and Tomlinson, F. (1980) *Cooperative and Community Group Dynamics*. Barefoot Books.

Reddy, M. (1987) *The Managers' Guide to Counselling at Work*. Leicester: British Psychological Society.

Reddy, M. (1993a) 'The counselling firmament: a short trip round the galaxy', *Counselling*, 4(1): 47–50.

Reddy, M. (ed.) (1993b) *EAPs and Counselling Provision in UK Organizations: An ICAS Report and Policy Guide*. Milton Keynes: ICAS.

Reddy, M. (1994) 'EAPs and their future in the UK: history repeating itself', *Personnel Review*, 23(7): 46–59.

Redman, (1995) *Counselling Your Staff*. London: Kogan Page.

Rest, J. (1984) 'Research on moral development: implications for training counseling psychologists', *The Counseling Psychologist*, 12(3): 19–29.

Rogers, C.J. (1961) *On Becoming a Person*. Boston, MA: Houghton Mifflin.

Roman, P.M. and Blum, T.C. (1985) 'Modes and levels of data management affecting the EAP practitioner', in S.H. Klarreich, J.L. Francek and C.E. Moore (eds), *The Human Resources Management Handbook: Principles and Practice of Employee Assistance Program*. New York: Praeger. pp. 203–21.

Ross, R.R. and Altmaier, E.M. (1994) *Intervention in Occupational Stress*. London: Sage.

Salt, H., Callow, S. and Bor, R. (1992) 'Confidentiality about health problems at work', *Employee Counselling Today*, 4(4): 10–14.

Sanders, G. (1990) 'Counselling models in the workplace', *Employee Counselling Today*, 2(2): 25–8.

Sexton, T.L. and Whiston, S.C. (1991) 'A review of the empirical basis of counselling: implications for practice and training', *Counselor Education and Supervision*, 30: 330–54.

de Shazer, S. (1985) *Keys to Solutions in Brief Therapy*. New York: Norton.

Smail, D. (1987) *Taking Care: An Alternative to Therapy*. London: Dent & Sons.

Smith, N.L. (1985) 'The certainty of judgments in health evaluation', in J.F. Dickman, W.G. Emener and W.S. Hutchison (eds), *Counseling the Troubled Person in Industry*. Springfield, IL: Charles C. Thomas. pp. 191–203.

Sonnenstuhl, W.J. and Trice, H.M. (1990) *Strategies for Employee Assistance Programs: The Crucial Balance*, 2nd edn. Cornell: ILR Press.

Stein, M. and Hollwitz, J. (eds) (1992) *Psyche at Work: Workplace Applications of Jungian Analytical Psychology*. Wilmette, IL: Chiron Publications.

Stiles, W.B., Shapiro, D.A. and Elliot, R. (1986) 'Are all psychotherapies equivalent?', *American Psychologist*, 41: 165–80.

Sugarman, L. (1992) 'Ethical issues in counselling at work', *Employee Counselling Today*, 4(4): 23–30.

Summerfield, J. and van Oudtshoorn, L. (1995) *Counselling in the Workplace*. London: Institute of Personnel and Development.

Swanson, N. and Murphy, L. (1991) 'Mental health counseling in industry', In C.L. Cooper and I.T. Robertson (eds), *International Review of Industrial and Organizational Psychology*. Chichester: Wiley. pp. 265–82.

Sworder, G. (1977) 'Counselling problems at work: where do we go from here?', in T. Watts (ed.), *Counselling at Work*. Plymouth: Bedford Square Press. pp. 79–83.

Tehrani, N. (1994) 'Business dimensions to organizational counselling', *Counselling Psychology Quarterly*, 7(3): 275–85.

Tehrani, N. (1995) 'The development of employee support', *Counselling Psychology Review*, 10(3): 2–7.

Toffler, A. (1970) *Future Shock*. New York: Bantam.

Tolley, K. and Rowland, N. (1995) *Evaluating the Cost-effectiveness of Counselling in Health Care*. London: Routledge.

Toomer, J.E. (1982) 'Counselling psychologists in business and industry', *The Counseling Psychologist*, 10(3): 9–18.

Torjman, S.R. (1985) 'Training referral agents for EAPs: knowledge, skills and attitudes', in S.H. Klarreich, J.L. Francek and C.E. Moore (eds), *The Human Resources Management Handbook: Principles and Practice of Employee Assistance Program*. New York: Praeger. pp. 188–200.

Turner, S. (1985) 'Assessment/referral', in S.H. Klarreich, J.L. Francek and C.E. Moore (eds), *The Human Resources Management Handbook: Principles and Practice of Employee Assistance Program*. New York: Praeger. pp. 69–79.

van Oudtshoorn, L. (1989) *Organization as a Nurturing Environment*. van Oudtshoorn Association: Oxford.

Verax (Human Synergistics) (1991) *Organizational Culture Inventory*. Hampshire: Verax.

Walker, V. (1992) 'Confidentiality – the personnel dilemma', *Employee Counselling Today*, 4(4): 15–22.

Watts, A.G. (ed.) (1977) *Counselling at Work*. Plymouth: Bedford Square Press.

242 *Workplace counselling*

Webb, W. (1990) 'Cognitive behaviour therapy: applications for employee assistance counselors', *Employee Assistance Quarterly*, 5(3): 55–65.

Welfel, E.R. and Lipsitz, N.E. (1983) 'Wanted: a comprehensive approach to ethics research and education', *Counselor Education and Supervision*, 22: 320–32.

White, E. (1993) 'The role of organizational social work in organizational change', private paper from Hogeschool Midden, The Netherlands.

Wilensky, J.L. and Wilensky, H.L. (1951) 'Personnel counseling: the Hawthorne case', *American Journal of Sociology*, 57: 265–80.

Williams, A. (1987) 'Parallel process in a course on counseling supervision', *Counselor Education and Supervision*, 26: 245–54.

World Health Organization (1992) *The ICD – 10: Classification of Mental and Behavioural Disorders*. Geneva: WHO.

Wray, G. (1992) 'Same sex counselling? A discussion on neutrality, social conditioning and issues of gender', unpublished thesis for Extra Mural Certificate in Counselling and Groupwork, University of Cambridge.

Wrich, J.T. (1985) 'Management's role in EAPs', in S.H. Klarreich, J.L. Francek and C.E. Moore (eds), *The Human Resources Management Handbook: Principles and Practice of Employee Assistance Program*. New York: Praeger. pp. 170–80.

Wright, D.A. (1985) 'Policies and procedures: the essential elements in an EAP', in S.H. Klarreich, J.L. Francek and C.E. Moore (eds), *The Human Resources Management Handbook: Principles and Practice of Employee Assistance Program*. New York: Praeger. pp. 13–23.

Yeager, J. (1983) 'A model for executive performance coaching', in James Manuso (ed.), *Occupational Clinical Psychology*. New York: Praeger. pp. 129–46.

Index